P9-CFU-730

The Myth of Separation

What is the correct relationship between Church and State?

A revealing look at what the Founders and early Courts _really_ said

by

David Barton

WallBuilder Press
PO Box 397
Aledo, TX 76008
817-441-6044

Nehemiah 2:17: "You see the distress that we are in...come, let us build the walls that we may no longer be a reproach."

Copyright © 1992 by David Barton
3rd Edition
5th Printing, July 1993
Over 100,000 in print

All Rights Reserved. No part of this book may be reproduced in any manner whatsoever without written permission of the publisher, except in the case of brief quotations in articles and reviews. For additional copies of this book, for information on other books, or to arrange for presentations of this material to groups, write WallBuilders, P.O. Box 397, Aledo, Texas, 76008, 817-441-6044.

Published by WallBuilder Press
P.O. Box 397
Aledo, Texas 76008
817-441-6044

Printed in the United States of America
ISBN 0-925279-18-8

Acknowledgments

While there were many special and hard-working individuals who participated in the formulation of this book, some should be individually honored. The first is my wife, Cheryl, who, while I was compiling and writing, patiently withstood months of my sixteen and eighteen hour work-days; she generously and consistently offered support and encouragement. My parents, Grady and Rose, had a significant impact in this work both by their editorial assistance and also through the habits and attitudes they instilled within me by their instruction and example. Kit Marshall spent hours—literally days—in the basements of law libraries meticulously searching through dusty storage boxes of old Court cases from across the decades in search of evidence to reveal the position of the Court on religion in government. Jeremiah Pent, for weeks on end passed entire days searching for quotes, statements, sometimes even single lines from early American documents in order to historically verify in the original documents what other historians had brought to our attention. Mike Ward was faced with the task of entering historical quotes and extensive portions of legal cases into the manuscript, as well as entering and reentering the numerous corrections and revisions made by the editors. There were numerous others involved in typing, running errands, compiling materials, editing text, etc., without whom this work might have taken years instead of months. A grateful thanks to them all!

One other group of individuals is worthy of special honor. This group includes men like Steven McDowell of the Providence Foundation, Dr. John Eidsmoe, Peter Marshall and David Manuel, Steve Dawson of the Plymouth Rock Foundation, Dr. Tim LaHaye, and many others who are faithfully presenting to the nation many of the portions of America's history which have been censored in recent years.

David Barton
Sept. 1991

Acknowledgments

Contents

Preface

This book will examine the doctrine behind the phrase "separation of church and state"—a phrase well-recognized by the citizens of the nation. Despite the fact that this phrase does not appear in our Constitution or Bill of Rights, recent studies show that up to two-thirds of the nation believe that it does.

The Courts' use of separation of church and state has enabled it to restructure significant aspects of national public affairs; activities which were part of American life for generations are now banned. Probably no other phrase used by the Courts has created such widespread and revolutionary changes in our culture.

Despite being so well recognized by the general public and so heavily utilized by the Courts, few know the origin of the phrase "separation of church and state," how it was originally applied, or even when it was introduced into contemporary American life. This book will examine that history and the evolution of that phrase.

In search of the truth about the separation of church and state, writings and statements from George Washington, John Jay, Alexander Hamilton, Benjamin Franklin, James Madison, Samuel Adams, John Adams, Roger Sherman, John Quincy Adams, Thomas Jefferson, Patrick Henry, and many other Founding Fathers will be examined. Additionally, excerpts from court rulings during the first 160 years under the Constitution also will be offered. Many of these decisions were handed down by Justices who had signed the founding documents. The rulings from these men—experts on our government—will show how the legal system originally viewed and applied the doctrine of separation of church and state.

Hundreds of court cases, beginning from as early as 1792, were researched for this book. The majority of the cases were from the United States Supreme Court, but also included are cases from State Supreme Courts, Federal Courts of Appeal, State District Courts, etc. Nearly eighty of those cases have been excerpted in this book, representing a broad and accurate view of the separation of church and state both past and present. While not every excerpt is from the Supreme Court, the excerpts used are taken from cases where final decisions had been rendered; cases where a higher court or the Supreme Court either refused to consider or refused to overturn the decision of the lower court. In other words, the quotes given represent the "final word" of the courts.

A note about the difference in usage between "Court" and "court" should be made. "Court" (capital "C") refers to the Supreme Court of the United States, whereas "court" (lower-case "c") indicates a State Supreme Court or any other court, whether federal or state. Similarly, "Courts" specifically refers to the decisions of collective U. S. Supreme Courts and "courts" refers to the judiciary in general, represented by its jurisdictions from the lowest level local courts through the Supreme Court of the United States.

In the original 1988 edition of this book, I cited from several contemporary authors (to whom I am gratefully indebted). However, in this present edition, I felt it preferable to quote original sources and primary source documents whenever possible—i.e., utilize the "best evidence." Consequently, the wordings and content of several of the quotes differ from the 1988 version and now conform to primary source documents.

Not only will the wordings in some of the quotes differ, but the spellings within those quotes will differ significantly, not only from our contemporary spellings, but also from the 1988 version. (For example, John Adams in his writings used the word "suppos" in lieu of "suppose," "accademies" instead of our customary "academies"; writings from the time of colonization often use "wisedome" rather than "wisdom," "meintayne" instead of "maintain," etc.). In an attempt to preserve historical accuracy, I chose not to "correct" the varied spellings and "incorrect" punctuation that appeared in the original works.

The bibliography and footnotes at the conclusion of this work will reflect the improvement in documentary sources; the dates of the writings will attest to the superior changes by the addition of many older and rare historical documents and writings. I believe this current edition to be much improved and to be a much more historically accurate product than the first edition (even down to the "misspellings").

Appendixes "A" and "B" at the end of this book contain a copy of the words of the Declaration of Independence and the Constitution of the United States. The reader is encouraged to read these two documents in their entirety and to refer to them when they are referenced or quoted in this book. Appendix "C" contains a complete citation list of the cases referenced in this book so that lawyers and others in the legal profession can locate these cases for their own use.

Foreword

We are a truth-conscious nation. Telling the truth is a virtue we impress on our children and a requirement we demand in our courts of law. Truth is so important that oaths are extracted from witnesses, binding them to tell the "truth, the whole truth, and nothing but the truth;" they are even threatened with criminal penalties for perjury if they do not declare the truth.

There is much to be said for knowing the truth about a subject. Truth has a very liberating effect—it brings a type of freedom. As Jesus once declared to His followers, "You will know the truth, and the truth will set you free" (John 8:32); Hosea 4:6 explains that people are destroyed for a lack of knowledge. Despite the popular axiom, ignorance is _not_ bliss! Therefore, it is important that we know the truth about the roots and foundations of this nation—we need to know what our Founders taught and what earlier courts ruled. This book will help us know and understand our national heritage.

The prophet Malachi once spoke of a "book of remembrance"—a record of those men who, in previous times, had "feared God and honored his name" (Malachi 3:16). That "book of remembrance" provided his people with three direct benefits. First, as they looked back into former years, they were able to discover and then to distinguish between right and wrong. This was important, because at their time, right and wrong were often confused and even reversed. Second, because they had read the "book of remembrance" and could now identify the difference between right and wrong, they were motivated to rise up and trample down the wrong. Third, the "book of remembrance" caused their hearts to be turned back toward their fathers.

This book is also a "book of remembrance" and can provide the same three benefits to the people of this nation. First, as people look back into the earlier years of the Supreme Court and the nation, they will understand and recognize what is right and wrong even though the two are now often reversed—what was previously unconstitutional for the Court is now its standard practice and what was previously embraced by the Court is now completely rejected by it. Second, after seeing how right and wrong have been reversed, the people may be motivated to rise up and trample down the wrong. Lastly, through this "book of remembrance," the hearts of the nation may again be turned back toward their fathers—their Founding Fathers.

~1~
The Way It Is

The First Amendment has erected a wall between church and state. That wall must be kept high and impregnable. We could not approve the slightest breach. [1]

This Supreme Court announcement from the 1947 case *Everson* v. *Board of Education* was the first occasion on which the Court declared there to be a separation of church and state in the First Amendment. Following that 1947 announcement, the Court began unraveling the fabric of American life by reversing long-standing national traditions. Notice what contemporary courts have now decreed:

☐ A verbal prayer offered in a school is unconstitutional, even if it is both voluntary and denominationally neutral. *Engel* v. *Vitale, 1962;* [2] *Abington* v. *Schempp, 1963;* [3] *Commissioner of Ed.* v. *School Committee of Leyden, 1971* [4]

☐ Freedom of speech and press is guaranteed to students unless the topic is religious, at which time such speech becomes unconstitutional. *Stein* v. *Oshinsky, 1965;* [5] *Collins* v. *Chandler Unified School Dist., 1981* [6]

☐ If a student prays over his lunch, it is unconstitutional for him to pray aloud. *Reed* v. *van Hoven, 1965* [7]

☐ It is unconstitutional for kindergarten students to recite: "We thank you for the flowers so sweet; We thank you for the food we eat; We thank you for the birds that sing; We thank you for everything." Even though the word "God" is not contained in it, someone might think it is a prayer. *DeSpain* v. *DeKalb County Community School Dist., 1967* [8]

☐ It is unconstitutional for a war memorial to be erected in the shape of a cross. *Lowe* v. *City of Eugene, 1969* [9]

☐ It is unconstitutional for students to arrive at school early to hear a student volunteer read prayers which had been offered by the chaplains in the chambers of the United States House of Representatives and Senate, even though those prayers are contained in the public *Congressional Record* published by the U.S. Government. *State Board of Educ.* v. *Board of Educ. of Netcong, 1970* [10]

- [ ] It is unconstitutional for a Board of Education to use or refer to the word "God" in any of its official writings. *State of Ohio* v. *Whisner, 1976* [11]

- [ ] It is unconstitutional for a kindergarten class to ask during a school assembly whose birthday is celebrated by Christmas. *Florey* v. *Sioux Falls School Dist., 1979* [12]

- [ ] It is unconstitutional for the Ten Commandments to hang on the walls of a classroom since the students might be lead to read them, meditate upon them, respect them, or obey them. *Stone* v. *Graham, 1980;* [13] *Ring* v. *Grand Forks Public School Dist., 1980;* [14] *Lanner* v. *Wimmer, 1981* [15]

- [ ] A bill becomes unconstitutional, even though the wording may be constitutionally acceptable, if the legislator who introduced the bill had a religious activity in his mind when he authored it. *Wallace* v. *Jaffree, 1985* [16]

- [ ] It is unconstitutional for a kindergarten class to recite: "God is great, God is good, let us thank Him for our food." *Wallace* v. *Jaffree, 1985* [17]

- [ ] It is unconstitutional for a school graduation ceremony to contain an opening or closing prayer. *Graham* v. *Central Community School Dist., 1985;* [18] *Kay* v. *Douglas School Dist., 1986* [19]

Numerous other judgments have proceeded from these types of court rulings:

> In the Alaska public schools [in 1987], students were told that they could not use the word "Christmas" in school because it had the word "Christ" in it. They were told that they could not have the word in their notebooks, or exchange Christmas cards or presents, or display anything with the word "Christmas" on it. In Virginia, a federal court has ruled that a homosexual newspaper may be distributed on a high school campus, but religious newspapers may not. [20]

> Recently public schools were barred from showing a film about the settlement of Jamestown, because the film depicted the erection of a cross at the settlement [despite the fact that] . . . according to historical facts, a cross *was* erected at the Jamestown settlement. [21]

This year [1987], a 185-year-old symbol of a Nevada city had to be changed because of its "religious significance" . . . [and] a fire station was forced to remove a cross, a Christian symbol in remembrance of a fellow fireman who lost his life in the line of duty. [22]

In December 1988, an elementary school principal in Denver removed the Bible from the school library and an elementary school music teacher in Colorado Springs stopped teaching Christmas carols because of alleged violations of the separation of church and state. [23]

In Omaha, Nebraska, 10-year-old James Gierke was prohibited from reading his Bible silently during free time . . . the boy was forbidden by his teacher to open his Bible at school and was told doing so was against the law. [24]

Why were these activities never declared unconstitutional prior to 1947? The Constitution is still the same; yet, somehow, its meaning now appears to be different! This is because the 1947 *Everson* Court used an unprecedented legal maneuver; a maneuver no previous Court had ever dared to make. This Court took the Fourteenth Amendment as a tool to apply the First Amendment *against* the states. Never before had the Fourteenth Amendment been used to forbid religious practices from the public affairs and public institutions of the individual states. This action by the 1947 Court was without precedent.

The Fourteenth Amendment was ratified in 1868 to guarantee that recently emancipated slaves would have civil rights in all states. It is a strange interpretation that takes an Amendment providing citizenship to former slaves and uses it to prohibit religious activity in the schools or public affairs of any state. It is no surprise that previous Courts had never applied the Fourteenth Amendment as the 1947 Court had done!

In *Walz* v. *Tax Commission, 1970,* the Court, in reviewing its use of the Fourteenth Amendment, admitted that by using the Amendment in such a manner, it had created an American revolution. The Court stated that this revolution:

Involved the imposition of new and far-reaching constitutional restraints on the States. Nationalization of many civil liberties has been the consequence of the Fourteenth Amendment, reversing the historic position that the foundations of those liberties rested largely in state law. . . . And so the revolution occasioned by the Fourteenth Amendment has progressed as Article after Article in the Bill of Rights has been incorporated in it and made applicable to the States. [25]

The Court has now given titles to the two religious portions of the First Amendment. The first portion, which it says contains the separation of church and state, it calls "The Establishment Clause." The second portion it entitles "The Free Exercise Clause." The Court purports the doctrine of separation to be a great American belief, present since the nation's birth. However, in *Walz* v. *Tax Commission, 1970,* the Court conceded that the separation doctrine is of recent origin, having been introduced into widespread legal use only through the revolution spawned by the Court's unprecedented use of the Fourteenth Amendment:

> The Establishment Clause [of the First Amendment] was not incorporated in the Fourteenth Amendment until *Everson* v. *Board of Education* was decided in 1947. . . . The meaning of the Establishment Clause and the Free Exercise Clause [has been] made applicable to the States for only a few decades at best. [26]

Although the Court announced its doctrine of separation in 1947, it was 15 years before it was applied widely in the Court's decisions, as evidenced by this statement from *Walz* v. *Tax Commission, 1970:*

> It was, for example, not until 1962 that . . . prayers were held to violate the Establishment Clause. [27]

That 1962 case *(Engel* v. *Vitale)* which declared voluntary non-denominational prayer in schools to be unconstitutional, was the first sweeping prohibition ever made by the Court in terms of separating religion from education. Notice this comment on that case from the *World Book Encyclopedia 1963 Yearbook:*

> The significance of the decision regarding this [school] prayer was enormous, for the whole thorny problem of religion in public education was thus inevitably raised. [28]

Even though the doctrine of separation had first been introduced in 1947, it had never been "raised" as an issue affecting education until the 1962 decision!

Following its initial 1947 announcement, the Court moved slowly and cautiously. In 1948 in *McCollum* v. *Board of Education* the Court did restrict some religious classes in public schools. However, it then desisted from any further restrictions on religious principles for the next 14 years, until it announced all-out and widespread war against religious principles in its 1962 *Engel* v. *Vitale* decision which first prohibited prayer in schools.

Imagine! Prior to 1962, there had been over 340 years of recorded history in this country concerning schools—170 of those years had occurred under the First Amendment of the Constitution! What schools and students were doing through those years had *never* been ruled unconstitutional!

The First Amendment, which the Court now uses to prohibit religious activities in public, simply states in reference to religion that:

> Congress shall make no law respecting an establishment of religion or prohibiting the free exercise thereof . . .

Neither the phrase "separation of church and state" nor the words "church" or "separation" are contained therein. The public's understanding (actually, misunderstanding) of this Amendment has been molded by the Court's oft-repeated usage of the phrase "separation of church and state."

Only 11 years after their 1947 announcement, the Court had already said so much so often about separation of church and state that it appeared some judges were already tired of hearing the phrase, as evidenced by this comment in *Baer* v. *Kolmorgen, 1958:*

> Much has been written in recent years concerning Thomas Jefferson's reference in 1802 to "a wall of separation between church and State." . . . Jefferson's figure of speech has received so much attention that one would almost think at times that it is to be found somewhere in our Constitution. [29]

Were there no controversies over religion before 1947? Is the Court's current use of the separation doctrine finally correcting a constitutional violation that should have been corrected decades earlier? Or did previous Courts rule differently on the same issues?

These questions can be answered by examining Supreme Court records from earlier years and comparing them with current Court decisions. The Framers of the Constitution also had much to say about the proper relationship between church and state. Their writings and statements will be examined as well as numerous Court decisions, some dating from as early as 1795. It can be easily determined if the application of the First Amendment by current courts is proper by using the standards applied by the Constitution's Framers.

It is important to know the intent of the Framers concerning the First Amendment. They had specific reasons for their decisions and intent. Only by following the plan upon which our government was founded can we hope to attain the results our Founders intended for us to enjoy. As President Woodrow Wilson stated:

> A nation which does not remember what it was yesterday, does not know what it is today, nor what it is trying to do. We are trying to do a futile thing if we do not know where we came from or what we have been about. [30]

It is significant that the 1947 *Everson* case, which introduced the phrase "separation of church and state," had to do with education. In fact, ten of the twelve case excerpts mentioned at the beginning of this chapter involved education. Education has become so important to the Court that the Court felt it worthwhile to review phrases that five-year-olds recite at school *(Wallace v. Jaffree, 1984).* [31] It is not by accident that education has become the focus of the separation of church and state. Abraham Lincoln expressed the principle so well understood by the current Court when he declared:

> The philosophy of the school room in one generation will be the philosophy of government in the next. [32]

In recent years, numerous cases similar to *Trietley v. Board of Ed., 1978,* [33] and *Brandon v. Board of Ed., 1980,* [34] have occurred. In the *Trietley* case, students were forbidden to form, on their own initiative, Bible clubs of voluntary membership in public high schools. In the *Brandon* case, members of a group called "Students for Voluntary Prayer" were prohibited from arriving early for prayer before the beginning of the school day. From the courts' rulings in these types of cases, it became obvious that there was no way, form, or fashion in which the courts were going to allow the First Amendment's latter statement on religion (. . . nor prohibit the free exercise thereof . . .) to occur in schools or public affairs, no matter how voluntary the activity, how widely supported it was by the community, nor how non-denominational it might be.

Such unilateral and consistent prohibitions by the courts caused public outcries. It was argued that if students *wanted* to participate voluntarily in prayer or Bible reading before school, they should be allowed to do so. After all, schools permitted rodeo clubs, homemaking clubs, journalism clubs, athletic clubs, and other types of clubs to meet before and after school. Why couldn't students form their own Bible clubs? Observers noted an obvious dichotomy in the court decisions:

> In many schools, baccalaureate or commencement speakers are free to expound on an endless variety of ideas, but are sometimes barred from speaking about religious subjects. In other schools teachers are free to use occult symbols such as witches and goblins at Halloween, but are prohibited from using Christian symbols at Christmas. Students are taught evolution but are not allowed to hear the evidence for special creation . . . teachers are free to force unwilling students to read semi-pornographic books but are sometimes prevented from sharing books about Jesus Christ. Taxpayer-funded student newspapers publish all sorts of materials, even if they contain foul language or anti-religious messages, but have been stopped from printing pro-religious material . . . The religious person has *less* freedom than the secular-minded person to publicly discuss and promulgate ideas that are important to him. [35]

Even to casual, disinterested observers, this was obvious religious discrimination by the courts. Following nationwide criticism of such inequities, Congress acted to guarantee to religious groups the same access to school facilities that was extended to others. The result was the passing of the Equal Access Bill of 1984. In an address delivered in December of 1984, President Reagan described the enactment of that bill:

> In 1962, the Supreme Court in the New York prayer case banned the . . . saying of prayers. In 1963, the Court banned the reading of the Bible in our public schools. From that point on, the courts pushed the meaning of the ruling ever outward, so that now our children are not allowed voluntary prayer. We even had to pass a law—pass a special law in the Congress just a few weeks ago—to allow student prayer groups the same access to school rooms after classes that a

Young Marxist Society, for example, would already enjoy with no opposition. [36]

With the Equal Access Bill thus providing a legitimate legal basis, student groups began to petition their schools for the right to use rooms before or after school. To their surprise, many of their requests were denied, despite the new law. Unable to reach agreements with their schools, several students pursued their desire to pray and have Bible clubs in school through legal challenges based on this new law.

Cases were filed against school districts, requesting the courts to instruct the schools to allow the access that had been provided through the Equal Access Law. In 1987, the *Harvard Journal on Legislation* reviewed the progress of the Equal Access Act through the courts. Were the courts willing to allow all students to have equal access?

All four courts of appeals which have ruled on the issue have held that granting equal access violates the Establishment Clause [of the First Amendment]. [37]

Although at the time of the 1987 review, no cases had yet reached the Supreme Court, the lower courts, in an insult to the form of government established by the Constitution, had refused to rule in favor of the students under the new law. The score to that point? According to information from the *Harvard Journal on Legislation*, it remained: the courts—12, students wanting to use a classroom—0. It was not until the *Westside* v. *Mergens* case [38] in 1990 that the Supreme Court held that Christian students did indeed have equal rights and deserved equal access to school activities and facilities.

Court rulings under the separation doctrine have even caused a censoring of history and social studies textbooks. Dr. Paul C. Vitz, conducting a study through the Department of Education, scrutinized the nation's most commonly used history and social studies books in all grade levels to see how they had dealt with religious events in history. One would expect there to be no deviation from factual written history. Even the Court, in the first two cases in which the separation doctrine was used to overturn long-standing school policies, had declared:

Religion has been closely identified with our history and government," *Abington School District, 1963,* and that "[t]he history of man is inseparable from the history of religion." *Engel* v. *Vitale, 1962* (quoted from *Stone* v. *Graham, 1980).* [39]

With even the Supreme Court acknowledging that American history is inseparable from religion, what did Dr. Vitz discover?

In the first part of the project a total of sixty representative social studies textbooks were carefully evaluated. . . . [n]one of the books . . . contain one word referring to any religious activity in contemporary American life. [40]

Not one of the . . . ten thousand pages had one *text* reference to a primary religious activity occurring in representative contemporary American life. [41]

An excellent illustration of the censorship of textbooks was provided through Vitz's description of an incident between the author of a short story and the textbook publisher who wanted to reprint it:

The issue centered on a children's story of hers [Barbara Cohen's] called "Molly's Pilgrim." . . . A major textbook publisher (Harcourt Brace Jovanovich) wanted to reprint part of the story for their third grade reader. But like most such stories, the publishers wanted to shorten it greatly and to rewrite parts to make it more acceptable. They phoned Ms. Cohen and asked for her permission to reprint their modified version. But her story wasn't just modified, it was maimed. . . . So Barbara Cohen refused to give them permission. They called back dismayed and tried to convince her to let them go ahead with the heavily censored version. They argued, "Try to understand. We have a lot of problems. If we mention God, some atheist will object. If we mention the Bible, someone will want to know why we don't give equal time to the Koran. Every time that happens, we lose sales." "But the Pilgrims did read the Bible," Barbara Cohen answered. "Yes, you know that and we know that, but we can't have anything in it that people object to," was the reply! . . . God and the Bible were "eternally unacceptable" and they had to go. The publisher claimed, "We'll get into terrible trouble if we mentioned the Bible." [42]

Textbooks form the basis for what students learn about the history of the nation. It is important that texts reflect historically accurate information. The story mentioned above dealt with Pilgrims—the Pilgrims *were* a religious group. The Mayflower Compact that they signed before they landed, and their history recorded in *Of Plymouth Plantation,* both affirm that the Pilgrims maintained a predominantly Christian focus in their activities. These facts about the Pilgrims are history, not religion! There is no reason to exclude this information from textbooks. Dr. Vitz revealed how important textbook content is for students:

> It is common in these books to treat Thanksgiving without explaining to whom the Pilgrims gave thanks . . . the Pilgrims are described *entirely* without any reference to religion; thus at the end of their first year they "wanted to give thanks for all they had" so they had the first Thanksgiving. But no mention is made of the fact that it was God they were thanking. . . . One mother wrote me that her first grade son was told by his teacher that at Thanksgiving the Pilgrims gave thanks to the Indians! When she complained to the principal that Thanksgiving was a feast to thank God . . . *the principal said that "they could only teach what was contained in the history books."* [43] (emphasis added)

While education has obviously been a target of the Supreme Court, other areas have not been exempt. President Reagan made an interesting observation on the repercussions of the widespread application of the separation doctrine to public policy:

> The 1962 decision opened the way to a flood of similar suits. Once religion had been made vulnerable, a series of assaults were made in one court after another, on one issue after another. Cases were started to argue against tax-exempt status for churches. Suits were brought to abolish the words "Under God" from the Pledge of Allegiance, and to remove "In God We Trust" from public documents and from our currency. [44]

The courts have restructured the traditions and habits that had formed part of American life since our nation's founding by their use of the First Amendment. Has the First Amendment always been understood as it is now? What is its history? When and how was it written, and under what circumstances?

~2~
The Way It Was—
Building the Constitution and
the First Amendment

The First Amendment has become the center of a controversy focusing on what the Supreme Court claims to be the intent—though not the wording—of the First Amendment: the "separation of church and state." The Court has used this interpretation of the First Amendment to restructure many of the traditions and habits which had long formed the fabric of American life. Since this Amendment is at the center of the controversy, it would be wise to review its history. When and how was it written, and under what circumstances?

Detailed records answering these questions have been carefully preserved. These accounts, revealing the proceedings surrounding the construction and wording of this Amendment, were officially recorded both by the individuals and by the Congress responsible for its framing.

Before considering the construction of the First Amendment, the process by which the Constitution itself was constructed should be noted. Those who attended the Constitutional Convention in Philadelphia in 1787 comprised a first-class team of statesmen, patriots, and thinkers. Professor Bradford, in his book *A Worthy Company*, provides an insightful mini-biography of each of the participants of the original Constitutional Convention. These biographies detail not only their distinguished political careers, but also the highlights of their private and educational backgrounds. Bradford described the public experience of the collective group with these words:

> There was no anomaly in the selection of this particular group to serve as delegates in Philadelphia. Thirty-six of the fifty-five had been members of the Continental Congress. Most of them had been or were to be called upon repeatedly by their neighbors and peers to fill other offices of trust. Twenty were at one time governors of states; twenty were United States Senators. Eight were Federal judges and thirteen were members of the United States House of Representatives. Washington and Madison were President of the United States, and Elbridge Gerry Vice-President. Several

served as diplomats in representing the Republic overseas. Others held cabinet posts. Their total political experience at the state and national level is so great as to suggest that as a company they are a dependable barometer of American attitudes and beliefs at the close of the eighteenth century. [1]

Until the time of the Constitutional Convention, the states had never actually functioned as a nation in the true sense of the word; they had always been individual states. Although joined together in a singular purpose for the Revolutionary War, they had not been required to relinquish any rights as individual states. The states were more like a confederation of several small, independent, neighboring nations on the same continent than a single, unified nation.

The states' first attempts at national government (the Articles of Association, followed by the Articles of Confederation) reflected their lack of commitment to any centralization of power that might divest them of their own rights.   The words "association" and "confederation" accurately described the states' relationship to the central government—a loose-knit voluntary alliance under a non-binding agreement.

Each of these forms of government had placed severe limitations on the central government. Decisions were not based on majority votes of the member states; votes had to be unanimous. A single state could block the action of the entire central government. It was difficult for the government to accomplish much, but the restrictions accurately portrayed the strength of the states' resolve concerning their own rights and sovereignty.

It was against this background that delegates were selected and sent to the Constitutional Convention. As a result of the War, the states recognized the need for a central government to perform functions they individually were not able to perform: for example, national defense. Although they remained individual states, they had become, by reason of common belief and common geography, united states (however, the emphasis was still more on the "states" than on the "united"). These delegates were intensely committed both to states' rights and to forming a workable national government. The difficulty facing them was to create a form of government to which the states would be committed, but which would not threaten their sovereignty.

There was obviously a sense of profound purpose as the states contemplated whom they would send to represent them in their effort to form a better national government. The men chosen as delegates were not random selections. There were clearly written laws within each state prescribing the qualifications of those who would serve in public affairs. Every delegate who attended the Constitutional Convention did so in a legal manner—he fulfilled the requirements mandated by his own state's constitution.

These written constitutional qualifications for holding public office were not obscure statements that had been developed decades earlier and were now lost to public awareness. Most of the state constitutions were less than a decade old; in many cases, those who went as delegates to the Convention had participated in the writing of their own state's constitution. Therefore, they were not only cognizant of the stipulations for public office in their states, but in several instances they had helped to formulate them—they were intimately aware of these requirements. What were some of the requirements? Consider those found in the constitution of Delaware:

> Article 22. Every person, who shall be chosen a member of either house, or appointed to any office or place of trust . . . shall . . . make and subscribe the following declaration, to wit: "I, _____, do profess faith in God the Father, and in Jesus Christ, His only Son, and in the Holy Ghost, one God, blessed for evermore; and I do acknowledge the holy scriptures of the Old and New Testament to be given by divine inspiration." [2]

These qualifications were not denominational qualifications [i.e., he must be a Baptist, a Lutheran, a Congregationalist, etc.]—they were simply general Christian qualifications, beliefs common to any orthodox Christian denomination. The delegates sent from Delaware to the Constitutional Convention had fulfilled these requirements. Notice the diversity of denominations from which they came: John Dickinson (Quaker/Episcopalian), George Read (Episcopalian), Richard Bassett (Methodist), Gunning Bedford (Presbyterian), and Jacob Broom (Lutheran). [3]

The Pennsylvania constitution contained similar requirements:

> Frame of Government, Section 10. And each member [of the legislature] before he takes his seat, shall make and subscribe the following declaration, viz: "I do believe in one God, the creator and governour of the universe, the rewarder of the good and the punisher of the wicked, and I do acknowledge the scriptures of the Old and New Testament to be given by divine inspiration." [4]

Again, the qualifications included any who embraced the tenets of general Christianity. The Pennsylvania delegates also represented many denominations: Benjamin Franklin (Deist), Robert Morris (Episcopalian), James Wilson (Episcopalian/Deist), Gouverneur Morris (Episcopalian), Thomas Mifflin (Quaker/Lutheran), George Clymer (Quaker/Episcopalian), Thomas FitzSimmons (Roman Catholic), and Jared Ingersoll (Presbyterian). [5]   Each of these delegates had fulfilled the state's requirements and was eligible to serve his state at the Convention.

Notice the similar requirements in the Massachusetts constitution:

> Chapter VI, Article I. [All persons elected to State office or to the Legislature must] make and subscribe the following declaration, viz. "I, _____, do declare, that I believe the Christian religion, and have firm persuasion of its truth." [6]

And the North Carolina provisions:

> Article XXXII. No person, who shall deny the being of God, or the truth of the Protestant religion, or the divine authority either of the Old or New Testaments, or who shall hold religious principles incompatible with the freedom and safety of the state, shall be capable of holding any office, or place of trust or profit in the civil department, within this state. [7]

And those of Maryland:

> Article XXXV. That no other test or qualification ought to be required . . . than such oath of support and fidelity to this state . . . and a declaration of a belief in the christian religion. [8]

Similar requirements from the other states' constitutions could also be noted. It becomes obvious that the delegates were not selected merely because they were good politicians; they were selected because they were good *Christian* politicians. Considering what was required for service in public office, it would be unreasonable to imagine that these men went to the Constitutional Convention with the design of separating church and state. After all, the delegates had not only voluntarily subscribed themselves to their state's stipulations, many of them had helped write the requirements. This group of statesmen and delegates was far from being religiously inactive:

> With no more than five exceptions (and perhaps no more than three), they were orthodox members of one of the estab-

lished Christian communions: approximately twenty-nine Anglicans, sixteen to eighteen Calvinists, two Methodists, two Lutherans, two Roman Catholics, one lapsed Quaker and sometime Anglican, and one open Deist—Dr. Franklin, who attended every kind of Christian worship, called for public prayer, and contributed to all denominations. [9]

The requirements for public service and the strong Christian commitment of those who attended the Convention were common knowledge to the people of that day, as well as to historians for the next 150 years. It has only been since the middle of this century that history books have ceased to carry any mention of the faith of our Founders. Nonetheless, this was such common knowledge during the Constitutional founding era, that statements like the following from Patrick Henry summarize what was already well known:

> It cannot be emphasized too strongly or too often that this great nation was founded, not by religionists, but by Christians, not on religions but on the gospel of Jesus Christ! For this very reason peoples of other faiths have been afforded asylum, prosperity, and freedom of worship here. [10]

While the Convention did produce a document that successfully created a new federal government, it ended on a divisive tone. Some prominent delegates refused to sign the new document because they strongly felt that not enough protection had been given to the rights of individuals or states. They feared that unless specific stipulations were placed on what the federal government could *not* do, it might give itself more and more unlimited power and swallow-up the rights of individuals and states.

Those who did sign felt that the power of the states was so obvious that it would be impossible for the federal government to usurp it. They further argued that if they began to list the specific rights retained by the states, they might inadvertently omit some, and thus they would not be protected. Despite this conflict, most of the delegates did sign the Constitution. It was then sent to the states for ratification.

The ratifying process among the states uncovered the same opposition that had been raised at the Convention. Massachusetts, South Carolina, New Hampshire, Virginia, and New York gave conditional approval to the Constitution, stipulating that some type of limitations be added to protect the states and citizens from the unlimited power that might someday be assumed by a central government. North Carolina flatly refused to ratify it until some express restrictions were included.

George Washington, in his inaugural address, urged Congress to move quickly to form some type of declaration of the rights of states and individuals to be added to the Constitution. James Madison, at that time a member of the U.S. House of Representatives, submitted nine articles to the Congress that expressed protection for fundamental rights. Madison's articles were passed on to the Committee of Eleven, a select committee in the House that included one member from each of the eleven states. The committee reviewed his nine articles and referred them to the House for full consideration. In the House, additions were made that resulted in seventeen total articles. Those seventeen were passed to the Senate which, after consideration, reduced the number to twelve.

A conference committee of the two houses convened to work out the differences in the two lists. James Madison led the House delegation and Oliver Ellsworth the Senate delegation. This committee agreed on final wording for twelve amendments and returned them to the full Congress for final approval. These twelve were first accepted by the House on September 24, 1789, and then by the Senate on September 25, 1789. They were then submitted to the states for ratification.

Of the twelve proposed amendments, the states approved only ten. On December 15, 1791, Virginia became the last state to ratify them. These ten articles were added as Amendments to the Constitution and are now known as the Bill of Rights—*a declaration of what the federal government could not do!* Thus, Congress had provided for the states the promise of state sovereignty and individual protection in at least ten specific Amendments.

The states had already stipulated that Christians were the ones who would serve in public office, and the federal Constitution had made no change in that. Had the federal Constitution made any attempt to violate or reverse the provisions of the states' constitutions, it would have been defeated by the delegates or rejected by the states.

The historical records of the drafting of the First Amendment show a strong reliance by the delegates on provisions from their own state constitutions. Notice the various proposals that led to the final House version of the First Amendment:

JUNE 8 [1789]. Initial proposals of James Madison. "The civil rights of none shall be abridged on account of religious belief or worship, nor shall any national religion be established, nor shall the full and equal rights of conscience be in any manner, or on any pretext infringed." [11]

AUGUST 15. House Select Committee. "No religion shall be established by law, nor shall the equal rights of conscience be infringed." Full day of debate with many alterations and additions, with some question, still, whether any such amendment was necessary. Following the suggestion of his own state's ratifying convention, Samuel Livermore of New Hampshire proposed: "Congress shall make no laws touching religion, or infringing the rights of conscience." [12]

AUGUST 20. Fisher Ames of Massachusetts moved that the following language be adopted by the House, and it was agreed: "Congress shall make no law establishing religion, or to prevent the free exercise thereof, or to infringe the rights of conscience." [13]

This last version was sent to the Senate, which began its own work on the wording: [14]

SEPTEMBER 3. Several versions proposed in quick succession.
"Congress shall not make any law infringing the rights of conscience, or establishing any religious sect or society."
"Congress shall make no law establishing any particular denomination of religion in preference to another, or prohibiting the free exercise thereof, nor shall the rights of conscience be infringed."
"Congress shall make no law establishing one religious society in preference to others, or to infringe on the rights of conscience."
Passed at the end of the day: "Congress shall make no law establishing religion, or prohibiting the free exercise thereof."
SEPTEMBER 9. "Congress shall make no law establishing articles of faith or a mode of worship, or prohibiting the free exercise of religion."

This version was sent back to the House where a Conference Committee convened to eliminate the differences in wording. This committee agreed that the final wording should be:

"Congress shall make no law respecting an establishment of religion, or prohibiting the free exercise thereof."

It was then returned to the full House and Senate, where it was approved as recommended by the Conference Committee. [15]

As evident from these records, the word "religion" was used interchangeably with "religious sect," "religious society," and "particular denomination." Today we would best understand the actual context of the First Amendment by saying, "Congress shall make no law establishing one Christian denomination as the national denomination."

Today when the First Amendment is discussed, there seems to be a general consensus that it was something unique and original for the time—a very progressive act by the members of Congress. This was not the case; recall the House records from August 15:

> AUGUST 15. Full day of debate with many alterations and additions, with some question, still, whether any such amendment was necessary. *Following the suggestion of his own state's ratifying convention,* Samuel Livermore of New Hampshire proposed: "Congress shall make no laws touching religion, or infringing the rights of conscience." [16]

The members of Congress relied on the precedent established in the wording of their own state's constitution when composing the First Amendment. The following excerpts from state constitutions not only reveal wording very similar to that proposed and used by Congress, but also the spirit behind the First Amendment:

> MASSACHUSETTS, 1780. Part I, Article II. It is the right, as well as the duty, of all men in society, publicly, and at stated seasons, to worship the Supreme Being, the Great Creator and Preserver of the Universe. And no subject shall be hurt, molested, or restrained, in his person, liberty, or estate, for worshiping God in the manner and season, most agreable to the dictates of his own conscience.
>
> Article III. *And every denomination of Christians demeaning themselves peaceably, and as good subjects of the commonwealth, shall be equally under the protection of the law: And no subordination of any one sect or denomination to another, shall ever be established by law.* [17] (emphasis added)

NEW HAMPSHIRE, 1783, 1792. Part One, Article I, Section V. Every individual has a natural and unalienable right to worship God according to the dictates of his own conscience, and reason . . .

Article I, Section VI. *And every denomination of Christians demeaning themselves quietly, and as good subjects of the state, shall be equally under the protection of the law: And no subordination of any one sect or denomination to another, shall ever be established by law.* [18] (emphasis added)

SOUTH CAROLINA, 1778. Article XXXVIII. That all persons and religious societies, who acknowledge that there is one God, and a future state of rewards and punishments, and that God is publicly to be worshipped, shall be freely tolerated. . . . *That all denominations of Christian[s]. . . in this State, demeaning themselves peaceably and faithfully, shall enjoy equal religious and civil privileges.* [19] (emphasis added)

There are similar provisions in the other state constitutions, but these are sufficient to show the primary intent of the First Amendment. The states themselves did not allow one denomination of Christianity to be the official denomination; it is certain they would not allow the federal government to do something they prohibited.

The intent of the First Amendment was not to separate Christianity and state—had that been the intent, it would never have been ratified. Even when the state constitutions stated that their citizens had a right to worship God according to their conscience, a statement immediately followed stipulating that it be within Christian standards. In other words, as long as someone was pursuing some form of orthodox Christianity, he was protected in his freedom of worship and conscience. The constitutions did not guarantee that freedom outside of traditional Christianity.

In today's application of the First Amendment, the Court states that since the First Amendment declares "Congress shall make no law respecting an establishment of religion . . . " that any group maintaining any type of religious belief, whether Christian or non-Christian, is protected under the First Amendment. Even atheism and secular humanism have been declared religions by the Court, and are therefore entitled (so says the Court), to the protection of the First Amendment. But how can atheism be a religion? According to the courts, the religious practice of atheists is the practice of *no* religious practice. That is, atheists religiously believe that there is no God and no religious duty; therefore, since they "religiously" believe these things, they are a "religion" and are entitled to constitutional protection. The legal usage of the word "religion" has now become so broad that the Court demands that atheism and secular humanism be co-equal with Christianity.

Such an interpretation defies the spirit and intent underlying the First Amendment. Additional evidence that the First Amendment did not provide protection to atheism or secular humanism is provided by the meaning of the word "religion." The original Webster's 1828 dictionary provides an insight into the meaning of the word as used in the First Amendment:

> RELIGION. Includes a belief in the being and perfections of God, in the revelation of his will to man, and in man's obligation to obey his commands, in a state of reward and punishment, and in man's accountableness to God; and also true godliness or piety of life, with the practice of all moral duties . . . the practice of moral duties without a belief in a divine lawgiver, and without reference to his will or commands, is not religion. [20]

This is the definition of religion that was commonly understood and used during the time the Constitution was being written. Notice the requirements to be a religion and to receive the protection of the First Amendment:

(1) Belief in the being and perfections of God;
(2) Belief in His revealed will to man;
(3) Belief in man's obligation to obey God's commands;
(4) Belief in accountability to God, with rewards and punishments;
(5) Belief in godliness, piety of life, and practice of moral duties.

Whatever is not a religion is not protected:

> The practice of moral duties without a belief in a divine lawgiver and without reference to his will or his commands *is not religion.* [21]

Neither atheism, secular humanism, nor other groups who have been granted the status of "religion" by the courts qualify for protection under the First Amendment. Further reinforcement that this was the common application of the word comes from Congressional investigations that occurred in the mid 1850's:

In the Senate of the United States, January 19, 1853, Mr. Badger made the following report . . . :—

The [First Amendment] clause speaks of "an establishment of religion." What is meant by that expression? It referred, without doubt, to that establishment which existed in the mother-country . . . endowment at the public expense, peculiar privileges to its members, or disadvantages or penalties upon those who should reject its doctrines or belong to other communions,—such law would be a "law respecting an establishment of religion". . . . They intended, by this amendment, to prohibit "an establishment of religion" such as the English Church presented, or any thing like it. But they had no fear or jealousy of religion itself, nor did they wish to see us an irreligious people . . . they did not intend to spread over all the public authorities and the whole public action of the nation the dead and revolting spectacle of atheistic apathy. Not so had the battles of the Revolution been fought and the deliberations of the Revolutionary Congress been conducted. [22]

March 27, 1854.   Mr. Meacham, from the [House] Committee on the Judiciary, made the following report:

What is an establishment of religion? It must have a creed, defining what a man must believe; it must have rites and ordinances, which believers must observe; it must have ministers of defined qualifications, to teach the doctrines and administer the rites; it must have tests for the submissive and penalties for the non-conformist. There never was an established religion without all these . . .

Had the people, during the Revolution, had a suspicion of any attempt to war against Christianity, that Revolution would have been strangled in its cradle. At the time of the adoption of the Constitution and the amendments, the universal sentiment was that Christianity should be encouraged, not any one sect [denomination]. Any attempt to level and discard all religion would have been viewed with universal indignation. [23]

The Founders understood that allowing and encouraging religious practice was not the same as establishing a religion. Because a man prayed, or an individual read the Scriptures, that did not establish a religion. An establishment of religion required the ingredients delineated in the reports: a defined creed, ordinances which believers must observe, official ministers to teach these doctrines, and penalties for those who do not conform. As the report said, "there never was an established religion without all these."

Yet today, the Court has ruled that allowing voluntary prayer establishes a national religion; allowing a manger scene to be viewed at Christmas establishes a national religion; allowing students to pray aloud over their lunch establishes a national religion; permitting them to read the Ten Commandments establishes a national religion; etc. This viewpoint holds that religious exercise is equal to establishing a national religion and thus is used to prevent any form of Christian activity.

This stand is exactly opposite to those taken by the first Supreme Court Justices, many of whom were members of the Constitutional Convention and of the state ratifying conventions. The following comments concerning the intent of the First Amendment are from Justice Joseph Story (appointed by James Madison—surely an ample endorsement of Story's Constitutional understanding):

> We are not to attribute this prohibition of a national religious establishment to an indifference to religion in general, and especially to Christianity (which none could hold in more reverence, than the framers of the Constitution). . . . Probably, at the time of the adoption of the Constitution, and of the amendment to it, now under consideration [the First Amendment], the general, if not the universal, sentiment in America was, that Christianity ought to receive encouragement from the State . . . . An attempt to level all religions, and to make it a matter of state policy to hold all in utter indifference, would have created universal disapprobation, if not universal indignation. [24]

Similar comments from several more Supreme Court Justices appointed by George Washington, John Adams, James Madison, etc., are presented in Chapter 4.

Another interesting comment on the widespread support of general Christianity in America's politics comes from Alexis de Tocqueville, a French historian who traveled extensively in America:

> The Americans combine the notions of Christianity and of liberty so intimately in their minds, that it is impossible to make them conceive the one without the other. [25]

In the United States, if a political character attacks a sect [denomination], this may not prevent even the partisans of that very sect, from supporting him; but if he attacks all the sects together [Christianity], every one abandons him and he remains alone. [26]

The consensus of recorded history requires that the Constitution and the First Amendment be interpreted within the understanding of Christianity. However, Article VI of the Constitution states:

No religious test shall ever be required as a qualification to any office or public trust under the United States.

Does Christianity then become a religious test of the type prohibited by Article VI of the Constitution? Our current understanding of what constitutes a religious test was considerably different from that of early Americans, as demonstrated by this excerpt from the 1796 Tennessee constitution:

Article VIII, Section II. No person who denies *the being of God, or a future state of rewards and punishments,* shall hold any office in the civil department of this State.
Article XI, Section IV. That no religious test shall ever be required as a qualification to any office or public trust under this state. [27]

A fixed set of religious beliefs for an office holder is prescribed in Article VIII, and then a religious test is prohibited in Article XI. Obviously, in their view, requiring a belief in God and in future rewards and punishments was *not* a religious test.

Currently, a religious test is perceived as something as simple as "Are you a Christian or an atheist?" This was not the question for our Founders. Prescribing a requirement professing "I, _____, do profess faith in God the Father, and in Jesus Christ, His only Son, and in the Holy Ghost, one God, blessed for evermore; and I do acknowledge the holy scriptures of the Old and New Testament to be given by divine inspiration [DELAWARE, 1776]" [28] was not considered a religious test. It was simply a qualification for office—a civil requirement. An unacceptable religious test to our Founders would be what we would now call a denominational test: "You must be an Anglican (Baptist, Presbyterian, Methodist, etc.) to hold office." A religious test did not pertain to Christian beliefs, but to specific denominational memberships. The fact that espousing Christianity was not considered an unconstitutional religious test is further illustrated by provisions from other state constitutions:

> MARYLAND, 1776. Article XXXV. That no other test or qualification ought to be required . . . than such oath of support and fidelity to this state . . . and a declaration of a belief in the Christian religion. [29]

> VERMONT, 1786. Frame of Government, Section 9. And each member [of the legislature], before he takes his seat, shall make and subscribe the following declaration, viz: "I do believe in one God, the Creator and Governor of the universe, the rewarder of the good and punisher of the wicked. And I do acknowledge the scriptures of the old and new testament to be given by divine inspiration, and own and profess the [Christian] religion."

> And no further or other religious test shall ever, hereafter, be required of any civil officer or magistrate in this State. [30]

Every individual was protected in his right to worship God according to his own conscience unless his mode of worship directly threatened the state, led to licentiousness, or caused physical injury to another. However, despite the fact that there was religious tolerance for individual citizens, there was a minimum belief that a *political* candidate must hold. The Founders were well aware that there were atheists and agnostics in that day; but they, or any individual with unorthodox Christian beliefs (relating to the inspiration of the Old and New Testaments, future rewards and punishments, and the acknowledgment of the Being of God) could *not* hold office in government. This exclusion was allowable and completely constitutional as evidenced by the fact that *it was part of their constitution.*

That the religious tests to which the constitutions referred were actually denominational tests is reflected in the manner in which Founders such as William Penn guided his state's government. This description of Penn appeared in the *Biographical Review* in London in 1819:

> It was his wish that every man who believed in God should partake of the rights of a citizen; and that every man who adored Him as a Christian, of whatever sect he might be, should be a partaker in authority. [31]

While rights for citizens were broad, the right of public service and public exercise of authority was extended only to those who were Christians. The denomination was irrelevant, only that he be Christian. An incident involving Roger Sherman is further demonstration that our Founders expected Christians to be the leaders in public office. Sherman has a unique and distinguished position among the Founding Fathers. He is the only one who signed the nation's four major founding documents: the Articles of Association in 1774, the Declaration of Independence in 1776, the Articles of Confederation in 1777, and the Constitution in 1787. With his intimate knowledge of our government, what was his view of Christians in government?

> In February 1776 [Sherman] was placed on a committee with Adams and George Wythe of Virginia to draw up instructions for an embassy going to Canada. . . . The instructions . . . included an interesting sentence: "You are further to declare that we hold sacred the rights of conscience, and may promise to the whole people, solemnly in our name, the free and undisturbed exercise of their religion." And . . . that all civil rights and *the right to hold office were to be extended to persons of any Christian denomination.* [32] (emphasis added)

Another Founder with extensive knowledge of the Constitution was John Jay. Jay had campaigned long and hard on behalf of the Constitution. It was he who, along with James Madison and Alexander Hamilton, authored *The Federalist Papers.* He was probably one of the three men most responsible for the ratification of the Constitution and was selected by George Washington as the first Chief Justice of the Supreme Court. With his Constitutional expertise, what did he say about Christians in office?

> Providence has given to our people the choice of their rulers, and it is the duty as well as the privilege and interest of our Christian nation to select and prefer Christians for their rulers. [33]

That this was the practice of the nation under the Constitution is underscored in the events surrounding the nation's second Presidential race between John Adams and Thomas Jefferson. The entire focus of the race was on whether or not Jefferson was actually a Christian. If he was not, he would not hold office.

> Jefferson was strongly attacked for his religious beliefs when he ran for President against John Adams in 1800. One of the

most powerful attacks came from Rev. William Linn, a Dutch Reformed minister in New York City. In the pamphlet *Serious Considerations on the Election of a President,* Linn asked, "Does Jefferson ever go to church? How does he spend the Lord's day? Is he known to worship with any denomination of Christians?" Linn continued: "Let the first magistrate to be a professed infidel, and infidels will surround him. Let him spend the sabbath . . . never in going to church; and to frequent public worship will become unfashionable . . . universal dissoluteness will follow. . . . Will you then, my fellow-citizens, with all this evidence . . . vote for Mr. Jefferson? . . . As to myself, were Mr. Jefferson connected with me by the nearest ties of blood, and did I owe him a thousand obligations, I would not, and could not vote for him. No; sooner than stretch forth my hand to place him at the head of the nation 'Let mine arms fall from my shoulder blade, and mine arm be broken from the bone.'"

John Adams, Jefferson's opponent, was much more orthodox in his Christian faith; Adam's wife, Abigail, joined the attack, charging that Jefferson was a deist: "Can the placing at the head of the nation two characters known to be Deists be productive of order, peace, and happiness?"

But supporters came to Jefferson's defense. Tunis Wortman wrote the pamphlet *A Solemn Address to the Christians and Patriots upon the Approaching Election of a President of the United States,* in which he declared, "That the charge of deism . . . is false, scandalous and malicious—That there is not a single passage in the *Notes on Virginia,* or any of Mr. Jefferson's writings, repugnant to Christianity; but on the contrary, in every respect, favourable to it." Dewitt Clinton also defended Jefferson by declaring, "we have the strongest reasons to believe that he is a real Christian." Clinton said, "I feel persuaded that he is a believer" and "I feel happy to hail him a Christian." He continued with: "And let me add . . . that he has for a long time supported out of his own private revenues, a worthy minister of the Christian church—an instance of liberality not to be met with in any of his rancorous enemies; whose love of religion seems principally to consist in their unremitted endeavors to degrade it into a handmaid of faction."

Two issues pinpointed in the debate deserve special mention. First, no one questioned the propriety of inquiry into a presidential candidate's religious beliefs. Second . . . the question was whether Jefferson was a deist or a Christian. [34]

A strong proof that the First Amendment was never intended to separate Christianity from public affairs came in the form of legislation approved by the same Congress which created the First Amendment. That legislation, originally entitled "An Ordinance for the Government of the Territory of the United States, North-West of the River Ohio" and later shortened to the "Northwest Ordinance," provided the procedure and requirements whereby territories could attain statehood in the newly United States. After all, there were thousands of Americans in the wilderness and the western territories across the Ohio River; provision must be made for them to enter the United States.

The Northwest Ordinance, originally approved by Congress on July 13, 1787, while the nation was still operating under the Articles of Confederation, was repassed by the Founders following the ratification of the Constitution so that it would remain effective under the new form of government. The Northwest Ordinance received final House approval on July 21, 1789, [35] Senate approval on August 4, 1789, [36] and was signed into law by President George Washington on August 7, 1789,[37] in the midst of the time that the same Congress was formulating the First Amendment (from June 7, 1789, to September 25, 1789).

That piece of legislation was neither an obscure nor an insignificant act in America's history. The *United States Code Annotated,* under the heading "The Organic Laws of the United States of America," lists our significant governmental instruments: the Articles of Confederation, the Declaration of Independence, the Constitution, and *the Northwest Ordinance!*

Article III of the Northwest Ordinance addressed the importance of religion to the territories. To establish the mindset of the Founders in that first Congress, one portion of Article III will be intentionally omitted; consider the word or phrase the Founders might have used to fill the following blank:

Article III: "Religion, morality, and knowledge, being necessary to good government and the happiness of mankind, _____ shall forever be encouraged." [38]

If the Founders considered religion and morality to be "necessary to good government and to the happiness of mankind" and that it "shall forever be encouraged," what vehicle would they utilize to achieve their goals? What would be the best and most effective institution for promoting religion and morality? A clear majority today would emphatically respond: "The Church!" Such a response indicates the degree to which our thinking has been distorted by the doctrine of the separation of church and state. Notice what our Founders felt should promote religion, morality, and knowledge:

> Article III: Religion, morality, and knowledge, being necessary to good government and the happiness of mankind, *schools and the means of education* shall forever be encouraged. [39] (emphasis added)

The Framers of the First Amendment felt that schools and educational systems were the proper means to encourage "religion, morality, and knowledge."

Following the passage of that legislation, Congressional enabling acts which allowed territories to organize and form a state government and ratify a state constitution required that those potential states adhere to the "Northwest Ordinance" as a requisite for admission. Consequently, the state constitutions of the newly admitted states frequently included exact wordings from portions of the "Northwest Ordinance," specifically Article III.

For example, on April 30, 1802, Congress passed the enabling act for Ohio, requiring that the territory form its government in a manner "not repugnant to the [Northwest] Ordinance." [40] Consequently, Article VIII, Section 3 of the November 1, 1802, Ohio constitution states:

> Religion, morality, and knowledge being essentially necessary to the good government and the happiness of mankind, schools and the means of instruction shall forever be encouraged by legislative provision. [41]

Of special note is the fact that this federally-mandated requirement, and the resulting Ohio state constitution, occurred under President Thomas Jefferson—a potent endorsement of its permissibility under the federal Constitution and the First Amendment. Similarly, Congress stipulated the same requirements while James Madison was President in the April 13, 1816, enabling act for Indiana. [42]

On March 1, 1817, Congress passed the Mississippi enabling act requiring that the territory form its government in a manner "not repugnant to the principles of the [Northwest] ordinance." [43] Consequently, Article IX, Section 16, of the 1817 Mississippi constitution states:

> Religion, morality, and knowledge, being necessary to good government, the preservation of liberty and the happiness of mankind, schools and the means of education shall be forever encouraged in this state. [44]

Since the same Congress which prohibited the federal government from the "establishment of religion" also required that religion be included in schools, the Framers obviously did not view a federal requirement to teach religion in schools as a violation of the First Amendment. Article III of the "Northwest Ordinance" was not only applied to the other early states, [45] it was also applied for decades after the Founders. For example, Article I, Section 4 of the June 12, 1875, Nebraska constitution required that:

> Religion, morality, and knowledge, however, being essential to good government, it shall be the duty of the legislature to pass suitable laws . . . to encourage schools and the means of instruction. [46]

What can be concluded from the records surrounding the Constitutional Convention and the framing of the First Amendment?

> The concept of a secular state was virtually non-existent in 1776 as well as in 1787, when the Constitution was written, and no less so when the Bill of Rights was adopted. To read the Constitution as the charter for a secular state is to misread history, and to misread it radically. The Constitution was designed to perpetuate a Christian order. [47]

In recent years, those advocating separation of church and state have argued that when the Constitution and First Amendment were ratified, they superseded and invalidated state constitutions and their religious stipulations. There are three grounds which disprove that assertion.

First, the records of the Constitutional Convention show that the First Amendment was modeled after many of the states' own provisions regarding "establishment of religion." From the delegates reliance on their states' documents, it is apparent that they were not attempting to repudiate them.

Second, the Constitutional Convention convened with proponents of, not opponents to, states' sovereignty. The concept of a new national constitution was not only novel, and thus tenuous, it was handled with great deference to the fears and concerns of the states. In order to gain the states' approval, a Bill of Rights, limiting the powers of the federal government and assuring the states that their own power would not be usurped, was added to the Constitution. Had the states perceived an attempt to overthrow or undermine the established fundamental principles of their own state governments, the new Constitution would have had no hope of ratification. The states perceived no threat to their own constitutions by the new federal Constitution.

Third, the Constitutional delegates had voluntarily subscribed themselves to the requirements of their own state's constitution regarding public service. These men had with their own lips confessed their belief in God, His Son, Jesus, the Holy Spirit, the Divine inspiration of the Old and New Testaments, and that there existed future rewards and punishments. They would have had to deny their own personal affirmations to allow the First Amendment to reverse the practice common throughout the states.

In order for those delegates to have achieved what the Supreme Court claims requires fantastic imagination, illogical conclusions, and a rejection of the documents existing from the time of the Constitutional Convention. Can our courts and politicians actually claim that we have a better understanding now of its intent than those who framed it, ratified it, and applied it in their governmental and judicial decisions? We are two centuries removed from its framing. Logic demands that if there is a conflict between the way the First Amendment is now applied and the manner in which our Founders applied it, the current application is the one in error.

The phrase "separation of church and state" is an over-used, misused, and abused phrase. It is a judicial and bureaucratic buzz-word now familiar to virtually the entire nation. Everyone knows it, yet few know its history. What is its history? Where did the phrase originate? How has it, in opposition to historical records, become the overriding judicial philosophy of this nation?

~3~
The Origin of the Phrase
"Separation of Church and State"

Most people are surprised when they find that the Constitution does not contain the words "separation of church and state." The common perception is that those words are the heart of the First Amendment and are included in it. Since that phrase does not appear in our Constitution, what is its origin?

At the time of the Constitution, although the states encouraged Christianity, no state allowed an exclusive state-sponsored denomination. However, many citizens did recall accounts from earlier years when one denomination ruled over and oppressed all others. Even though those past abuses were not current history in 1802, the fear of a recurrence still lingered in some minds.

It was in this context that the Danbury Baptist Association of Danbury, Connecticut, wrote to President Jefferson. Although the statesmen and patriots who framed the Constitution had made it clear that no one Christian denomination would become the official denomination, the Danbury Baptists expressed their concern over a rumor that a particular denomination was soon to be recognized as the national denomination. On January 1, 1802, President Jefferson responded to the Danbury Baptists in a letter. He calmed their fears by using the now infamous phrase to assure them that the federal government would not establish any single denomination of Christianity as the national denomination:

> I contemplate with solemn reverence that act of the whole American people which declared that their legislature should "make no law respecting an establishment of religion, or prohibiting the free exercise thereof," thus building a wall of separation between Church and State. [1]

Since this phrase was not recorded in the discussions of the Constitutional Convention nor in the records of the subsequent Congress that produced the First Amendment and the Bill of Rights, why did Jefferson select this particular phrase to reassure them?

Recall that he was addressing a group of Baptists, a denomination of which he was not a member. In writing to them, he sought to establish the common ground necessary between an author and the group he is addressing. By using the phrase "a wall of separation," he was actually borrowing the words of one of the Baptist's own prominent ministers: Roger Williams. Williams' words had been:

> "When they have opened a gap in the hedge or wall of separation between the garden of the church and the wilderness of the world, God hath ever broke down the wall itself . . . . And that there fore if He will eer please to restore His garden and paradise again, it must of necessity be walled in peculiarly unto Himself from the world . . . " According to Williams, the "wall of separation" was to protect the "garden of the church" from the "wilderness of the world." [2]

That "wall" was originally introduced as, and understood to be, a one-directional wall protecting the church from the government. This was also Jefferson's understanding, as conveyed through statements he made concerning the First Amendment—statements now ignored by the Court:

> *Kentucky Resolutions of 1798:* No power over the freedom of religion . . . [is] delegated to the United States by the Constitution. [3]

> *Second Inaugural Address, 1805:* In matters of religion I have considered that its free exercise is placed by the Constitution independent of the powers of the General [federal] Government. [4]

> *Letter to Samuel Miller, 1808:* I consider the government of the United States as interdicted [prohibited] by the Constitution from intermeddling with religious institutions, their doctrines, discipline, or exercises. This results not only from the provision that no law shall be made respecting the establishment or free exercise of religion, but from that also which reserves to the States the powers not delegated to the United States [10th Amendment]. Certainly, no power to prescribe any religious exercise, or to assume authority in religious discipline, has been delegated to the General Government. It must then rest with the States, as far as it can be in any human authority. [5]

Contrary to Jefferson's explanation of the intent, such power no longer rests with the states. In 1947, in *Everson* v. *Board of Educ.,* [6] the Court reversed 150 years of established legal practice under the Constitution and decided that it *did* have the right to rule on an individual state's decisions regarding religious practice. Prior to that reversal, the Courts had left the decisions as Jefferson and all other Founders had planned it—"rest[ing] with the states." State legislatures had been passing laws since the 1600's allowing the free exercise of religious practices in schools and public affairs: voluntary prayer, Bible reading, the use of the Ten Commandments, etc. These laws had been enacted "with the consent of the governed" and through representatives elected "of the people, by the people, and for the people."

Jefferson's words of assurance to the Danbury Baptist Association were soon forgotten since the rumor never became fact. Jefferson's letter remained in obscurity, as is usual with most presidential addresses delivered to specific audiences, until 76 years later when it appeared in the 1878 case of *Reynolds* v. *United States*. [7] In that case, a lengthy excerpt from Jefferson's letter was used, and its context clearly presented. In that case, the Court did *not* use Jefferson's letter to attempt to separate church and state, but used it in an opposite manner.

The opportunity for the Court to use Jefferson's letter arose in 1878 when the Mormons claimed that the First Amendment's "free exercise of religion" promise and the "separation of church and state" principle should keep the United States government from making laws prohibiting their "religious" exercise of polygamy. Using Jefferson's letter, the Court showed that while the government was *not* free to interfere with opinions on religion, which is what frequently distinguishes one denomination from another, it *was* responsible to enforce civil laws according to general Christian standards. In other words, separation of church and state pertained to denominational differences, not to basic Christian principles. Therefore, and on that basis, the Court ruled that the Mormon practice of polygamy and bigamy was a violation of the Constitution because it was a violation of basic Christian principles.

Nearly 70 years after the *Reynolds* case, in the 1947 *Everson* case, the Court excerpted eight words out of Jefferson's letter ("a wall of separation between church and state") and adopted that phrase as its new battle cry. It announced for the first time the *new* meaning of separation of church and state—a separation of basic religious principles from public arenas. When the Court excerpted Jefferson's words in the *Everson* case, it did not bother to present the context in which the phrase had originally been used, nor reveal that it had been applied in an opposite manner in previous Supreme Court cases.

Those eight words, now taken out of context, concisely articulated the Court's plan to divorce Christianity from public affairs.

Once the Court adopted the portion of Jefferson's words with which it agreed and ignored their intent, it began declaring state laws unconstitutional. It struck down voluntary prayer laws in Maryland, Pennsylvania, Florida, Alabama, New Jersey, and a host of other states. Statutes allowing religious practice in public affairs were overturned in nearly every state in the Union. Laws no longer were being enacted or removed by the people through their elected representatives; it was now occurring through unelected Justices. If as few as five Justices agreed (the majority of the Court), they could overturn the people's will that had been expressed through Constitutionally correct legislative means.

There is probably no other instance in America's history where words spoken by an individual have become the law of the land. Jefferson's remark now carries more weight in judicial circles than does the writing of any other Founder. That Jefferson's letter to the Danbury Baptists should become a national legal policy is absurd when considering:

> Jefferson made the statement in 1802, thirteen years after Congress passed the First Amendment. Jefferson was not a delegate to the 1787 Constitutional Convention, nor was he a member of Congress in 1789 [which framed the First Amendment], nor was he a member of any state legislature or ratifying convention at any time relevant to the passage of the First Amendment; he was serving as U.S. Minister to France throughout this time. [8]

Doesn't it seem unreasonable that the Justices had to bypass all the other Founding Fathers in order to find some words with which they could agree? And even then, they selected someone who was *not* a part of the Constitutional proceedings or even in the nation at the time. And on top of that, they used his words in a manner in which he never would have approved!

George Washington had much to say about the relationship of Christianity to schools and government. He was President of the Convention that formed the Constitution and then President of the United States when the First Amendment was created and ratified. Why doesn't the Court quote him? Amazingly, the Court seems to have lost the records on George Washington, as well as those on

John Adams, Patrick Henry, Samuel Adams, John Jay, and a host of other Founders! (Don't worry—we found them and will present them in Chapter 5!) The simple explanation is that the Justices have found in Jefferson's eight words what they want the First Amendment to say, not what our Founders framed it to say, and not even what Jefferson understood it to say.

There is no "wall of separation" in the Constitution, unless it is a wall intended by the Founding Fathers to keep the government out of the church. Jefferson's words have been twisted to mean just the opposite; now, the state must be "protected" from the church!

> If the American people have ever adopted the principle of complete separation of church and state, we should find the evidence of it in the federal Constitution, in the acts of Congress, or in the constitutions or laws of the several states. There is no such evidence in existence. In its absence, the mere opinion of private individuals or groups that *there should be absolute separation of church and state* . . . does not create "a great American principle." [9]

As a note of interest, while the phrase "separation of church and state" is not found in the United States Constitution, it is found in another prominent document—the Constitution of the former Soviet Union:

> Article 52: The church in the USSR is separated from the state, and the school from the church. [10]

It seems that, because of the current Court's rulings, we have more similarities with the Soviet Union than we might have thought; although they seem to have more religious practice in schools under their Constitution than we do under ours:

> Who would have believed that the Supreme Court in 1980 would uphold the decision of a Kentucky school board (in *Stone* v. *Graham)* that the Ten Commandments, the basis of English law and the most important code of laws ever written, were illegal to display on the walls of the public schools because they represented a religious symbol? Ironically, just a few weeks before the court's decision, some Polish high school students had demonstrated openly against their country's communist authorities for ordering the

removal of the Catholic crucifix that still adorned the walls of their public schools—and the government backed down. Americans cheered the courage of those young people for speaking out against their repressive government. Yet when our atheistically dominated Supreme Court removed the Ten Commandments from our halls, not a whimper was heard. [11]

William James is considered by many to be the father of modern psychology. He was a strong advocate and early pioneer of the "separation" doctrine. Perhaps a statement credited to him reveals the reason that Jefferson's misapplied phrase has had so much impact on the nation's public policy:

There is nothing so absurd but if you repeat it often enough people will believe it.

The doctrine of separation of church and state is absurd; it has been repeated often; and people have believed it. It is amazing what continually hearing about separation of church and state can do to a nation!

~4~
The Court's Early Rulings—
We Are A *Christian* Nation

In recent years, courts have often declared a need to understand the intent of the First Amendment before pronouncing a ruling on a pending case. The legal profession wrestles with intent because it is now more than two centuries removed from the minds of the Framers.

Is there nothing to document the intent of the Founders? It would be logical that any rulings made by the courts in the years immediately following the framing of the Constitution would accurately reflect the Founders' intent. Are those early accounts still available?

Fortunately, they are. This chapter will examine several of those rulings, some dating back to 1795. In many of these cases, justices on the courts had personally participated in drafting and ratifying the Constitution. When ruling on a case, they did not have to struggle with intent—they knew their own intentions!

In its rulings over the past three decades, the Court has implied that the Founders were vehemently opposed *en masse* to involving Christian principles in schools and government. If that is true, it will be reflected in the rulings of the early courts. The early decisions and commentaries will verify whether there is any validity to the doctrine of separation of church and state as now enforced by the Court.

Excerpts from fifteen early cases will be presented. These fifteen, representing hundreds of similar cases, illustrate the spirit and conclusions that pervade them all. This chapter will establish, by court record, that our Founders would *never* have tolerated the separation of church and state as it now exists. Only in a nightmare could the Founders have envisioned what the Court is now doing with the First Amendment!

Church of the Holy Trinity *v.* United States, 1892
United States Supreme Court

This case provides a good starting point, for it cites several of the earlier cases. This case centered on an 1885 federal law concerning immigration which declared:

> It shall be unlawful for any person, company, partnership, or corporation, in any manner whatsoever . . . to in any way assist or encourage the importation . . . of any alien or . . .

foreigners, into the United States . . . under contract or agreement . . . to perform labor or service of any kind. [1]

Two years later, in 1887, the Church of the Holy Trinity in
New York employed a clergyman from England as its pastor.
That employment was challenged by the United States Attorney
General's office as a violation of the law. The case eventually
reached the Supreme Court.

The first half of the Court's decision dealt with what it termed
"absurd" application of laws. The Court was not saying that the
legislation was absurd, for in the early years the Court rarely criti-
cized the legislature since it was the voice of the people. "Absurd"
referred to cases where an interpretation by the letter of the law and
not by the spirit or intent of its framers would lead to absurd results.

The Court examined the Congressional records of the hearings
surrounding this legislation and established, from the legislators'
own testimony, that the law was enacted solely to preclude an
influx of cheap and unskilled labor for work on the railroads.
Although the church's alleged violation was certainly within the
letter of the law, it was not within its spirit. The Court concluded
that only an "absurd" application of the Constitution would allow
a restriction on Christianity:

> No purpose of action against religion can be imputed to any
> legislation, state or national, because this is a religious
> people. . . . This is a Christian nation. [2]

The Court resolved the legal question within the first half of its
written ruling and devoted the remainder to establishing that this
nation is indeed Christian and why it would be constitutionally
"absurd" and legally impossible to legislate any restrictions on
Christianity. Despite the Court's use of only brief historical quotations, its references comprised eight of the sixteen pages in the
decision. Justice Brewer, who delivered the opinion of the Court,
gave the basis for the Court's conclusion:

> This is a religious people. This is historically true. From the
> discovery of this continent to the present hour, there is a single
> voice making this affirmation. The commission to Christo-
> pher Columbus . . . [recited] that "it is hoped that by God's
> assistance some of the continents and islands in the ocean will
> be discovered . . . ." The first colonial grant made to Sir Walter

Raleigh in 1584 . . . and the grant authorizing him to enact statutes for the government of the proposed colony provided that "they be not against the true Christian faith . . . ." The first charter of Virginia, granted by King James I in 1606 . . . commenced the grant in these words: " . . . in propagating of Christian Religion to such People as yet live in Darkness . . . ."

Language of similar import may be found in the subsequent charters of that colony . . . in 1609 and 1611; and the same is true of the various charters granted to the other colonies. In language more or less emphatic is the establishment of the Christian religion declared to be one of the purposes of the grant. The celebrated compact made by the Pilgrims in the Mayflower, 1620, recites: "Having undertaken for the Glory of God, and advancement of the Christian faith . . . a voyage to plant the first colony in the northern parts of Virginia . . . ."

The fundamental orders of Connecticut, under which a provisional government was instituted in 1638-1639, commence with this declaration: " . . . And well knowing where a people are gathered together the word of God requires that to maintain the peace and union . . . there should be an orderly and decent government established according to God . . . to maintain and preserve the liberty and purity of the gospel of our Lord Jesus which we now profess . . . of the said gospel [which] is now practiced amongst us."

In the charter of privileges granted by William Penn to the province of Pennsylvania, in 1701, it is recited: " . . . no people can be truly happy, though under the greatest enjoyment of civil liberties, if abridged of . . . their religious profession and worship . . . ."

Coming nearer to the present time, the Declaration of Independence recognizes the presence of the Divine in human affairs in these words: "We hold these truths to be self-evident, that all men are created equal, that they are endowed by their Creator with certain unalienable Rights . . . "; " . . . appealing to the Supreme Judge of the world for the rectitude of our intentions . . . "; "And for the support of this Declaration, with a firm reliance on the Protection of Divine Providence, we mutually pledge to each other our Lives, our Fortunes, and our sacred Honor." [3]

The Court continued with example after example, citing portions from the forty-four state constitutions (the number of states in 1892), using many of the same excerpts given in this book in earlier chapters. The Court's historical discourse continued for several pages until finally summarizing its findings:

> There is no dissonance in these declarations. There is a universal language pervading them all, having one meaning; they affirm and reaffirm that this is a religious nation. These are not individual sayings, declarations of private persons: they are organic utterances; they speak the voice of the entire people. While because of a general recognition of this truth the question has seldom been presented to the courts, yet we find that in *Updegraph* v. *The Commonwealth*, it was decided that, "Christianity, general Christianity, is, and always has been, a part of the common law . . . not Christianity with an established church . . . but Christianity with liberty of conscience to all men." And in *The People* v. *Ruggles*, Chancellor Kent, the great commentator on American law, speaking as Chief Justice of the Supreme Court of New York, said: "The people of this State, in common with the people of this country, profess the general doctrines of Christianity, as the rule of their faith and practice. . . . We are a Christian people, and the morality of the country is deeply engrafted upon Christianity, and not upon the doctrines or worship of those impostors [other religions]." And in the famous case of *Vidal* v. *Girard's Executors*, this Court . . . observed: "It is also said, and truly, that the Christian religion is a part of the common law . . . ." These, and many other matters which might be noticed, add a volume of unofficial declarations to the mass of organic utterances that this is a Christian nation. 4

This stands as quite a convincing and broad-based argument! The Court quoted directly from eighteen sources, alluded to over forty others, and acknowledged "many other" and "a volume" more from which selections could have been made.

The Court cited *People* v. *Ruggles*, *Updegraph* v. *Commonwealth*, and *Vidal* v. *Girard's Executors* in establishing its conclusion. The *Ruggles* case was decided by the Supreme Court of New York in 1811, *Updegraph* by the Supreme Court of Pennsylvania in 1826, and *Vidal* by the United States Supreme Court in 1844. Before reviewing these three cases, an observation needs to be made about cases stemming from state supreme courts.

Currently, the federal Supreme Court is very high profile and affects national and private life through its far-reaching decisions. Consequently, a state's supreme court is now perceived as a less credible source than the federal Supreme Court. However, this was not the attitude of earlier years. For 150 years after the ratification of the Constitution, the states were considered the highest source of authority. Most disputes went no higher than state courts, and only unusual circumstances would cause a case to go to the federal Supreme Court (i.e., disputes between states, cases involving federal territories not yet states, cases not involving a jury decision, etc.).

Therefore, on items concerning religion and Christianity, the federal courts were considered *less* of an authority than the state courts. As the Court itself had noted in the *Holy Trinity* case, it had few occasions in which to decide on issues affecting Christianity:

> While because of a general recognition of this truth [that we are a Christian nation], the question has seldom been presented to the courts. [5]

When the federal Court did render a decision touching Christianity, it frequently cited the decisions of the state supreme courts, as it did in *Holy Trinity*. It is helpful to keep this background information in mind when examining the following cases.

Updegraph v. The Commonwealth, 1824
Supreme Court of Pennsylvania

This was the first case cited in *Holy Trinity*. The following is the description of the grand jury's indictment and the facts of the case:

> Abner Updegraph . . . on the 12th day of December [1821] . . . not having the fear of God before his eyes . . . contriving and intending to scandalize, and bring into disrepute, and vilify the Christian religion and the scriptures of truth, in the presence and hearing of several persons . . . did unlawfully, wickedly and premeditatively, despitefully and blasphemously say . . . : "That the Holy Scriptures were a mere fable: that they were a contradiction, and that although they contained a number of good things, yet they contained a great many lies." To the great dishonor of Almighty God, to the great scandal of the profession of the Christian religion. [6]

Since the indictment was for blasphemy, the court needed to establish a legal definition of the word. It turned to the writings of Sir
William Blackstone:

> Blasphemy against the Almighty is denying his being or
> providence, or uttering contumelious reproaches on our
> Savior Christ. It is punished, at common law by fine and
> imprisonment, for Christianity is part of the laws of the land. [7]

Blackstone was an oft-quoted authority among lawyers of that
day. According to Congressman Robert K. Dornan, in his book
Judicial Supremacy:

> Since colonial America had no regular schools of law, and
> lawyers educated in England were few, Blackstone's four-
> volume *Commentaries on the Laws of England (1765-1769)*
> served as the bible of American lawyers for generations.
> Indeed, nearly as many copies of Blackstone were sold in the
> colonies as in England, despite disparity in population. It
> was from Blackstone that most Americans, including John
> Marshall, acquired their knowledge of natural law. [8]

Legal Professor John Eidsmoe, in his book *Christianity and the
Constitution,* says of Blackstone that:

> His *Commentaries* were in the offices of every lawyer in
> the land, that candidates for the bar were routinely
> examined on Blackstone, that he was cited authoritatively
> in the Courts, and that a quotation from Blackstone settled
> many a legal argument. [9]

Further evidence of Blackstone's influence in America comes from
a ten-year research of 15,000 articles written during the founding era
(1760-1805). This research reveals that Blackstone was one of the
two men quoted most frequently by our Founders. [10] The number of
times that our Founders quoted Blackstone testifies to the impact that
he had on their thinking and to the respect they paid him.

The Updegraph case went to trial, and the jury found Updegraph
guilty. The attorney for the defendant submitted to the court his
reasons that the jury's verdict should be overturned. He pointed out
that Updegraph was a member of a debating association which
convened weekly and that what he had said was uttered in the course
of argument on a religious question. Wilkins argued that both the

state and federal Constitution protected freedom of speech, and that if any state law against blasphemy did exist, the federal Constitution had done away with it—that Christianity was no longer part of the law.

Undoubtedly, had this case been tried today, the defense would differ little. Arguments for unlimited freedom of speech and against the constitutionality of laws limiting expression have been used since courts existed. Notice how the court responded to these arguments:

> The jury . . . finds a malicious intention in the speaker to vilify the Christian religion and the scriptures, and this court cannot look beyond the record, nor take any notice of the allegation, that the words were uttered by the defendant, a member of a debating association, which convened weekly for discussion and mutual information. . . . That there is an association in which so serious a subject is treated with so much levity, indecency and scurrility . . . I am sorry to hear, for it would prove a nursery of vice, a school of preparation to qualify young men for the gallows, and young women for the brothel, and there is not a skeptic of decent manners and good morals, who would not consider such debating clubs as a common nuisance and disgrace to the city. . . . It was the out-pouring of an invective, so vulgarly shocking and insulting, that the lowest grade of civil authority ought not to be subject to it, but when spoken in a Christian land, and to a Christian audience, the highest offence *contra bonos mores*; and even if Christianity was not part of the law of the land, it is the popular religion of the country, an insult on which would be indictable. [11]

Having sustained the jury's verdict and the legality of laws on blasphemy, the court turned its attention to the objections raised by the defense attorney:

> The assertion is once more made, that Christianity never was received as part of the common law of this Christian land; and it is added, that if it was, it was virtually repealed by the constitution of the United States, and of this state. . . . If the argument be worth anything, all the laws which have Christianity for their object—all would be carried away at one fell swoop—the act against cursing and swearing, and breach of the Lord's day; the act forbidding incestuous marriages,

perjury by taking a false oath upon the book, fornication and adultery . . . —for all these are founded on Christianity—for all these are restraints upon civil liberty. . . .

We will first dispose of what is considered the grand objection—the constitutionality of Christianity—for, in effect, that is the question. Christianity, general Christianity, is and always has been a part of the common law . . . not Christianity founded on any particular religious tenets; not Christianity with an established church . . . but Christianity with liberty of conscience to all men.

Thus this wise legislature framed this great body of laws, for a Christian country and Christian people. This is the Christianity of the common law . . . and thus, it is irrefragably proved, that the laws and institutions of this state are built on the foundation of reverence for Christianity. . . . In this the constitution of the United States has made no alteration, nor in the great body of the laws which was an incorporation of the common-law doctrine of Christianity . . . without which no free government can long exist.

To prohibit the open, public and explicit denial of the popular religion of a country is a necessary measure to preserve the tranquillity of a government. Of this, no person in a Christian country can complain. . . . In the Supreme Court of New York it was solemnly determined, that Christianity was part of the law of the land, and that to revile the Holy Scriptures was an indictable offence. The case assumes, says Chief Justice Kent, that we are a Christian people, and the morality of the country is deeply engrafted on Christianity. *The People* v. *Ruggles.*

No society can tolerate a wilful and despiteful attempt to subvert its religion, no more than it would to break down its laws—a general, malicious and deliberate intent to overthrow Christianity, general Christianity.

Without these restraints no free government could long exist. It is liberty run mad to declaim against the punishment of these offences, or to assert that the punishment is hostile to the spirit and genius of our government. They are far from being true friends to liberty who support this doctrine, and the promulgation of such opinions, and general receipt of them among the people, would be the sure forerunners of anarchy, and finally, of despotism.

No free government now exists in the world unless where Christianity is acknowledged, and is the religion of the country. . . . Its foundations are broad and strong, and deep . . . it is the purest system of morality, the firmest auxiliary, and only stable support of all human laws. . . .

Christianity is part of the common law; the act against blasphemy is neither obsolete nor virtually repealed; nor is Christianity inconsistent with our free governments or the genius of the people.

While our own free constitution secures liberty of conscience and freedom of religious worship to all, it is not necessary to maintain that any man should have the right publicly to vilify the religion of his neighbors and of the country; these two privileges are directly opposed. [12]

The People *v.* Ruggles, 1811
Supreme Court of New York

This case was not only cited in the previous case, it was also the second case cited in *Holy Trinity*. The offense and surrounding facts are described from the case:

The defendant was indicted . . . in December, 1810, for that he did, on the 2nd day of September, 1810 . . . wickedly, maliciously, and blasphemously, utter, and with a loud voice publish, in the presence and hearing of divers good and Christian people, of and concerning the Christian religion, and of and concerning Jesus Christ, the false, scandalous, malicious, wicked and blasphemous words following: "Jesus Christ was a bastard, and his mother must be a whore," in contempt of the Christian religion. . . . The defendant was tried and found guilty, and was sentenced by the court to be imprisoned for three months, and to pay a fine of $500. [13]

The attorney for the prisoner presented his defense:

There are no statutes concerning religion. . . . The constitution allows a free toleration to all religions and all kinds of worship. . . . Judaism and Mahometanism may be preached here, without any legal animadversion. . . . The prisoner may have been a Jew, a Mahometan, or a Socinian: and if so, he had a right, by the constitution, to declare his opinions. [14]

The prosecuting attorney countered:

> While the constitution of the State has saved the rights of
> conscience, and allowed a free and fair discussion of all points
> of controversy among religious sects, it has left the principal
> engrafted on the body of our common law, that Christianity is
> part of the laws of the State, untouched and unimpaired. [15]

The Chief Justice of the New York Supreme Court during this case
was Chancellor James Kent, author of *Commentaries on American
Law*. There were few purely American legal precedents or writings
in the young nation on which to rely in its early years; consequently,
lawyers and judges studied and applied the writings of Sir William
Blackstone, an English judge and author of *Blackstone's Commentaries on the Law*. However, as time progressed and experience
accumulated in the young nation, American writings and standards
were developed. These were due, in large part, to the four-volume
work written by James Kent: *Commentaries on American Law*.
Kent's writings, while heavily dependent upon Blackstone, eventually replaced Blackstone's as the standard in America.

In addition to producing his *Commentaries,* Kent also originated
the practice of written decisions in New York. After his years in that
state's supreme court, he went on to a nine-year term as the head of
the Court of Chancery—a specialized court dealing with complicated
and intricate situations that regular courts were unable to handle.
James Kent was much more than an average judge in a northeastern
state—he was one of the premier individuals in the development of
legal practice in the United States. His words on law carry significant weight and importance. Notice his decision in this case:

> Such words uttered with such a disposition were an offense at
> common law. In *Taylor's* case the defendant was convicted
> upon information of speaking similar words, and the Court . . .
> said that Christianity was parcel of the law, and to cast contu-
> melious reproaches upon it, tended to weaken the foundation
> of moral obligation, and the efficacy of oaths. And in the case
> of *Rex* v. *Woolston,* on a like conviction, the Court said . . . that
> whatever strikes at the root of Christianity tends manifestly to
> the dissolution of civil government. . . . The authorities show
> that blasphemy against God and . . . profane ridicule of Christ
> or the Holy Scriptures (which are equally treated as

blasphemy), are offenses punishable at common law, whether uttered by words or writings ... because it tends to corrupt the morals of the people, and to destroy good order. Such offenses have always been considered independent of any religious establishment or the rights of the Church. They are treated as affecting the essential interests of civil society. ...

We stand equally in need, now as formerly, of all the moral discipline, and of those principles of virtue, which help to bind society together. The people of this State, in common with the people of this country, profess the general doctrines of Christianity, as the rule of their faith and practice; and to scandalize the author of these doctrines is not only . . . impious, but . . . is a gross violation of decency and good order. Nothing could be more offensive to the virtuous part of the community, or more injurious to the tender morals of the young, than to declare such profanity lawful. ...

The free, equal, and undisturbed enjoyment of religious opinion, whatever it may be, and free and decent discussions on any religious subject, is granted and secured; but to revile . . . the religion professed by almost the whole community, is an abuse of that right. ... We are a Christian people, and the morality of the country is deeply engrafted upon Christianity, and not upon the doctrines or worship of those impostors [other religions]. ... [We are] people whose manners . . . and whose morals have been elevated and inspired ... by means of the Christian religion.

Though the constitution has discarded religious establishments, it does not forbid judicial cognizance of those offenses against religion and morality which have no reference to any such establishment. . . . This [constitutional] declaration (noble and magnanimous as it is, when duly understood) never meant to withdraw religion in general, and with it the best sanctions of moral and social obligation from all consideration and notice of the law. ... To construe it as breaking down the common law barriers against licentious, wanton, and impious attacks upon Christianity itself, would be an enormous perversion of its meaning. ...

Christianity, in its enlarged sense, as a religion revealed and taught in the Bible, is not unknown to our law. ...

The Court are accordingly of opinion that the judgment below must be affirmed: [that blasphemy against God, and contumelious reproaches, and profane ridicule of Christ or the Holy Scriptures, are offenses punishable at the common law, whether uttered by words or writings]. [16]

These are powerful words, written by one of the fathers of American legal practice! His specific statement concerning Christianity and the Constitution bears repeating:

To construe it [the Constitution] as breaking down the common law barriers against licentious, wanton, and impious attacks upon Christianity itself, would be an enormous perversion of its meaning. [17]

Commonwealth *v.* Abner Kneeland, 1838
Supreme Court of Massachusetts

This case also involved an attack against God and Christianity, but unlike the previous cases, these attacks had been published. Not surprisingly, the publisher claimed "freedom of the press" in his defense. The legal indictment against him was for "willfully blaspheming the holy name of God" and for a public disavowal of Christ. The indictment revealed his published statements:

"The Universalists believe in a god which I do not; but believe that their god, with all his moral attributes . . . is nothing more than a chimera of their own imagination"; "Universalists believe in Christ, which I do not; but believe that the whole story concerning him is . . . a fable and a fiction . . . "; etc. . . . the language was . . . a willful denial of the existence of God . . . so as to bring it within the statute. [18]

An interesting term was used in the indictment, a term unknown to contemporary courts when used in connection with God:

The defendant admitted the writing and publishing of the _libel_. [19]

"Libel" is a familiar term when used concerning other persons. It means to intentionally declare things about them that are false and would publicly injure their reputation or expose them to public ridicule. Such attacks on individuals were, and still are, illegal and subject to litigation. Yet, in previous years, attacks on God and Christ fell under the same laws constructed to protect reputations: the laws against libel.

The defendant explained to the court the reasons his conviction should be overturned. First, he claimed he did not deny a belief in

God; he was a pantheist and only denied the belief in *a* God; he felt that everything was god. Therefore, he asserted no law had been broken. Second, he argued that the law under which he was convicted had been superseded and overturned by the Constitution's guarantee of religious freedom. Lastly, he believed the laws against blasphemy were a violation of the freedom of the press. He felt the Constitution:

> Guarantees to me the strict right of propagating my senti-
> ments, by way of argument or discussion, on religion or any
> other subject. [20]

The court addressed the defendant's first argument, that he had broken no law:

> The statute, on which the question arises is as follows: "That
> if any person shall willfully blaspheme the holy name of God,
> by denying, cursing, or contumeliously reproaching God, his
> creation, government, or final judging of the world," &c. . . .
>   In general, blasphemy [that is, libel against God] may be
> described, as consisting in speaking evil of the Deity . . . to
> alienate the minds of others from the love and reverence of
> God. It is purposely using words concerning God . . . to
> impair and destroy the reverence, respect, and confidence
> due to him. . . . It is a wilful and malicious attempt to lessen
> men's reverence of God by denying his existence, or his
> attributes as an intelligent creator, governor and judge of
> men, and to prevent their having confidence in him. [21]

The court reviewed the history of blasphemy laws in America from 1646 until the then current 1782 version of the law. After summarizing the intent of each of those laws and establishing their legal validity, the Chief Justice upheld the jury's verdict finding the defendant guilty of blasphemy and libel. Having disposed of the defendant's first position, the court addressed the issue of the consti-tutionality of the law:

> But another ground for arresting the judgment, and one
> apparently most relied on and urged by the defendant, is, that
> this statute itself is repugnant to the constitution . . . and
> therefore wholly void. . . .
>   [This law] was passed very soon *after* the adoption of the
> constitution, and no doubt, many members of the convention

which framed the constitution, were members of the legislature which passed this law. [22]

The court showed how that Massachusetts laws against blasphemy were compatible with similar provisions in the constitutions of other states whose constitutions also granted religious freedom, and thus were constitutionally valid laws:

> In New Hampshire, the constitution of which State has a similar declaration of [religious] rights, the open denial of the being and existence of God or of the Supreme Being is prohibited by statute, and declared to be blasphemy.
>
> In Vermont, with a similar declaration of rights, a statute was passed in 1797, by which it was enacted, that if any person shall publicly deny the being and existence of God or the Supreme Being, or shall contumeliously reproach his providence and government, he shall be deemed a disturber of the peace and tranquility of the State, and an offender against the good morals and manners of society, and shall be punishable by fine. . . .
>
> The State of Maine also, having adopted the same constitutional provision with that of Massachusetts, in her declaration of rights, in respect to religious freedom, immediately after the adoption of the constitution reenacted, the Massachusetts statute against blasphemy. . . .
>
> In New York the universal toleration of all religious professions and sentiments, is secured in the most ample manner. It is declared in the constitution . . . that the free exercise and enjoyment of religious worship, without discrimination or preference, shall for ever be allowed in this State to all mankind. . . . Notwithstanding this constitutional declaration carrying the doctrine of unlimited toleration as far as the peace and safety of any community will allow, the courts have decided that blasphemy was a crime at common law and was not abrogated by the constitution [People v. Ruggles]. [23]

The court lastly addressed the "freedom of the press" issue raised by the defendant and concluded that there was much that could not be protected by "freedom of the press":

> According to the argument . . . every act, however injurious or criminal, which can be committed by the use of language,

may be committed . . . if such language is printed. Not only therefore would the article in question become a general license for scandal, calumny and falsehood against individuals, institutions and governments, in the form of publication . . . but all incitation to treason, assassination, and all other crimes however atrocious, if conveyed in printed language, would be dispunishable. [24]

Vidal *v.* Girard's Executors, 1844
United States Supreme Court

This was the third case cited in *Holy Trinity*. This case involved the probate of the will of Stephen Girard, a native of France. He arrived in America before the Declaration of Independence was written and settled in the city of Philadelphia, where he lived until his death in 1831. He bequeathed his entire estate and personal property, valued at over $7 million, to the city of Philadelphia. The provisions of his will required the city to construct both an orphanage and a college according to his specific stipulations.

Girard's heirs (the plaintiffs) filed suit claiming that a trust could be given only to an individual, not to a city. The suit centered on who would take possession of the estate: the city or the plaintiffs. While the case was eventually decided in favor of Philadelphia, an ancillary issue was raised during the trial that is of interest to this study (it was this issue which received the Court's attention in the *Holy Trinity* case). Girard had stipulated:

I enjoin and require that no ecclesiastic, missionary, or minister of any sect whatsoever, shall ever hold or exercise any station or duty whatever in the said college; nor shall any such person ever be admitted for any purpose, or as a visitor, within the premises. . . . My desire is, that all the instructors and teachers in the college shall take pains to instil into the minds of the scholars the purest principles of morality. [25]

Such a requirement was unprecedented in America. The lawyers for the plaintiffs complained:

The plan of education proposed is anti-christian, and therefore repugnant to the law. [26]

The city's attorneys agreed, but said that the plaintiffs should not have sued on the issue of the trust; instead, they should have:

> Joined with us in asking the state to cut off the obnoxious clause [prohibiting teaching religion]. [27]

The city's attorneys further pointed out:

> The purest principles of morality are to be taught. Where are they found? Whoever searches for them must go to the source from which a Christian man derives his faith—the Bible. . . . There is an obligation to teach what the Bible alone can teach, viz. a pure system of morality. [28]

The plaintiff's attorneys offered the final argument:

> Both in the Old and New Testaments [religious instruction's] importance is recognized. In the Old it is said, "Thou shalt diligently teach them to thy children," and in the New, "Suffer little children to come unto me and forbid them not. . . . " No fault can be found with Girard for wishing a marble college to bear his name for ever, but it is not valuable unless it has a fragrance of Christianity about it. [29]

The unanimous opinion of the Supreme Court was delivered by Justice Joseph Story—appointed to the Court by President James Madison, the "Chief Architect of the Constitution," (a sufficient endorsement of Story's understanding of the Constitution both in its technical aspects and in its intent):

> Christianity . . . is not to be maliciously and openly reviled and blasphemed against, to the annoyance of believers or the injury of the public. . . . It is unnecessary for us, however, to consider the establishment of a school or college, for the propagation of . . . Deism, or any other form of infidelity. *Such a case is not to be presumed to exist in a Christian country.* [30] (emphasis added)

The Court continued, pointing out that the will, by prohibiting clergy, had not prohibited Christian instruction, and was therefore still acceptable under the Constitution:

> Why may not laymen instruct in the general principles of Christianity as well as ecclesiastics. . . . And we cannot overlook the blessings, which such [lay]men by their conduct, as well as their instructions, may, nay *must* impart to their youthful pupils. Why may not the Bible,

and *especially* the New Testament, without note or comment, be read and taught as a divine revelation in the [school]—its general precepts expounded, its evidences explained and its glorious principles of morality inculcated? . . . Where can the purest principles of morality be learned so clearly or so perfectly as from the New Testament? [31] (emphasis added)

On this issue, all parties involved in the case agreed! The plaintiff's lawyers said separating Christianity from education was "repugnant," the city's lawyers declared it "obnoxious," and the Court said it couldn't be done—moral principles *must* be taught from the Bible!

John M'Creery's Lessee vs. Allender, 1799
Supreme Court of Maryland

Thomas M'Creery, a native of Ireland, had emigrated to the United States. Upon his death, he left the estate he had acquired in this nation to his relative, John M'Creery, still a resident in Ireland. It was doubted that an alien could leave an estate in the United States to another alien outside the States. In order to resolve the dispute in M'Creery's favor, it would have to be proven that Thomas M'Creery, had become a citizen of the United States. A certificate was produced which settled the case by showing that M'Creery had indeed been naturalized before Justice Samuel Chase.

Samuel Chase, like so many of the other men cited in this chapter, was a well-respected Justice with great legal influence. He was a signer of the Declaration of Independence and was appointed by George Washington to serve as a Justice on the United States Supreme Court. Below is an excerpt from the document Chase executed in the naturalization of M'Creery:

Thomas M'Creery, in order to become . . . naturalized according to the Act of Assembly . . . on the 30th of September, 1795, took the oath . . . before the Honorable Samuel Chase, Esquire, then being the Chief Judge of the State of Maryland . . . and did then and there receive from the said Chief Judge, a certificate thereof . . . : "Maryland; I, Samuel Chase, Chief Judge of the State of Maryland, do hereby certify all whom it may concern, that . . . personally appeared before me Thomas M'Creery, and did repeat and subscribe a declaration of his belief in the Christian Religion, and take the oath required by the Act of Assembly of this State, entitled, 'An Act for Naturalization.' [32]

What was a requirement for naturalization of immigrants?

Repeat and subscribe a declaration of his belief in the Christian Religion. [33]

Runkel *v.* Winemiller, 1799
Supreme Court of Maryland

This case involved a conflict between a minister of the German Reformed Christian Church and the church from which he had been dispossessed. In the introduction to the case, the judge who delivered the ruling noted that it was a decision in which all of the justices unanimously concurred. What was it upon which they all unanimously concurred?

Religion is of general and public concern, and on its support depend, in great measure, the peace and good order of government, the safety and happiness of the people. By our form of government, the Christian religion is the established religion; and all sects and denominations of Christians are placed upon the same equal footing, and are equally entitled to protection in their religious liberty. [34]

Again, the same recurring theme: general Christianity—but not denominational Christianity—is part of government in this nation.

The Commonwealth *v.* Sharpless and others, 1815
Supreme Court of Pennsylvania

This case, and two following it, will deal with "morality." Today's oft-repeated assertion that "Morality cannot be legislated!" was not accepted by our Founders. They believed that morality *could* be legislated and had found the Bible to be the perfect example of moral legislation. Evidently no one had told God He couldn't legislate morality— He had done so and in the opinion of our Founders, had done so quite successfully! Consequently, when the courts made decisions concerning moral values, they relied on Biblical guidelines.

Dr. Sterling Lacy, in his book *Valley of Decision*, accurately identifies what now occurs in the struggle to legislate standards for morality:

"Morality" is defined as the condition of conforming with right principles. It pits right against wrong. To "legislate" means to make a law. Law imposes rules of conduct and enforces them with authority. What law has ever been enacted by any government in the history of man that has not named something wrong and its opposite right? [35]

Every law establishes and legislates morality. What today's critics are saying is, "We don't want God to have anything to do with today's morality. We want to determine what is right and wrong without God. . . . "

America has become the battleground between the world's two oldest religions. The first religion to appear in the history of mankind worships God. The second worships man. In America, the first is expressed primarily by Christianity. The second by humanism.

It is not a question of whether morality can or should be legislated. It is a question of which religious guidelines will undergird the legislation: religious guidelines that deify God, or religious guidelines that deify man? [36]

The following cases illustrate how the courts upheld Congress' legislation of moral standards—standards based on the Bible. The indictment delivered by the grand jury in *Commonwealth* v. *Sharpless* describes the offense:

Jesse Sharpless . . . John Haines . . . George Haines . . . John Steel . . . Ephraim Martin . . . and —— Mayo . . . designing, contriving, and intending the morals, as well of youth as of divers other citizens of this commonwealth, to debauch and corrupt, and to raise and create in their minds inordinate and lustful desires . . . in a certain house there . . . scandalously did exhibit and show for money . . . a certain lewd . . . obscene painting, representing a man in an obscene . . . and indecent posture with a woman, to the manifest corruption and subversion of youth, and other citizens of this commonwealth . . . offending . . . [the] dignity of the Commonwealth of Pennsylvania. [37]

Here we have a classic description of a porno case, yet this one occurred in 1815! The defense claimed that this was not an indictable offense since it was only a "home viewing," and not a "public porno shop." The court, with Judge Duncan delivering the opinion, addressed these arguments, stating that many things occurring in private have a public effect and are therefore punishable:

> The defendants have been convicted, upon their own confession, of conduct indicative of great moral depravity. . . . This court is . . . invested with power to punish not only open violations of decency and morality, but also whatever secretly tends to undermine the principles of society. . . . Whatever tends to the destruction of morality, in general, may be punished criminally. Crimes are public offences, not because they are perpetrated publicly, but because their effect is to injure the public. Burglary, though done in secret, is a public offense; and secretly destroying fences is indictable.
>
> Hence, it follows, that an offence may be punishable, if in its nature and by its example, it tends to the corruption of morals; although it be not committed in public.
>
> The defendants are charged with exhibiting and showing . . . for money, a lewd . . . and obscene painting. A picture tends to excite lust, as strongly as a writing; and the showing of a picture is as much a publication as the selling of a book. . . . If the privacy of the room was a protection, all the youth of the city might be corrupted, by taking them, one by one, into a chamber, and there inflaming their passions by the exhibition of lascivious pictures. In the eye of the law, this would be a publication, and a most pernicious one. [38]

The court, by referring to other laws not specifically related to this case, had noted that the law did not allow lascivious, lewd, or obscene publications—the types of publications that are widely distributed today. This is another example of moral legislation based on Biblical standards. In an act unusual for that period, a second Justice, Judge Yeates, also delivered a statement:

> Although every immoral act, such as lying, etc., is not indictable, yet where the offence charged is destructive of morality in general . . . it is punishable at common law. The destruction of morality renders the power of the government invalid. . . . The corruption of the public mind, in general, and debauching the manners of youth, in particular, by lewd and obscene pictures exhibited to view, must necessarily be

attended with the most injurious consequences. . . . No man is permitted to corrupt the morals of the people; secret poison cannot be thus disseminated. [39]

These rulings and opinions clash sharply with those of current courts who refuse to oppose such materials or even to take any stands that would involve having to define "morality." When objective standards for right and wrong are disallowed (i.e., the Bible), the standards for morality become variable and individually determined. By refusing to sustain standards of morality, the courts have, by default, installed immorality as the acceptable and prevalent standard.

Davis v. Beason, 1889
United States Supreme Court

In this case, it was argued that what was immoral for one group might be moral for another. To further complicate the case, the alleged immorality was claimed to be part of a religious belief and therefore protected under the "free exercise" portion of the First Amendment. Specifically, this case involved bigamy and polygamy among Mormons in the western territories.

Under United States laws, bigamy and polygamy were crimes, but an Idaho statute went further and made it illegal for anyone who even taught or encouraged it, much less committed it, to vote or to hold any public office within the territory. Samuel Davis was convicted of bigamy and polygamy and was fined and sentenced to a jail term.

Following his conviction, he argued that his imprisonment was solely by virtue of his religious belief. He claimed that the law under which he had been convicted was a violation of the First Amendment, which prohibited laws respecting an establishment of religion or prohibiting their free exercise. He therefore requested that the court release him. He was freed by a court order, pending the outcome of the hearing on his arguments.

In arguments before the Supreme Court, his defense attorneys raised three issues. First, they contended that the laws on bigamy and polygamy were a violation of the First Amendment because they interfered with the religious beliefs of Davis and other Mormons. Second, they argued that the laws were a violation of the Fourteenth Amendment, which prohibited the states from making laws that interfered with the rights of their citizens. Third, they claimed the laws violated Article VI of the Constitution, which forbids a religious test as a requirement for office.

Justice Stephen Field, who was appointed to the Supreme Court by President Abraham Lincoln in 1863, and who was also on the Court during the *Holy Trinity* case, delivered the Court's ruling in a very straightforward statement:

> Bigamy and polygamy are crimes by the laws of all civilized and Christian countries. They are crimes by the laws of the United States, and they are crimes by the laws of Idaho. They tend to destroy the purity of the marriage relation, to disturb the peace of families, to degrade woman and to debase man. . . . To extend exemption from punishment for such crimes would be to shock the moral judgment of the community. To call their advocacy a tenet of religion is to offend the common sense of mankind.
>
> There have been sects which denied as a part of their religious tenets that there should be any marriage tie, and advocated promiscuous intercourse of the sexes as prompted by the passions of its members. . . . Should a sect of either of these kinds ever find its way into this country, swift punishment would follow the carrying into effect of its doctrines, and no heed would be given to the pretence that . . . their supporters could be protected in their exercise by the Constitution of the United States. Probably never before in the history of this country has it been seriously contended that the whole punitive power of the government for acts, recognized by the general consent of the Christian world . . . must be suspended in order that the tenets of a religious sect . . . may be carried out without hindrance.
>
> The constitutions of several States, in providing for religious freedom, have declared expressly that such freedom shall not be construed to excuse acts of licentiousness. . . . The constitution of New York of 1777 provided: "The free exercise and enjoyment of religious profession and worship, without discrimination or preference, shall forever hereafter be allowed, within this State, to all mankind: *Provided,* That the liberty of conscience, hereby granted, shall not be so construed as to excuse acts of licentiousness. . . . The constitutions of California, Colorado, Connecticut, Florida, Georgia, Illinois, Maryland, Minnesota, Mississippi, Missouri, Nevada and South Carolina contain a similar declaration. [40]

The defendant contended that his actions were not licentious—at least in his view. Yet, the basis for the Supreme Court's rejection of the defendant's argument was that they are crimes by the laws of "Christian countries." Notice further what the Court said would happen if some group advocating promiscuous intercourse of the sexes should appear in the United States:

> Swift punishment would follow the carrying into effect of its doctrines, and no heed would be given to the pretence that . . . their supporters could be protected in their exercise by the Constitution of the United States. [41]

This was the belief when legislation and judicial rulings were still God-centered and not man-centered. As is obvious from the Court's comments, it never envisioned it would be any other way. Our Founders would be shocked to see what courts protect today!

Literally hundreds of magazine, film publishers, and other groups "advocating promiscuous intercourse of the sexes" now operate under the Court's "constitutional" protection. For example, consider these excerpts from books and materials that *Planned Parenthood* recommends for adolescents: [42]

Boys and Sex: [43]

> More and more people are coming to understand that having sex is a joyful and enriching experience at any age. (p. 2)

> Playing with girls sexually before adolescence . . . increases the chances for a satisfactory sex life when a boy grows up. (p. 38)

> Premarital intercourse does have its definite values as a training ground for marriage . . . boys and girls who start having intercourse when they're adolescents . . . will find that it's a big help . . . it's like taking a car out on a test run before you buy it. (p. 117)

> Premarital intercourse among adolescents is often helpful in later life because it's easier to learn things in our earlier years. (p. 118)

> When people want to get close to each other, intercourse is the closest they can get. (p. 129)

Girls and Sex: [44]

> Girls understand now that they are far more likely to make good social and sexual adjustments to life if they learn to be

warm, open, responsive, and sexually unafraid. They're learning to be sexual partners of men. (p. 10-11)

Everyone's agreed . . . that teenage sex should be a learning experience. (p. 15)

Sex play with boys . . . can be exciting, pleasurable, and even worthwhile . . . it will help later sexual adjustment. (p. 48)

For those who plan on marriage eventually, early intercourse can also be a training ground. (p. 95)

Another reason for intercourse is the fact that . . . it's a means of learning how to live with people. (p. 96)

You've Changed the Combination: [45]

There are only two basic kinds of sex: sex with victims and sex without. Sex with victims is always wrong. Sex without is always right. (p. 10)

One way to avoid having victims is, of course, to have sexual relationships only with your friends. (p. 12)

It has been estimated that up to 80 percent of American public schools use materials available from *Planned Parenthood*. Publications are provided to adolescents, complete with photographs, illustrations, and graphics showing how to accomplish sexual activity easily, even encouraging types of sexual activity that are still illegal in many states today. The effect that groups like *Planned Parenthood* have had on the nation in recent years (under Court protection) is seen through statistics published in *Parade* on December 18, 1988:

Two-thirds of America's 11 million teenage boys say they have had sex with a girl . . . The first time for most of them was when they were around 15. By the time they are 18, on the average, boys have had sex with five girls.

The contemporary Court is a party to the decline of America's morality. It has upheld the "rights" of groups to propagate teachings on immorality and has prohibited schools from presenting Biblical teachings on morality. With the Court protecting groups who "advocate promiscuous intercourse," immorality has become so much a part of our society that, according to the same article:

There are 20,000 scenes with suggested sexual acts on television each year, all of them without regard to outcome.

A study conducted by Lou Harris, entitled "Sexual Material on American Network Television During the 1987-1988 Season," found the number of sexual instances on television tallied over 27 per hour.

The Court had protected morality based on Biblical standards for more than a century-and-a-half based on the beliefs of the Founders that morality provides our government its greatest protection. As Abraham Lincoln expressed it:

> The only assurance of our nation's safety is to lay our foundation in morality and religion. [46]

Lincoln continued:

> At what point then is the approach of danger to be expected? I answer, if it ever reach us, it must spring up amongst us; it cannot come from abroad. If destruction be our lot we must ourselves be its author and finisher. As a nation of freemen we must live through all time, or die by suicide. [47]

Murphy *v.* Ramsey & Others, 1885
United States Supreme Court

This case also dealt with polygamy, but this time in the territory of Utah. Would the Court use the standards of traditional Biblical morality, or discard them? The Court again upheld God's standards. Notice the Court's strong declaration on the importance of upholding legislation protecting the family according to Biblical teachings:

> Certainly no legislation can be supposed more wholesome and necessary in the founding of a free, self-governing commonwealth . . . than that which seeks to establish it on the basis of the idea of the family, as consisting in and springing from the union for life of one man and one woman in the holy estate of matrimony; [the family is] the sure foundation of all that is stable and noble in our civilization; the best guarantee of that reverent morality which is the source of all beneficent progress in social and political improvement. [48]

Ironically, legal action now goes directly against establishing family on "the union for life of one man and one woman in the holy estate of matrimony."

For example, in 1988, California was considering adopting legislation requiring that whenever sex education was taught in public schools that:

> Course material and instruction shall stress that monogamous heterosexual [one man and one woman] intercourse within marriage is a traditional American value. [49]

The Senator promoting this bill received a letter from an active legal organization protesting this provision. The excerpt below is from a copy of their letter; the letterhead bears the logo of the ACLU and is dated April 18, 1988. Why did the ACLU oppose the bill?

> It is our position that teaching that monogamous, heterosexual intercourse within marriage as a traditional American value is an unconstitutional establishment of a religious doctrine in public schools.   There are various religions which hold contrary beliefs with respect to marriage and monogamy. We believe SB 2394 violates the First Amendment.

As in previous cases, the argument is again raised that *any* moral standard is protected under the "free exercise" of religion; the difference is that the contemporary courts sustain this argument! Groups who claim Jefferson and Madison as their heroes because he allegedly advanced religious "toleration" and the complete separation of religious principles from the state would probably be horrified to read what the Court stated in many of the polygamy cases (this particular excerpt is from *Reynolds* v. *United States, 1878, United States Supreme Court):*

> It is a significant fact that on the 8th of December, 1788, after the passage of the act establishing religious freedom, and after the convention of Virginia had recommended as an amendment to the Constitution of the United States the declaration in a bill of rights that "all men have an equal, natural, and unalienable right to the free exercise of religion, according to the dictates of conscience," the legislature of that State substantially enacted the . . . death penalty . . . [for polygamy]. [50]

Jefferson and Madison, the men many idolize as heroes who allegedly argued free conscience for any and all religious beliefs, were party to enacting the death penalty for bigamy and polygamy! Traditional Biblical morality had always been embodied in our Founder's legislation and upheld by the courts.

City of Charleston *v.* S. A. Benjamin, 1846
Supreme Court of South Carolina

This controversy focused on the violation of a law best described by a quotation from the case:

> "An Ordinance for the better observance of the Lord's day, commonly called Sunday." . . . [Specifically:] "No person or persons whatsoever shall publicly expose to sale, or sell . . . any goods, wares or merchandise whatsoever upon the Lord's day." [51]

The defendant was accused of selling a pair of gloves in his shop on a Sunday. The defense used in the case is one that is frequently raised today: laws that prefer or support Christianity are a violation of the religious rights of others. The defense attorney argued that the Sunday law was a violation of the Constitution and an infringement on his client's religious rights because the defendant was a Jew, and observed the seventh day of the week. On the other side, the city's attorneys responded that:

> Christianity is a part of the common law of the land, with liberty of conscience to all. It has always been so recognized. . . . If Christianity is a part of the common law, its disturbance is punishable at common law. The U.S. Constitution allows it as a part of the common law. The President is allowed ten days [to sign a bill], with the exception of Sunday. The Legislature does not sit, public offices are closed, and the Government recognizes the day in all things. . . . The observance of Sunday is one of the usages of the common law, recognized by our U.S. and State Governments. . . . The Sabbath is still to be supported; Christianity is part and parcel of the common law. . . . *Christianity has reference to the principles of right and wrong . . . it is the foundation of those morals and manners upon which our society is formed; it is their basis. Remove this and they would fall. . . . [Morality] has grown upon the basis of Christianity.* [52] (emphasis added)

The court commended the defendant for his religious devotion, but pointed out that in the United States, Sunday is a particularly important day because Sunday is . . .

The Lord's day, the day of the Resurrection, is to us, who are called Christians, the day of rest after finishing a new creation. It is the day of the first visible triumph over death, hell and the grave! It was the birth day of the believer in Christ, to whom and through whom it opened up the way which, by repentance and faith, leads unto everlasting life and eternal happiness! On that day we rest, and to us it is the Sabbath of the Lord—its decent observance, in a Christian community, is that which ought to be expected. [53]

Then, addressing the defendant's assertion that all religions are to be treated equally under the Constitution, the judge directed attention to the source of the tolerance described in the Constitution:

What gave to us this noble safeguard of religious toleration...? It was Christianity. . . . But this toleration, thus granted, is a religious toleration; it is the free exercise and enjoyment of religious profession and worship, with two provisos, one of which, that which guards against acts of licentiousness, testifies to the Christian construction, which this section should receive! What are acts "of licentiousness" within the meaning of this section? Must they not be such public acts, as are calculated to shock the moral sense of the community where they take place? The orgies of Bacchus, among the ancients, were not offensive! At a later day, the Carnivals of Venice went off without note or observation. Such could not be allowed now! Why? Public opinion, based on Christian morality, would not suffer it!

What constitutes the standard of good morals? Is it not Christianity? There certainly is none other. Say that cannot be appealed to, and I don't know what would be good morals. The day of moral virtue in which we live would, in an instant, if that standard were abolished, lapse into the dark and murky night of Pagan immorality.

In the Courts over which we preside, we daily acknowledge Christianity as the most solemn part of our administration. A Christian witness, having no religious scruples about placing his hand upon the book, is sworn upon the holy Evangelists—the books of the New Testament, which testify of our Savior's birth, life, death, and resurrection; this is so common a matter, that it is little thought of as an evidence of the part which Christianity has in the common law.

I agree fully to what is beautifully and appropriately said in *Updegraph* v. *The Commonwealth* ... —Christianity, general Christianity, is, and always has been, a part of the common law: "not Christianity founded on any particular religious tenets; not Christianity with an established church . . . but Christianity with liberty of conscience to all men." [54] (emphasis added)

Since Christianity was the source of the religious tolerance found both in the United States and in its Constitution, the court could not allow it to become an equal among other religions; Christianity must remain foremost in the laws and statutes. The court then addressed the charge that laws preferring Christianity violated the free exercise of religion:

It is said [that a Sunday law] violates the free exercise and enjoyment of the religious profession and worship of the Israelite. Why? It does not require him to desecrate his own Sabbath. It does not say, "you must worship God on the Christian Sabbath." On the contrary, it leaves him free on all these matters. His evening sacrifice and his morning worship, constituting the 7th day, he publicly and freely offers up, and there is none to make him afraid. His Sundays are spent as he pleases, so far as religion is concerned.

It is however fancied that in some way this law is in derogation of the Hebrew's religion, inasmuch as by his faith and this statute, he is compelled to keep two Sabbaths. There is the mistake. He has his own, free and undiminished! Sunday is to us our day of rest. We say to him, simply, respect us, by ceasing on this day from the pursuit of that trade and business in which you, by the security and protection given to you by our [Christian] laws, make great gain. . . .

There is therefore no violation of the Hebrew's religion, in requiring him to cease from labor on another day than his Sabbath, if he be left free to observe the latter according to his religion. [55]

The Commonwealth *v.* Wolf, 1817
Supreme Court of Pennsylvania

Though this case occurred nearly three decades before *Charleston* v. *Benjamin*, the circumstances in the two cases were almost identical, as were the defense arguments. The court, in addressing the seventh day sabbath of the Jewish religion vs. the first day sabbath of the Christian religion, returned to the Scriptures to show that it could not be argued that Saturday, or any other day, was *the* day commanded by the Scripture—the Sabbath could be any day, as long as it occurred every seventh. However, the court emphasized the importance of a uniform national sabbath, in this, a Christian nation, Sunday was to be that day:

> Laws cannot be administered in any civilized government unless the people are taught to revere the sanctity of an oath, and look to a future state of rewards and punishments for the deeds of this life. It is of the utmost moment, therefore, that they should be reminded of their religious duties at stated periods. . . . A wise policy would naturally lead to the formation of laws calculated to subserve those salutary purposes. The invaluable privilege of the rights of conscience secured to us by the constitution of the commonwealth, was never intended to shelter those persons, who, out of mere caprice, would directly oppose those laws for the pleasure of showing their contempt and abhorrence of the religious opinions of the great mass of the citizens. [56]

Again, the same conclusion was reached as in the previous cases. The court concluded that the rights of conscience and free exercise of religion do not shelter those opposed to Christianity; rights and beliefs were protected insofar as they did not oppose the advancement of Christianity.

United States *v.* Macintosh, 1931
United States Supreme Court

This case, concerning a Canadian who was applying for naturalization in the United States, occurred more than 140 years after the ratification of the Constitution, yet the Court was still articulating the same message:

> We are a Christian people . . . according to one another the equal right of religious freedom, and acknowledging with reverence the duty of obedience to the will of God. [57]

Zorach v. Clauson, 1952
United States Supreme Court

Although this case occurred after the 1947 case *Everson* v. *Board of Education* (the case in which the Court announced, for the first time in its history, that it would pursue "a wall of separation between church and state"), the Court did not deviate completely from the longstanding practice of commingling Christianity with education. The Court upheld the constitutionality of students receiving religious instruction during the school day. However, the Court did take a step toward separation and away from historical precedent by declaring that the instruction must occur off campus. Nonetheless, its ruling was still light-years away from the position now held by the Court. Notice these comments during what was still the adolescent stage of the Court's now well-developed position on separation:

> The First Amendment, however, does not say that in every and all respects there shall be a separation of Church and State. . . . Otherwise the state and religion would be aliens to each other—hostile, suspicious, and even unfriendly. . . .
>
> We are a religious people whose institutions presuppose a Supreme Being. . . . When the state encourages religious instruction or cooperates with religious authorities by adjusting the schedule of public events to sectarian needs, it follows the best of our traditions. For it then respects the religious nature of our people and accommodates the public service to their spiritual needs. To hold that it may not would be to find in the Constitution a requirement that the government show a callous indifference to religious groups. That would be preferring those who believe in no religion over those who do believe. . . . We find no constitutional requirement which makes it necessary for government to be hostile to religion and to throw its weight against efforts to widen the effective scope of religious influence. [58]

The Court concluded that the argument for separation of church and state did not apply to religious instruction for school students during school hours . . .

> Unless separation of Church and State means that public institutions can make no adjustments of their schedules to accommodate the religious needs of the people. We cannot read into the Bill of Rights such a philosophy of hostility to religion. [59]

The fifteen cases excerpted above are only a few of hundreds of similar cases. Contemporary courts lack no legal precedents to help establish the constitutional intent of the First Amendment. The simple fact is that the historical precedents disprove what the Court wishes to enact, and therefore are disregarded or avoided!

Early Supreme Court Justices

In addition to the extensive number of early cases available, there are also records providing the opinions of many of the earliest Justices who served on the Supreme Court. Their individual statements are as clear and concise as were the early court's.

For example, consider the statements of John Jay, the first Chief Justice of the first Supreme Court. Jay was appointed by President George Washington, which is in itself probably an ample endorsement of Jay. As President of the Constitutional Convention, Washington was intimately aware of the intent of our Constitution and those he selected as Justices were not only those best qualified to serve, but were also those who would help establish the ideas birthed in Constitution Hall in Philadelphia. Even though his selection by Washington was a high commendation, Jay could properly stand on his own accomplishments.

Jay, along with James Madison and Alexander Hamilton, authored *The Federalist Papers*. These three men, through their writings, probably did more to secure the ratification of the Constitution than any other group of men. They explained to America what would be achieved through the new form of government and how it would function to benefit the entire nation. If there were "heroes" in the effort to establish a new national government, John Jay would have to be placed near the top. Notice what this first Chief Justice of the Supreme Court declared:

> Providence has given to our people the choice of their rulers, and it is the duty as well as the privilege and interest of our Christian nation to select and prefer Christians for their rulers. [60]

Another Justice appointed by George Washington, James Wilson, was one of only six men who signed both the Declaration of Independence and the Constitution. He was extremely active at the Constitutional Convention, speaking 168 times, second only to Gouverneur Morris' 173 times. This particular quote concerning

Judge Wilson appeared in the Pennsylvania Supreme Court records of *Updegraph* v. *Commonwealth, 1826:*

> The late Judge Wilson, of the Supreme Court of the United States, Professor of Law in the College in Philadelphia, was appointed in 1791, unanimously, by the House of Representatives of this state. . . . He had just risen from his seat in the convention which formed the constitution of the United States, and of this state; and it is well known, that for our present form of government we are greatly indebted to his exertions and influence. With his fresh recollections of both constitutions, in his Course of Lectures (3d vol. of his Works, 122), he states that . . . Christianity is part of the common-law. [61]

Quite impressive credentials! Not only did he participate in the birth of the nation and in its constitutional establishment, he was unanimously confirmed as George Washington's choice to serve on the Supreme Court. Having helped frame the Constitution, he was intimately aware of its intent, and he explicitly stated that Christianity is part of the "common law." (The "common law" is the basis on which all other laws are built; it is the foundation). According to Justice James Wilson, our foundation is Christianity. It is ludicrous for anyone to assert that since the building is now complete, it would cause no damage to remove its foundation!

Another early Justice was Joseph Story. Justice Story was appointed by President James Madison and served on the Supreme Court for 34 years. Logic assures us that James Madison, as the "Chief Architect of the Constitution," would not have selected someone opposed to the principles of the new Constitution. Notice what Justice Story, who was also a professor at Harvard Law School, wrote concerning the First Amendment in his *Commentaries on the Constitution* and his *A Familiar Exposition of the Constitution of the United States:*

> We are not to attribute this prohibition of a national religious establishment [in the First Amendment] to an indifference to religion in general, and especially to Christianity, *(which none could hold in more reverence than the framers of the Constitution)*. . . . Probably, at the time of the adoption of the Constitution, and of the Amendments to it . . . the general, if not the universal, sentiment in America was, that Christianity ought to receive encouragement from the State. . . . An attempt to level all religions, and to make it a matter of state policy to hold all in

utter indifference, would have created universal disapprobation, if not universal indignation. [62] (emphasis added)

It yet remains a problem to be solved in human affairs, whether any free government can be permanent, where the public worship of God, and the support of religion, constitute no part of the policy or duty of the state in any assignable shape. [63]

His statement is worth repeating: "Christianity ought to receive encouragement from the state" because it is doubted "whether any free government can be permanent" where "the support of religion constitute[s] no part of the policy or duty of the state."

Perhaps the most famous of all Chief Justices of the Supreme Court has been John Marshall. Marshall was active in the Revolutionary War as a captain, fought in many campaigns in several states, and went through the infamous winter of 1777-1778 at Valley Forge with General George Washington. He was active with James Madison in urging ratification of the Constitution at Virginia's ratifying convention. Marshall served in the House of Representatives and declined an appointment from George Washington to be Attorney General. Before being appointed by President John Adams as Chief Justice of the Supreme Court, he was Adams' Secretary of State.

Marshall served on the Court for 34 years. It was through his efforts that the Court moved from its fledgling beginnings to its position as a viable third branch of government. Elegant carvings of Marshall, which now adorn the outside of the Supreme Court building, commemorate his years of distinguished service to the Court. The following story about Chief Justice John Marshall was originally published in the *Winchester Republican* concerning an incident which occurred at McGuire's hotel in Winchester after Marshall had suffered a mishap on the road nearby:

The shafts of his ancient gig were broken and "held together by withes formed from the bark of a hickory sapling"; he was negligently dressed, his knee buckles loosened. In the tavern a discussion arose among some young men concerning "the merits of the Christian religion." The debate grew warm and lasted "from six o'clock until eleven." No one knew Marshall, who sat quietly listening. Finally one of the youthful combatants turned to him and said: "Well, my old gentleman, what think you of these things?" Marshall responded with a "most eloquent and unanswerable appeal."

He talked for an hour, answering "every argument urged against" the teachings of Jesus. "In the whole lecture, there was so much simplicity and energy, pathos and sublimity, that not another word was uttered." The listeners wondered who the old man could be. Some thought him a preacher, and great was their surprise when they learned afterwards that he was the Chief Justice of the United States. [64]

Observers from the Outside

In addition to the records of the Supreme Court Justices, there are interesting observations recorded by visitors to this nation in its early years. The observations of one of these visitors, Alexis de Tocqueville, are preserved in his famous work *Democracy in America*. He was more than a mere "tourist" visiting America:

It is not, then, merely to satisfy a legitimate curiosity that I have examined America; my wish has been to find instruction by which we may ourselves profit. [65]

De Tocqueville, a French historian, traveled the length and breadth of the nation, observing and recording what made America so distinctive and great among the nations of the world. Pertinent to this chapter is an observation he made on the judicial system in the United States:

While I was in America, a witness, who happened to be called at the assizes of the county of Chester (state of New York), declared that he did not believe in the existence of God or in the immortality of the soul. The judge refused to admit his evidence, on the ground that the witness had destroyed beforehand all the confidence of the court in what he was about to say. The newspapers related the fact without any farther comment. The New York *Spectator* of August 23d, 1831, relates the fact in the following terms:

The court of common pleas of Chester county (New York), a few days since rejected a witness who declared his disbelief in the existence of God. The presiding judge remarked, that he had not before been aware that there was a man living who did not believe in the existence of God; that this belief constituted the sanction of all testimony in a court of justice: and that he knew of no cause in a Christian country, where a witness had been permitted to testify without such belief. [66]

De Tocqueville's observations again confirm the Christian standards which were applied in America's courts from its founding.

The cases presented in this chapter, representing only the "tip of the iceberg," accurately portray what was typical in America's courts and legal system during its first 150 years under our Constitution. These cases (and hundreds like them), the records of the early Supreme Court Justices, and the writings of the pioneers of American legal practice, leave no doubt where our Founders stood on Christian principles in government, education, and public affairs. Our Fathers intended that this nation should be a Christian nation, not because all who lived in it were Christians, but because it was founded on and would be governed and guided by Christian principles.

~ 5 ~
Other "Organic Utterances"

In the previous chapter, many legal records establishing this country as a Christian nation were examined. In *Church of the Holy Trinity* v. *United States*, 1892, the Court stated:

> This is a religious people. This is historically true. From the discovery of this continent to the present hour, there is a single voice making this affirmation . . . these are not individual sayings, declarations of private persons: they are organic utterances; they speak the voice of the entire people . . . these and many other matters which might be noticed, add a volume of unofficial declarations to the mass of organic utterances that this is a Christian nation. [1]

The Court explained that it was the "organic utterances" which proved that this was a Christian nation. "Organic," in a legal sense, simply means "belonging to the fundamental or constitutional law" and can be comprised of both historical information and of previous legal rulings based on such historical information. "Organic utterances" are the base on which laws are built and are therefore part of the law—they are what judges term the "common law." The Court noted that the "mass of organic utterances" provided "a volume of unofficial declarations," prompting their official conclusion that "this is a Christian nation." This chapter will present some of that "volume" and "mass of organic utterances."

The quantity of organic utterances (historical material) available for proving that this is a Christian nation are such that one might be tempted to say, as did the Apostle John when writing about Jesus, that if everything "were written down, I suppose that even the whole world would not have room for the books that would be written" (John 21:25). Even though this chapter is filled with numerous selections typical of the mass, they still only "skim the surface" of that which is available. The reader can become his own investigator of history and quickly discover how much more could be added to that which is presented here.

The following selections are presented in the same chronological order utilized by the Court: "from the discovery of the continent to the present hour." The historical records from each era, when combined together in this chapter, indeed form a choir of resounding

voices affirming Christianity to be the base of our nation, government, and educational system. The reader will soon be convinced of
what the Supreme Court declared: "this is a Christian nation."

America's Discovery

The decision by Columbus to embark on an unprecedented and
obviously dangerous journey could not have been an easy one to
make.   Professional opinion assured Columbus that dragons and
death awaited him beyond the charted waters. Surely he must have
considered the possibility that such a belief might be correct. Why,
then, did he set out at such risk and peril? Excerpts from his own
writings provide the answer:

> Our Lord opened . . . my understanding (I could feel his hand
> upon me), so it became clear to me that it was feasible to
> navigate from here to [there]. . . . All those who heard about
> my enterprise rejected it with laughter, scoffing at me. . . .
> Who doubts that this illumination was from the Holy Spirit? I
> attest that he, with marvelous rays of light, consoled me
> through the holy and sacred Scriptures . . . they inflame me
> with a sense of great urgency. . . . No one should be afraid to
> take on any enterprise in the name of our Savior, if it is right
> and if the purpose is purely for his holy service. . . . And I say
> that the sign which convinces me . . . is the preaching of the
> Gospel recently in so many lands. [2]

America's First Colonies

Following Columbus' discovery of the western lands, other
explorers ventured onto the new continent, making property claims
for their own nations. Soon, groups of prospective colonists began to
approach their sovereign and request land charters in the new nation.
In 1606, a charter was obtained from King James I for a permanent
settlement in the new world in Virginia. That charter reveals the
colonists' declared reasons for traveling to the new world:

> To make Habitation . . . and to deduce a colony of sundry of
> our People into that part of America commonly called
> Virginia . . . in propagating of Christian religion to such
> People, as yet live in Darkness . . . [to] bring . . . a settled and
> quiet Government. [3]

In 1609, another charter was granted for Virginia:

> Because the principal Effect which we can desire or expect of
> this Action, is the Conversion . . . of the people in those Parts
> unto the true Worship of God and Christian Religion. [4]

The Pilgrims arrived in America on the Mayflower in November
of 1620. Before disembarking, they drafted and signed the
Mayflower Compact, the first plan of government formed solely in
America. That government compact was brief and concise,
proclaiming their purpose for coming to America and affirming their
commitment to that purpose:

> Having undertaken for the Glory of God, and Advancement
> of the Christian Faith . . . a Voyage to plant the first colony
> in the northern Parts of Virginia . . . [we] combine ourselves
> together into a civil Body Politick, for . . . Furtherance of the
> Ends aforesaid. [5]

The First Charter of Massachusetts, dated March 1629, reflected
similar goals. It was granted so that:

> Our said People . . . may be soe religiously, peaceablie, and
> civilly governed, as their good Life and orderlie Conversacon
> maie wynn and incite the Natives of [that] Country, to the
> Knowledg and Obedience of the onlie true God and Sauior of
> Mankinde, and the Christian fayth, which in our Royall
> Intencon . . . is the principall Ende of this Plantacon. [6]

The Puritans arrived nearly a decade after the Pilgrims. During
their journey to America, their leader, John Winthrop, authored a
work which described their intended role in America—*A Model of
Christian Charity:*

> Wee are a Company professing our selues fellow members of
> Christ . . . knitt together by this bond of loue. . . . Wee are
> entered into Covenant with him for this worke. [7]

Winthrop warned that since they were declaring to the world that
they were witnesses of the Christian lifestyle, there was an awesome
responsibility resting upon them:

> For wee must Consider that wee shall be as a Citty vpon a
> Hill, the eies of all people are vppon vs; soe that if wee shall
> deale falsely with our god in this worke wee haue vndertaken

and soe cause him to withdrawe his present help from vs, wee shall be made a story and a by-word through the world. [8]

That warning is still pertinent for America today.

The charters of other early colonies reflected similar commitments. In 1632, the Charter of Maryland issued by King Charles described Lord Baltimore and his goals for the Colony:

> Our well beloved and right trusty subject Cœcilius Calvert, Baron of Baltimore . . . being animated with a laudable, and pious Zeal for extending the Christian Religion . . . hath humbly besought Leave of Us that he may transport . . . a numerous Colony of the English Nation, to a certain Region . . . having no Knowledge of the Divine Being. [9]

On March 25, 1634, Lord Baltimore and his group arrived on the land designated by the charter. One of the members of the expedition, Father White, recorded what occurred on their arrival:

> We celebrated the mass. . . . This had never been done before in this part of the world. After we had completed the [mass], we took on our shoulders a great cross, which we had hewn out of a tree, and advancing in order to the appointed place, with the assistance of the Governor and his associates . . . we erected a trophy to Christ the Savior. [10]

In 1647, William Bradford, the leader of the Pilgrims, collected his notes from earlier years and compiled them into the historical work *History of Plymouth Plantation.* Bradford explained why the Pilgrims came to the new world:

> [A] great hope & inward zeall they had of laying some good foundation, or at least to make some way therunto, for ye propagating & advancing ye gospell of ye kingdom of Christ in those remote parts of ye world. [11]

Quakers and other Christian groups began to settle in North Carolina in 1653. Several years later, in 1662, they obtained a charter confirming what was already obvious—that the settlement had been established because the colonists were:

> Excited with a laudable and pious zeal for the propagation of the Christian faith . . . in the parts of America not yet cultivated or planted, and only inhabited by . . . people, who have no knowledge of Almighty God. [12]

The Charter of Rhode Island, granted by King Charles II in July 1663, reflected the same goals as the other charters:

> That they pursuing with peace and loyal mindes, their sober, serious and religious intentions . . . in the holy Christian faith . . . a most flourishing civil state may stand, and best be maintained . . . grounded upon gospel principles. [13]

In 1731, some 100 settlers moved into the Georgia area and were soon followed by the Moravians and other Christian groups. What did they do on their arrival in the new territory?

> When they touched shore, [they] kneeled in thanks to God. They said, "Our end in leaving our native country is not to gain riches and honor, but singly this: to live wholly to the glory of God." The object . . . was "to make Georgia a religious colony" and so . . . they invited John and Charles Wesley and Rev. George Whitefield over to serve as chaplains, oversee Indian affairs and build orphanages, etc. When Whitefield died, the legislature attempted to have him buried there at public cost in honor of his influence. [14]

The charters of Connecticut,[15] New Hampshire,[16] and New Jersey [17] were virtually a restatement of the Christian goals reflected in the other charters.

America's First Governments

As the number of colonists and settlements increased, so did the need for government. Even though each colony relied heavily on the personal self-control and integrity of its individual members, the colonists recognized the benefit of civil regulations. They thus produced the first constitution ever written in the United States: the Fundamental Orders of Connecticut. This constitution, written primarily by Puritan minister Thomas Hooker, was the beginning of American government. According to historians, our own federal Constitution is "in lineal descent more nearly related to that of Connecticut than to that of any of the other thirteen colonies." [18] The charge delivered to the committee which convened to frame these laws was to make them: "As near the law of God as they can be." [19]

On January 14, 1639, the men from Hartford, Wethersfield, and Windsor gathered in Hartford and adopted this new constitution. Its preamble proclaimed their reason for establishing this government:

> Well knowing when a people are gathered together the word of God requires, that to meinteine the peace and union of such a people, there should bee an orderly and decent govemement established according to God. [20]

It further explained how this was to be attained:

> Enter into combination and confederation together, to meinteine and preserve the libberty and purity of the gospell of our Lord Jesus which we now profess . . . . Which, according to the truth of the said Gospell, is now practised amongst us; as allso, in our civill affaires to be guided and governed according to such lawes, rules, orders, and decrees. [21]

When the colonists of Exeter, New Hampshire, established their government seven months later, they expressed the same rationale:

> Considering with ourselves the holy Will of God and our own Necessity that we should not live without wholesome Lawes and Civil Government among us of which we are altogether destitute; do in the name of Christ and in the Sight of God combine ourselves together to erect and set up among us such Government as shall be to our best discerning agreeable to the Will of God. [22]

A similar proclamation was made when Massachusetts, Connecticut, New Plymouth, and New Haven formed the New England Confederation in 1643:

> We all came into these parts of America, with one and the same end and aim, namely, to advance the Kingdom of our Lord Jesus Christ. [23]

In 1644, the New Haven Colony adopted rules for their courts:

> The judicial laws of God as they were delivered by Moses . . . [are to] be a rule to all the courts in this jurisdiction. [24]

In 1669, the Fundamental Constitutions of Carolina was drawn up by John Locke. [25] It required people to: (1) believe that there is a God, (2) in court, recognize Divine justice and human responsibility, and (3) be a church member in order to be a freeman of the colony. [26]

In 1665 the New York legislature passed an act to uphold "the public worship of God" and instruction of "the people in the true religion." [27]

In 1681, the Quaker minister William Penn received a land grant giving him the land between New York and Maryland, the area later called Pennsylvania. On receiving this new land, Penn, in a letter on January 1, 1681, professed:

> God that has given it me . . . will, I believe, bless and make it the seed of a nation. [28]

The following year, Penn wrote the Frame of Government for this new territory. It was to:

> Make and establish such laws as shall best preserve true Christian and civil liberty, in all opposition to all unchristian . . . practices. [29]

The laws were very simple—whatever was Christian was legal, whatever was not Christian was illegal. Penn also told the Russian Czar, Peter the Great, that:

> "If thou wouldst rule well, thou must rule for God, and to do that, thou must be ruled by him." Penn also said that "those who will not be governed by God will be ruled by tyrants." [30]

An article on Penn that appeared in the 1819 London *Biographical Review* stated that he:

> Established an absolute toleration; it was his wish that every man who believed in God should partake of the rights of a citizen; and that every man who adored Him as a Christian, of whatever sect he might be, should be a partaker in authority. [31]

The differentiation was clear: anyone who believed in God could be a citizen, but only Christians could be part of the civil authority. The "absolute toleration" was reflected in the inclusion of Christians in government "of whatever sect they might be." As with so many of the Founders, Penn felt the issue was not whether an individual was from the proper denomination, but whether he was Christian.

In 1697, the New Jersey governor made a proclamation "in obedience to the laws of God" which enacted statutes "encouraging of religion and virtue, particularly the observance of the Lord's day." [32] The influence of Christianity and the Bible on New Jersey is seen even in the inscription that appeared on the 1665 seal of the East Jersey Colony: Proverbs 14:34—"Righteousness exalteth a nation." [33]

Christianity was the essential ingredient in the early growth and orderly development of the new world in its colonization, government, and education. Virtually every significant achievement of our early years was accomplished under the influence of Christianity.

The Founding of Education in America

In Europe, the Reformation had occurred because men like Martin Luther had desired that the common man be able to read the Scriptures for himself. It had been the illiteracy of the people—and thus their inability to judge the practices of the civil government against the teachings of the Bible—which had permitted so many civil abuses to occur under the banner of "Christianity." Those civil atrocities were not ancient history to the settlers in America; they were still fresh in their minds.

The settlers wanted to preclude the possibility of any such repetition in America. Therefore, one of the first laws providing public education for children of colonists was enacted in 1642 first in Massachusetts, then in 1647 in both Massachusetts and Connecticut. It was a calculated attempt to prevent illiteracy and to avert the abuse of power which can be imposed on a Biblically illiterate people. The 1647 law (titled the "Old Deluder Satan Law"), as did the 1642 law, had a specific declared intent:

> It being one chiefe project of that old deluder, Sathan, to keepe men from the knowledge of the scriptures, as in former time. . . . It is therefore ordered . . . [that] after the Lord hath increased [the settlement] to the number of fifty howshoulders, [they] shall then forthwith appointe one within theire towne, to teach all such children as shall resorte to him, to write and read. . . . And it is further ordered, That where any towne shall increase to the number of one hundred families or howshoulders, they shall sett up a grammar schoole . . . to instruct youths, so farr as they may bee fitted for the university. [34]

Both the 1642 and the 1647 laws enacted the establishment of schools to ensure that students would know how to read the Bible. The inseparability of Christianity from public education in America was seen not simply in grammar schools, but at every level of American education. Consider, for example, America's first college: Harvard

College in Massachusetts, established by the Puritans less than a decade after their arrival in America. A pamphlet made available to prospective students delineated the rules to be observed by every student who chose to attend Harvard. Notice some of the requirements:

2. Let every Student be plainly instructed, and earnestly pressed to consider well the maine end of his life and studies is, *to know God and Jesus Christ which is eternal life,* Joh. 17.3. and therefore to lay *Christ* in the bottome, as the only foundation of all sound knowledge and Learning.

And seeing the Lord only giveth wisedome, Let every one seriously set himselfe by prayer in secret to seeke it of him. *Prov* 2, 3.

3. Every one shall so exercise himselfe in reading the Scriptures twice a day, that he shall be ready to give such an account of his proficiency therein. [35]

The official motto of Harvard was "For Christ and the Church" and prior to the Revolution, ten of its twelve presidents were ministers. [36]

In 1692, the College of William & Mary was founded in Williamsburg, Virginia, through the efforts of the Rev. James Blair. It was chartered that:

The youth may be piously enacted in good letters and manners, and that the Christian faith may be propagated . . . to the glory of God. [37]

In 1701, Yale was founded in Connecticut by ten Congregational ministers. Until 1898, every president of Yale was a minister. Its purpose was:

To plant, and under ye Divine blessing to propagate in this Wilderness, the blessed Reformed, Protestant religion. [38]

Yale, like Harvard, had requirements for its students:

Seeing God is the giver of all wisdom, every scholar, besides private or secret prayer, where all we are bound to ask wisdom, shall be present morning and evening at public prayer in the hall at the accustomed hour. . . . [39]

The Scriptures . . . morning and Evening [are] to be read by the Students at the times of prayer in the School . . . studiously Indeavor[ing] in the Education of s^d students to promote the power and Purity of Religion. [40]

In 1746, Princeton was founded by Presbyterians with the official motto "Under God's Power She Flourishes." The Rev. Jonathan Dickinson became its first president, declaring, "Cursed be all that learning that is contrary to the cross of Christ!" [41] Until 1902, every president after him was a minister.

In 1766, through the efforts of Rev. Theodore Frelinghuysen, Rutgers University was founded. Its official motto, "Son of Righteousness, Shine upon the West also," was an adaptation of the Netherlands' University of Utrecht motto: "Son of Righteouness, Shine upon Us." [42]

In 1779, George Washington confirmed the central role of Christianity in education. Chiefs from the Delaware Indian tribe visited him at his military encampment and brought him three Indian youth to be trained in American schools. On May 12, 1779, Washington assured the chiefs that "Congress . . . will look upon them as their own Children." [43] Washington then commended them:

> You do well to wish to learn our arts and ways of life, and above all, the religion of Jesus Christ. These will make you a greater and happier people than you are. Congress will do every thing they can to assist you in this wise intention. [44]

What would these youth learn in America's schools "above all"? "The religion of Jesus Christ"! These were neither aberrations nor isolated examples—these represented the norm:

> One hundred and six of the first one hundred and eight colleges in America were founded on the Christian faith. By the time of the Civil War, non-religious universities could be counted on one hand. College presidents were almost always clergymen until around 1900. A study entitled *"An Appraisal of Church and Four-year Colleges"* (1955) stated that "nearly all of those institutions which have exerted a decided influence, even in our literary and political history, were established by evangelical Christians." [45]

To substantiate that Christian education "exerted a decided influence . . . in our . . . political history," one needs to investigate no further than John Witherspoon, President of Princeton. Witherspoon not only signed the Declaration of Independence, he served on over 100 committees in Congress. He also trained many of the nation's leaders while at Princeton, including:

1 President, 1 Vice-President, 3 Supreme Court Justices, 10 Cabinet members, 12 Governors, 60 Congressmen (21 Senators and 39 Representatives), plus many members of the Constitutional Convention and many state congressmen. [46]

Each of these men had been trained in the college which had declared "Cursed be all learning that is contrary to the cross of Christ!" And this is only one example from one college! Christian education trained our statesmen and patriots; to it we owe the form of government that established this nation as a world leader.

The Struggle for Independence

During the era of independence, there was probably no individual more influential than Samuel Adams, "The Father of the American Revolution." He was a tireless patriot and an unparalleled leader in the cause of liberty for over 20 years, helping America understand not only the oppression it was under, but also the solution to that tyranny.

In the years immediately preceding the Revolution, when English oppression was mounting and injustices were increasing, there was no reliable source from which the Colonists could receive accurate information or patriotic inspiration. It was to meet this need that Samuel Adams formed Committees of Correspondence. The original Committee in Boston had a three-fold goal: (1) to delineate the rights the Colonists had as men, as Christians, and as subjects of the crown, (2) to detail how these rights had been violated, and (3) to publicize throughout the Colonies the first two items.

This Committee was replicated in numerous other localities, and it was through this network of Committees that their three primary goals and other "news flashes" were uniformly communicated throughout the towns and parishes in each state by an early "pony express" system. These Committees provided the unity and cohesion necessary for the Colonies to stand united during a time when communication was difficult and unreliable.

Samuel Adams assumed personal responsibility for the first goal of the Committees: the exposition of their rights. His resulting work, "The Rights of the Colonists," was circulated in 1772. In explaining their rights as Christians, Adams declared:

These may be best understood by reading and carefully studying the institutes of the great Law Giver and Head of the Christian Church, which are to be found clearly written and promulgated in the New Testament. [47]

Adams reminded them that their rights could be understood from the New Testament; to bring about proper change they needed to study the laws of Christianity. Not only did Adams believe Christianity to be vital to the birth of the nation, he believed it vital to its longevity:

> While the people are virtuous they cannot be subdued; but when once they lose their virtue they will be ready to surrender their liberties to the first external or internal invader. . . . If virtue and knowledge are diffused among the people, they will never be enslaved. This will be their great security. [48]

Adams never separated the struggle for freedom from Biblical principles. During conflicts between the American provincial congresses and the British crown-governors, Adams would set aside days of prayer and fasting to seek the Lord and His intervention on America's behalf. [49] For Samuel Adams there was no separation between "political" service and "spiritual" activities.

However, the sentiments of the provincial congresses were no different than those held by Adams. They proclaimed to the nation:

> "Our cause is just;" and it was . . . a Christian duty to defend it. [50]

As Americans responded to their "Christian duty" to defend the "cause," they organized into small militia groups. These groups were frequently comprised of the men in a local church and became known as the "Minutemen." A deacon of the local church, or even the pastor, was generally responsible for drilling the men. Their military duty was not separated from their spiritual responsibilities:

> On the days of drill the citizen soldiers sometimes went from the parade-ground to the church, where they listened to exhortation and prayer. [51]

The charge given to the Minutemen by the Provincial Congress indicates how closely national policy was intertwined with Christian principles:

> You . . . are placed by Providence in the post of honor, because it is the post of danger. . . . The eyes not only of North America

and the whole British Empire, but of all Europe, are upon you. Let us be, therefore, altogether solicitous that no disorderly behavior, nothing unbecoming our characters as Americans, as citizens and Christians, be justly chargeable to us. [52]

Here was a governmental charge to the military to remember their Christian witness during the struggle! Congress did not want any opportunity for an accusation of misbehavior to be lodged against Christianity in the United States.

That the patriots were strongly influenced by Christianity is evidenced by a letter written from Abigail Adams to Mercy Warren in late 1775:

A patriot without religion in my estimation is as great a paradox, as an honest Man without the fear of God. . . . The Scriptures tell us righteousness exalteth a Nation. [53]

On May 2, 1778, Commander-in-chief George Washington expressed similar sentiments to his troops at Valley Forge when he declared:

To the distinguished character of Patriot, it should be our highest Glory to add the more distinguished Character of Christian. [54]

Civil liberties were so inseparable from religious principles that the description of the inhabitants of a town in Massachusetts seemed to describe the entire nation:

Civil and religious principles [were] the sweetest and essential part of their lives, without which the remainder was scarcely worth preserving. [55]

In December 1773, in opposition to taxes, the Colonists held the infamous Boston Tea Party. Tensions escalated rapidly and led to open reprisals between the Colonies and Great Britain. In early 1774, Parliament passed the Boston Port Bill to blockade Boston harbor and eliminate all trade to or from the port. The Committee of Correspondence quickly instructed its members to inform the rest of the Colonies of the plight facing Bostonians. How did the other Colonies respond?

The first action of the colonies was to call for a Day of Fasting and Prayer for June 1, 1774, the day on which the Boston Port blockade would take effect. Thus the colonies

turned immediately "to seek divine direction and aid."
Secondly, the cities and towns of the sister colonies
responded to Boston with letters affirming their support and
sending them whatever supplies they could. Every colony
contributed something for a period of over six months—
voluntarily—to strangers. Third, there was an immediate
move to join together in a general Congress in Philadelphia
on September 5, 1774. [56]

By August, the men of Pepperell, Massachusetts, had already
sent many loads of rye. Their leader, William Prescott, must
have summed up the feelings of a great many Americans,
when he wrote to the men of Boston:

> We heartily sympathize with you, and are always ready
> to do all in our power for your support, comfort and
> relief; knowing that Providence has placed you where
> you must stand the first shock. We consider we are all
> embarked in [the same boat] and must sink or swim
> together. We think if we submit to these regulations, all
> is gone. Our forefathers passed the vast Atlantic, spent
> their blood and treasure, that they might enjoy their
> liberties, both civil and religious, and transmit them to
> their posterity. . . . Now if we should give them up, can
> our children rise up and call us blessed? . . . Let us all
> be of one heart, and stand fast in the liberty wherewith
> Christ has made us free; and may he, of his infinite
> mercy grant us deliverance out of all our troubles. [57]

Boston gratefully responded to this outpouring of spiritual encouragement and material support:

> The Christian sympathy and generosity of our friends through
> the Continent cannot fail to inspire the inhabitants of this
> town with patience, resignation, and firmness, while we trust
> in the Supreme Ruler of the universe, that he will graciously
> hear our cries, and in his time free us from our present
> bondage and make us rejoice in his great salvation. [58]

Such open declarations of the Colonists' reliance on Christ
evidently caused one Crown-appointed governor to write to the
Board of Trade in England explaining to them:

> If you ask an American, who is his master? He will tell you
> he has none, nor any governor but Jesus Christ. [59]

That letter may well have given rise to the cry soon passed by the Committees of Correspondence throughout the Colonies:

"No King but King Jesus!" [60]

As time progressed, the inevitable became obvious: peaceful reconciliation with Great Britain was impossible. Armed hostility had already erupted at Lexington and Concord; a complete separation was the only solution. Thus, on July 2, 1776, the Declaration of Independence was approved in principle and on July 4, 1776, the distinguished representatives from throughout the Colonies officially approved their separation from Great Britain. Those patriots were not foolish; they realized that they were facing a monumental, and perhaps impossible, task by facing up to Britain's superior, well-honed fighting machine. They already knew they could *not* win this struggle solely through their own efforts. They would need help, and they knew just where to go to receive it; they announced the source of their aid in the final sentence of the Declaration of Independence:

> For the support of this Declaration, *with a firm reliance on the protection of Divine Providence,* we mutually pledge to each other our Lives, our Fortunes, and our sacred Honor. (emphasis added)

They entered into this commitment with more than just a token acknowledgment of God, they had a "*firm* reliance on the protection of Divine Providence."

Congress, in fact, had not been content with Jefferson's original version of the Declaration; after all, this was a declaration to the world. Consequently, the original draft was changed in several places to further reflect their commitment to God:

> While reviewing Thomas Jefferson's original draft of the Declaration, the committee assigned to the task added the words, "they are endowed by their Creator with certain unalienable rights." Then, when the Declaration was debated before Congress, they added the phrase, "appealing to the Supreme Judge of the World, for the rectitude of our intentions," as well as the words "with a firm reliance on the protection of divine Providence." [61]

Though much of the remainder of Jefferson's draft remained intact, these revisions reflected Congress' firm conviction that God and civil government were inseparable. That document was actually a dual declaration: a Declaration of *Independence* from Britain and a Declaration of *Dependence* on God!

The day following Congress' approval of the Declaration, John Adams wrote Abigail about the importance of that special July day in 1776:

> I am apt to believe that it will be celebrated by succeeding generations as the great anniversary Festival. It ought to be commemorated, as the day of deliverance, by solemn acts of devotion to God Almighty. [62]

On July 8th, the Declaration was read publicly outside Independence Hall, and on July 19th, Congress ordered that the Declaration be engrossed in beautiful script on parchment so that it could be signed by the entire Congress. On August 2, 1776, the members of the Congress placed their hands to that document in its support. As it was being signed, Samuel Adams summarized the prevalent sentiment when he declared:

> We have this day restored the Sovereign to whom alone men ought to be obedient. . . . From the rising to the setting sun may his kingdom come. [63]

The "shot heard 'round the world" had been fired between the Colonists and the British on April 19, 1775, more than a year before the Declaration was approved. Congress, knowing they were facing a protracted war, contemplated their choice for a qualified leader for their "military."

On June 12th, Congress declared a day of prayer and fasting, [64] and on June 14th, 1775, George Washington was nominated as Commander-in-chief of the Continental Army. [65] The next day, the 15th, Congress unanimously approved Washington, [66] and on the 16th he gave his acceptance speech. [67] Congress could have made no finer choice to command the disorganized and fledgling army.

Washington's first general order to his troops on July 9, 1776, contained an admonition similar to the one Congress had delivered to the Minutemen. He called on:

> Every officer and man . . . to live, and act, as becomes a Christian Soldier defending the dearest Rights and Liberties of his country. [68]

Throughout the Revolution, miraculous interventions frequently accompanied the new American army. Somehow they avoided situations where they should have been crushed by the British. On one occasion, an unexplained thick fog appeared, allowing the Americans to escape from certain defeat at the powerful, closing jaws of the Redcoat army. On other occasions, unexplained storms and torrential downpours appeared from nowhere to halt British retreats and prevent their escape, thus allowing the Continentals to surround them. Several such instances are thoroughly documented in *The Light and the Glory* by Peter Marshall and David Manuel. So obvious was the help that America received from their "firm reliance on Divine Providence" that when George Washington wrote Thomas Nelson on August 20, 1778, he declared:

> The hand of Providence has been so conspicuous in all this, that he must be worse than an infidel that lacks faith, and more than wicked, that has not gratitude enough to acknowledge his obligations. [69]

At the conclusion of the War, Washington, in a 1783 circular letter addressed to the Governors of all the states, told them:

> I now make it my earnest prayer, that God would have you, and the State over which you preside, in his holy protection . . . that he would most graciously be pleased to dispose us all to do justice, to love mercy, and to demean ourselves with that charity, humility, and pacific temper of mind, which were the characteristics of the Divine Author of our blessed religion, and without an humble imitation of whose example in these things, we can never hope to be a happy nation. [70]

What an unusual way to close a war! It would have been appropriate for Washington to express exultant joy or to extend deserved congratulations, yet he chose to conclude the War by praying for the Governors and their states, and by reminding them that without the "humble imitation" of Christ, "we can . . . never be a happy nation."

Washington, the "Father of Our Country," could not have successfully led the nation had it not concurred with him and his beliefs. His spirit and beliefs were typical of the entire nation, as confirmed by a pamphlet written by Benjamin Franklin while he was serving as emissary in France. The pamphlet, *Information to Those Who Would Remove to America*, was written for those Frenchmen who were considering a move to America, or who might send their children there for studies or further opportunity. Franklin was in France—home of the "enlightenment," land of the rejection of religion, bastion of atheism and marital infidelity; notice his description of America for the French:

Bad examples to youth are more rare in America, which must be a comfortable consideration to parents. To this may be truly added, that serious religion, under its various denominations, is not only tolerated, but respected and practised. Atheism is unknown there; infidelity rare and secret; so that persons may live to a great age in that country without having their piety shocked by meeting with either an Atheist or an Infidel. [71]

One of the most famous and recognizable symbols of the American Revolution is the Liberty Bell. It rang, proclaiming liberty, when the Declaration of Independence was first read publicly on July 8, 1776. But why was it rung in conjunction with the reading of the Declaration of Independence? How does this bell symbolize freedom? The answer lies in the inscription emblazoned on its side. Most do not even realize that the Liberty Bell bears an inscription, much less that the inscription is a Bible verse:

Proclaim liberty throughout the land unto all the inhabitants thereof. LEVITICUS 25:10

The symbol most closely associated with the Revolution proclaims that the Bible and civil government were bound together.

Official Acts of Continental Congress

Just as the records of individuals from the Revolutionary era are both interesting and revealing, so also are the official Congressional records from that time. For example, when the representatives to the *very first* Continental Congress met together for the *very first* time, what was the *very first* act of these patriots?

Tuesday, September 6, 1774. *Resolved,* That the Rev[d]. Mr. Duché be desired to open the Congress tomorrow morning with prayers, at the Carpenter's Hall, at 9 o'Clock. [72]

The next day, the records of Congress reported:

Wednesday, September 7, 1774, 9 o'clock a. m. Agreeable to the resolve of yesterday, the meeting was opened with prayers by the Rev^d. Mr. Duché. *Voted*, That the thanks of Congress be given to Mr. Duché . . . for performing divine Service, and for the excellent prayer, which he composed and delivered on the occasion. [73]

John Adams, in a letter to his wife Abigail, described what happened that Wednesday morning:

Accordingly, next morning [the Rev. Mr. Duché] appeared with his clerk and in his pontificals, and read several prayers in the established form, and read the collect for the seventh day of September, which was the thirty-fifth Psalm. You must remember, this was the next morning after we heard the horrible rumor of the cannonade of Boston. I never saw a greater effect upon an audience. It seemed as if heaven had ordained that Psalm to be read on that morning. After this, Mr. Duché, unexpectedly to every body, struck out into an extemporary prayer, which filled the bosom of every man present. I must confess, I never heard a better prayer, or one so well pronounced. Episcopalian as he is, Dr. Cooper himself [Adam's personal pastor] never prayed with such fervor, such ardor, such earnestness and pathos, and in language so elegant and sublime, for America, for the Congress, for the province of Massachusetts Bay, and especially the town of Boston. It has had an excellent effect upon every body here. I must beg you to read that Psalm. [74]

Information taken from an historical poster in the Library of Congress and based on collected reports from the various patriots in attendance provides further insights both into the prayer offered by Mr. Duché and the effect that it had upon the first Congress:

"Be Thou present, O God of Wisdom, and direct the councils of this honorable assembly. Enable them to settle things on the best and surest foundation; that the scenes of blood may be speedily closed, that order, harmony, and peace, may be effectually restored, and truth and justice, religion and piety, prevail and flourish among Thy people. Preserve the health of their bodie, and the vigor of their minds; shower down on them and the millions they here represent, such temporal blessings as Thou seest expedient for them in this world, and crown them with everlasting glory in the world to come. All this we ask, in the name, and through the merits of Jesus Christ, Thy Son, and our Savior, Amen!" [75]

Washington was kneeling there, and Henry, Randolph, and Rutledge, and Lee, and Jay; and by their side there stood, bowed down in deference, the Puritan Patriots of New England, who at that moment had reason to believe that an armed soldiery was wasting their humble households. . . . They prayed fervently for "America, for the Congress, for the province of Massachusetts Bay, and especially for the town of Boston:" and who can realize the emotions with which they turned imploringly to heaven for divine interposition and aid. It was enough . . . to melt a heart of stone. I saw the tears gush into the eyes of the old, grave, pacific Quakers of Philadelphia. [76]

Times of dedicated prayer was part and parcel of the men who guided the nation through the Revolution. Both the national and the state congresses regularly called for days of prayer and fasting or prayer and thanksgiving. Their proclamations were far from pluralistic—they were Christian. Notice this Massachusetts proclamation, given when the ominous storm clouds of war were evident to the entire nation:

Concord, April 15, 1775. . . .

In circumstances dark as these, it becomes us, as men and christians, to reflect, that whilst every prudent measure should be taken to ward off the impending judgments . . . all confidence must be withheld from the means we use, and reposed only on that God, who rules in the armies of heaven, and without whose blessing, the best human councils are but foolishness, and all created power vanity;

It is the happiness of his church, that when the powers of earth and hell combine against it . . . then the throne of grace is of the easiest access, and its appeal thither is graciously invited by that Father of mercies, who has assured it that when his children ask bread he will not give them a stone. . . .

Resolved, That it be, and hereby is, recommended to the good people of this colony, of all denominations, that Thursday, the eleventh day of May next, be set apart as a day of public humiliation, fasting and prayer . . . to confess the sins . . . to implore the forgiveness of all our transgressions . . . and a blessing on the husbandry, manufactures, and other lawful employments of this people; and especially, that the union of the American colonies in defence of their rights, for which, hitherto, we desire to thank Almighty God, may be preserved and confirmed. . . . And that America may soon behold a gracious interposition of Heaven.

[By Order of the Massachusetts Provincial Congress, John Hancock, President.] [77]

The national Congress maintained a firm reliance on God and a steady participation in religious activities, as indicated by this excerpt from the July 19th, 1775, *Journals of Congress:*

Agreed, That the Congress meet here to Morrow morning, at half after 9 o'Clock, in order to attend divine service at Mr. Duché's Church; and that in the afternoon they meet here to go from this place and attend divine service at Doct[r] Allison's church. [78]

In the weeks preceding the official separation from Great Britain, Congress continued to encourage the national pursuit of God. Foreseeing the commencement of a full-scale war, Congress was determined that the nation not enter such a conflict unless it was in a proper relationship with God Almighty. Consequently, on May 16, 1776, Congress proclaimed:

The Congress . . . . Desirous . . . to have people of all ranks and degrees duly impressed with a solemn sense of God's superintending providence, and of their duty, devoutly to rely . . . on his aid and direction . . . Do earnestly recommend . . . a day of humiliation, fasting, and prayer; that we may, with united hearts, confess and bewail our manifold sins and transgressions, and, by a sincere repentance and amendment of life . . . and, through the merits and mediation of Jesus Christ, obtain his pardon and forgiveness. [79]

The day following the public reading of the Declaration of Independence, Congress again moved quickly to secure prayer as a regular part of the daily proceedings of the new nation:

> *Resolved,* That the Rev. Mr. J. Duché be appointed chaplain
> to Congress, and that he be desired to attend every morning
> at 9 o'Clock. [80]

A committee was then appointed—a committee composed of John
Adams, Thomas Jefferson, and Ben Franklin—to draft a seal for the
newly united states which would characterize the spirit of the new
nation. Even though Congress eventually delayed the adoption of
any seal, the suggestions offered by the members of that committee
again reveal their belief that the Bible was inseparable from civil
government. Franklin proposed:

> Moses lifting up his wand, and dividing the red sea, and
> Pharaoh in his chariot overwhelmed with the waters. This
> motto: "Rebellion to tyrants is obedience to God." [81]

Jefferson proposed:

> The children of Israel in the wilderness, led by a cloud by
> day, and a pillar of fire by night. [82]

Recall that Congress, as its first official act, had authorized
chaplains to open Congressional meetings. When the Continental
Army became the responsibility of Congress, Congress quickly
authorized chaplains for the Army. Washington responded promptly
and on July 9, 1776, he appointed chaplains for each regiment. [83]

By 1777, the impact from having lost Britain as the Colonies'
major trading partner was being felt. There was a shortage of
several important commodities, including the Bible. Since the
arrival of the original Colonists, the Bible had been an integral part
of America, both in public and personal realms. Therefore, a
request was placed before Congress either to print or to import
more. The request was referred to a special committee which
examined the possibilities and then reported:

> That the use of the Bible is so universal, and its importance
> so great . . . your Committee recommend[s] that Congress
> will order the Committee of Commerce to import 20,000
> Bibles from Holland, Scotland, or elsewhere, into the
> different parts of the States of the Union. Whereupon, the
> Congress was moved, to order the Committee of Commerce
> to import twenty-thousand copies of the Bible. [84]

Congress not only acted to provide Bibles throughout the nation, it continued to promote prayer. On November 1, 1777, Congress called for a national day of thanksgiving and prayer for the victory at Saratoga. As with its previous proclamations, this one was neither pluralistic nor religiously "neutral":

> Forasmuch as it is the indispensable duty of all men to adore the superintending providence of Almighty God; to acknowledge with gratitude their obligation to him for benefits received and to implore such farther blessings as they stand in need of . . . [to offer] humble and earnest supplication that it may please God, through the merits of Jesus Christ, mercifully to forgive and blot [our sins] out of remembrance . . . and to prosper the means of religion for the promotion and enlargement of that kingdom which consisteth "in righteousness, peace, and joy in the Holy Ghost." [85]

As the war progressed, continuing evidences of God's aid to the nation were recognized and gratefully acknowledged. The following series of documents shows how America's leaders reacted to the discovery of the plot by Benedict Arnold to betray them to the British. The first is a message from George Washington delivered to his troops:

> General Orders—Head Quarters, Orangetown, September 26, 1780, Tuesday.

> Treason of the blackest dye was yesterday discovered! General Arnold who commanded at Westpoint, lost to every sentiment of honor, of public and private obligation, was about to deliver up that important Post into the hands of the enemy. Such an event must have given the American cause a deadly wound if not a fatal stab. Happily the treason has been timely discovered to prevent the fatal misfortune. The providential train of circumstances which led to it affords the most convincing proof that the Liberties of America are the object of divine Protection. [86]

The Congressional response followed on October 18, 1780:

> Whereas it hath pleased Almighty God, the Father of all mercies, amidst the vicissitudes and calamities of war, to bestow blessings on the people of these states, which call for their devout and thankful acknowledgments, more especially in the late remarkable interposition of his watchful provi-

dence, in rescuing the person of our Commander in Chief and the army from imminent dangers, at the moment when treason was ripened for execution. . . . It is therefore recommended to the several states . . . a day of public thanksgiving and prayer; that all the people may assemble on that day to celebrate the praises of our Divine Benefactor; to confess our unworthiness of the least of his favours, and to offer our fervent supplications to the God of all grace . . . to cause the knowledge of Christianity to spread over all the earth. [87]

As the Revolution continued, for a second time a shortage of Bibles occurred. On January 21, 1781, Robert Aitken, publisher of *The Pennsylvania Magazine,* petitioned Congress for permission to print the Bibles, pointing out that his Bible would be "a neat edition of the Holy Scriptures for the use of schools." [88] Congress approved his request, and the next year the Bibles rolled off the press. That edition is now called the "Bible of the Revolution" and is one of the world's rarest books, being a purely American printing. On September 10, 1782, Congress issued its endorsement—an endorsement printed in the front of the new Bible:

Whereupon, Resolved, That the United States in Congress assembled . . . recommend this edition of the Bible to the inhabitants of the United States, and hereby authorize [Robert Aitken] to publish this recommendation in the manner he shall think proper. [89]

Congress, composed of America's premier group of statesmen and patriots, was neither ashamed of nor reticent about placing their whole-hearted endorsement on the use of the Bible for schools and citizens.

Individual states, as well as the national Congress, had encouraged the principles of Christianity. On November 8, 1783, at the conclusion of the War, Governor John Hancock of Massachusetts issued this proclamation:

John Hancock, Esquire
Governor of the Commonwealth of Massachusetts

A Proclamation for a Day of Thanksgiving:
   Whereas . . . these United States are not only happily rescued from the Danger and Calamities to which they have been so long exposed, but their Freedom, Sovereignty and Independence ultimately acknowledged.

And whereas . . . the Interposition of Divine Providence in our Favor hath been most abundantly and most graciously manifested, and the Citizens of these United States have every Reason for Praise and Gratitude to the God of their salvation.

Impressed therefore with an exalted Sense of the Blessings by which we are surrounded, and of our entire Dependence on that Almighty Being from whose Goodness and Bounty they are derived;

I do by and with the Advice of the Council appoint *Thursday the Eleventh Day of* December *next* (the Day recommended by the Congress to all the States) to be *relig- iously* observed as a Day of Thanksgiving and Prayer, that all the People may then assemble to celebrate . . . that he hath been pleased to continue to us the Light of the blessed Gospel;. . . . That we also offer up fervent Supplications . . . to cause pure Religion and Virtue to flourish . . . and to fill the World with his glory. [90] (emphasis added)

Establishing a Stronger Government

With the cessation of hostilities and the victorious conclusion of the campaign against Great Britain, it was time for the legislators to turn their full attention toward securing their nation's newly gained freedom and liberty. The Declaration of Independence had only declared their rights; now it was time to safeguard them.

To respond to this need, delegates from each state arrived in Philadelphia to revise the Articles of Confederation under which the government had been functioning. It soon became evident to the attending delegates that revising the Articles would not be sufficient; a completely new pact of government was needed. Although the convention had not convened to write a new constitution, it ultimately did, and therefore became known historically as the Constitutional Convention.

The Convention had begun in a manner quite different from the original Congress whose first act had been to seek God. Even though that same attitude of reliance on God had been carried throughout the Revolution, now, perhaps as a consequence of the nation's successes, the delegates did not commence this endeavor as their previous ones: they neither formally requested God's aid nor acknowledged their dependence on Him.

From all historical accounts, there had been very little progress in their effort to establish a new government until one specific incident provided a new spirit for their endeavors. James Madison, who kept fastidious personal records of the Convention's events and debates, described the turning point in the Convention—a stinging rebuke delivered by the 81 year-old Ben Franklin on Thursday, June 28, 1787.

At the time of Franklin's address, the delegates were embroiled in a heated debate over how each state would be represented in the new government. The dispute had caused great animosity, pitting the larger states against the smaller ones and creating bitter and hostile feelings between the state delegations. Addressing George Washington, President of the Convention, Franklin declared:

Mr. President:

The small progress we have made after 4 or five weeks close attendance & continual reasonings with each other—our different sentiments on almost every question, several of the last producing as many noes as ayes, is methinks a melancholy proof of the imperfection of the Human Understanding. We indeed seem to feel our own want of political wisdom, since we have been running about in search of it. We have gone back to ancient history for models of government, and examined the different forms of those Republics which having been formed with the seeds of their own dissolution now no longer exist. And we have viewed Modern States all round Europe, but find none of their Constitutions suitable to our circumstances.

In this situation of this Assembly, groping as it were in the dark to find political truth, and scarce able to distinguish it when presented to us, how has it happened, Sir, that we have not hitherto once thought of humbly applying to the Father of lights to illuminate our understanding? In the beginning of the Contest with G. Britain, when we were sensible of danger we had daily prayer in this room for the divine protection.—Our prayers, Sir, were heard, & they were graciously answered. All of us who were engaged in the struggle must have observed frequent instances of a superintending providence in our favor. To that kind providence we owe this happy opportunity of consulting in peace on the means of establishing our future national felicity. And have we now forgotten that powerful Friend? or do we imagine we no longer need his assistance?

I have lived, Sir, a long time, and the longer I live, the more convincing proofs I see of this truth—*that God Governs in the affairs of men.* And if a sparrow cannot fall to the ground without his notice, is it probable that an empire can rise without his aid? We have been assured, Sir, in the sacred writings, that "except the Lord build the House, they labor in vain that build it." I firmly believe this; and I also believe that without his concurring aid we shall succeed in this political building no better, than the Builders of Babel: We shall be divided by our partial local interests; our projects will be confounded, and we ourselves shall become a reproach and bye word down to future ages. And what is worse, mankind may hereafter from this unfortunate instance, despair of establishing Governments by Human wisdom and leave it to chance, war and conquest.

I therefore beg leave to move—that henceforth prayers imploring the assistance of Heaven, and its blessings on our deliberations, be held in this Assembly every morning before we proceed to business, and that one or more of the clergy of this city be requested to officiate in that service. [91]

How did the delegates respond to this rebuff? One of them, Jonathan Dayton of New Jersey, reported:

The Doctor sat down; and never did I behold a countenance at once so dignified and delighted as was that of Washington, at the close of the address; nor were the members of the convention, generally, less affected. The words of the venerable Franklin fell upon our ears with a weight and authority, even greater than we may suppose an oracle to have had in a Roman senate! [92]

Roger Sherman of Connecticut seconded Franklin's motion for prayer. [93] Edmund Jennings Randolph of Virginia further proposed:

That a sermon be preached at the request of the convention on 4th of July, the anniversary of Independence; & thenceforward prayers be used in ye Convention every morning. [94]

It was then pointed out that the Convention had no funds and therefore could not pay the clergy. Notwithstanding, some clergy of the city, in response to the delegates' desire to convene with prayer—

and having no desire for monetary remuneration—responded affirmatively to their request. These measures had a profound effect on the Convention. Notice Dayton's records for July 2, after they had turned their attention toward God:

> We assembled again; and . . . every unfriendly feeling had been expelled, and a spirit of conciliation had been cultivated. [95]

On July 4, in accordance with the proposal by Edmund Jennings Randolph, the entire Convention assembled in the Reformed Calvinistic Church and heard a sermon by Rev. William Rogers. His prayer reflected the sentiment which had gripped the delegates following Franklin's admonition:

> We fervently recommend to thy fatherly notice . . . our federal convention. . . . Favor them, from day to day, with thy inspiring presence; be their wisdom and strength; enable them to devise such measures as may prove happy instruments in healing all divisions and prove the good of the great whole; . . . that the United States of America may form one example of a free and virtuous government. . . . May we . . . continue, under the influence of republican virtue, to partake of all the blessings of cultivated and Christian society. [96]

Franklin's admonition—and the delegates response to it—had been the turning point not only for the Convention, but also for the future of the nation. While neglecting God, their efforts had been characterized by frustration and selfishness. With their repentance came a desire to begin each morning of official government business with prayer and even to attend church *en masse,* as government officials, to hear a minister inspire and challenge them. After returning God to their deliberations, were they effective in their efforts to frame a new government?

> "We, the people of the United States . . . " Thus begins what has become the oldest written constitution still in effect today. . . . The greatest legal minds of two centuries have continued to marvel at it as being almost beyond the scope and dimension of human wisdom. When one stops to consider the enormous problems the Constitution somehow anticipated and the challenges and testings it foresaw, that statement appears more understated than exaggerated. For

not even the collective genius of the fledgling United States of America could claim credit for the fantastic strength, resilience, balance, and timelessness of the Constitution. And most of them knew it. [97]

As seen in the last chapter, Justices who participated in the founding and initial development of the nation unequivocally declared that Christianity was part of and the basis for the Constitution. But did Christianity really have any effect on our form of government? Would it have made any difference if our Founders had embraced the enlightenment philosophy so prevalent in France— the philosophy which advocated the complete separation of religious principle from government and education?

> If our Founding Fathers had been smitten with the idealism of the Enlightenment . . . we would have established the same unstable form of government experienced by France, which has endured seven different governmental systems during the two hundred years that America has enjoyed only one. [98]

Additional evidence that Christianity was the basis of the Constitution is seen in Article 1, Section 7, Paragraph 2, which states that the President shall have ten days to consider a bill, "Sundays excepted." To most people today, the provision of "Sundays excepted" does not declare a strong Christian construction of the Constitution. However, that was not the sentiment in earlier years, as evidenced by this excerpt from a January 19, 1853, Senate Judiciary Committee report commenting on the "Sundays excepted" provision:

> In the law, Sunday is a *"dies non;"* . . . . The executive departments, the public establishments, are all closed on Sundays; on that day neither House of Congress sits. . . . Here is a recognition by law, and by universal usage, not only of a Sabbath, but of the Christian Sabbath, in exclusion of the Jewish or Mohammedan Sabbath. . . . The recognition of the Christian Sabbath [by the Constitution] is complete and perfect. [99]

Not only did the Senate view Sunday recognition as an important aspect indicating the Christian basis of the government, even the courts declared the national importance of Sunday. Recall the *Charleston* case from the previous chapter:

The Lord's day, the day of the Resurrection to us who are
called Christians, the day of rest after finishing a new
creation. It is the day of the first visible triumph over death,
hell and the grave! It is the birth day of the believer in
Christ, to whom and through whom it opened up the way
which, by repentance and faith, leads unto everlasting life
and eternal happiness! On that day we rest, and to us it is the
Sabbath of the Lord. [100]

For the most part, citizens of the United States no longer see
Sunday as a major reflection of Christianity. In *McGowan* v.
Maryland, 1960, the Court said Sunday closing laws had no real religious significance, but only represented a national day of rest, relaxa-
tion, and recreation [101] (which contradicts even the case just quoted).
Understanding Sunday's importance in former years establishes why
earlier courts and Congresses viewed the "Sundays excepted" provision as a clear declaration of Christianity in the government.

The evidence of Christianity's infusion into governmental affairs
was apparent in the activities surrounding the inauguration of George
Washington. The April 23, 1789, *Daily Advertiser* reported:

On the morning of the day on which our illustrious President
will be invested with his office, the bells will ring at nine
o'clock, when the people may go up and in a solemn manner
commit the new Government, with its important train of
consequences, to the holy protection and blessings of the
Most High. An early hour is prudently fixed for this peculiar
act of devotion, and it is designed wholly for prayer. [102]

On April 27, 1789, three days before the Inauguration, the
Senate acted:

Resolved, That after the oath shall have been administered to
the President, he, attended by the Vice President, and
members of the Senate, and House of Representatives,
proceed to St. Paul's Chapel, to hear divine service, to be
performed by the Chaplain of Congress already appointed. [103]

On April 29th, the House approved that resolution. [104] The next
day, April 30th, 1789, George Washington delivered his inaugural
speech to a joint session of Congress. That speech reflected the
same spirit and conviction which had characterized every previous
act of government:

It would be peculiarly improper to omit, in this first official act my fervent supplications to that Almighty Being who rules over the universe, who presides in the councils of nations, and whose providential aids can supply every human defect. . . . No people can be bound to acknowledge and adore the Invisible Hand which conducts the affairs of men more than those of the United States. Every step by which they have advanced to the character of an independent nation seems to have been distinguished by some token of providential agency. . . . We ought to be no less persuaded that the propitious smiles of Heaven can never be expected on a nation that disregards the eternal rules of order and right which Heaven itself has ordained. [105]

The *Annals of Congress* record what happened following Washington's Inaugural Address:

The President, the Vice President, the Senate, and House of Representatives, &c., then proceeded to St. Paul's Chapel, where divine service was performed by the Chaplains of Congress. [106]

Shortly after Washington's election as the first President, the United Baptist Churches in Virginia sent him a letter of congratulations. Washington's reply to them on May 10, 1789, confirms the sentiments prevalent among the delegates to the Constitutional Convention:

If I could have entertained the slightest apprehension, that the Constitution framed in the Convention, where I had the honor to preside, might possibly endanger the religious rights of any ecclesiastical Society, certainly I would never have placed my signature to it. [107]

As President, Washington continued his custom of earlier years; he remained outspoken and adamant in his promotion of the importance of Christianity to government. For example, in an October 9, 1789, letter to the Synod of the Dutch Reformed Church in North America, Washington declared:

While just government protects all in their religious rights, true religion affords to government its surest support. [108]

He further declared:

It is impossible to rightly govern . . . without God and the Bible. [109]

Washington was convinced of God's importance to this nation. In a letter on March 11, 1792, he explained:

> I am sure there never was a people, who had more reason to acknowledge a divine interposition in their affairs, than those of the United States; and I should be pained to believe, that they have forgotten that agency, which was so often manifested during our revolution, or that they failed to consider the omnipotence of that God, who is alone able to protect them. [110]

In Washington's first year in office, Congress debated whether to request that Washington declare a day for a national thanksgiving. The *Journals of Congress* record the discussion on this issue:

> Mr. Sherman justified the practice of thanksgiving, on any signal event, not only as a laudable one in itself, but as warranted by a number of precedents in Holy Writ: for instance, the solemn thanksgivings and rejoicings which took place in the time of Solomon, after the building of the temple, was a case in point. This example, he thought, worthy of Christian imitation on the present occasion. [111]

Since a time of thanksgiving was precedented in the Scriptures, the Congress thought it worthy of emulation for the United States. They unanimously adopted the following resolution and delivered it to President Washington:

> Friday, September 25, [1789]. Day of Thanksgiving.

> *Resolved.* That a joint committee of both Houses . . . request that [President Washington] recommend to the people of the United States a day of public thanksgiving and prayer, to be observed by acknowledging, with grateful hearts, the many signal favors of Almighty God, especially by affording them an opportunity peaceably to establish a constitution of government for their safety and happiness. [112]

Washington heartily concurred with the request of Congress and issued the following proclamation:

> Whereas it is the duty of all nations to acknowledge the providence of Almighty God, to obey His will, to be grateful for his benefits, and humbly to implore His protection and

favor. . . . Now, therefore, I do recommend and assign Thursday, the twenty-sixth day of November next, to be devoted by the people of these United States . . . that we then may all unite unto him our sincere and humble thanks for His kind care and protection of the people of this country previous to their becoming a nation; for the signal and manifold mercies and the favorable interpositions of His providence in the course and conclusion of the late war; for the great degree of tranquility, union, and plenty which we have since enjoyed; for the peaceable and rational manner in which we have been enabled to establish constitutions of government for our safety and happiness, and particularly the national one now lately instituted; for the civil and religious liberty with which we are blessed. . . .

And also that we may then unite in most humbly offering our prayers and supplications to the great Lord and Ruler of Nations, and beseech Him to pardon our national and other transgressions . . . to promote the knowledge and practice of true religion and virtue. . . .

Given under my hand, at the city of New York, the 3rd of October, A. D. 1789.

G⁰ Washington. [113]

During his years as President, Washington skillfully guided the nation through many tenuous situations and precarious circumstances. Probably no one else could have secured the nation in overall peace and stability.

In addition to traversing many stressful situations, he personally observed many others. The French Revolution, with its proponents of amorality and atheism, had become a bloodbath and spectacle of horrors. Not only did Washington never want to see anything similar in the United States, he also did not want to see the philosophy which had caused it ever to infiltrate the thinking of Americans. Therefore, in his Farewell Address on September 19, 1796, he delivered an articulate warning which summarized the difference between the successful American experiment and the embarrassing French spectacle:

Of all the dispositions and habits which lead to political prosperity, religion and morality are indispensable supports. In vain would that man claim the tribute of patriotism, who should labor to subvert these great pillars of human happiness. . . . The mere politician . . . ought to respect and to cherish them. A volume could not trace all their connections with private and public felicity. Let it simply be asked, Where is the security for property, for reputation, for life, if the sense of religious obligation desert . . . ? And let us with caution indulge the supposition that morality can be maintained without religion. Whatever may be conceded to the influence of refined education on minds . . . reason and experience both forbid us to expect that national morality can prevail, in exclusion of religious principle. [114]

Famous Founding Fathers

The records from each era of America's history have already declared this to be a Christian nation, and there still remain volumes of additional evidence. For example, the writings of prominent Founding Fathers add yet more to the volume of "organic utterances" already confirming the Court's 1892 declaration that "this is a Christian nation."

SAMUEL ADAMS

Samuel Adams not only organized the Committees of Correspondence, he also instigated the Boston Tea Party, signed the Declaration of Independence, called for the first Continental Congress in 1774, and served as a member of those Congresses until 1781. His participation in politics continued well after the War. He was active in Massachusetts, helping draft that state's constitution, serving as a delegate to the state's ratifying convention for the federal Constitution, serving as Lieutenant Governor under John Hancock, and then becoming Governor. Having given over two decades of his life and energy to the cause of America and liberty, he wanted to ensure that America never lost the things for which it had fought. He described the nation's true enemy:

A general dissolution of principles and manners will more surely overthrow the liberties of America than the whole force of the common enemy. While the people are virtuous they cannot be subdued; but when once they lose their virtue they will be ready to surrender their liberties to the first external or internal invader. . . . If virtue and knowledge are diffused among the people, they will never be enslaved. This will be their great security. [115]

Since virtue and knowledge were the chief protection against the loss of liberties, how could they be diffused among the people? What means should they use—and what standard would they use for virtue? Samuel Adams proposed the simple solution in a letter to his cousin John Adams on October 4, 1790:

> Let divines and philosophers, statesmen and patriots, unite their endeavors to renovate the age, by impressing the minds of men with the importance of educating their little boys and girls, of inculcating in the minds of youth the fear and love of the Deity ... and, in subordination to these great principles, the love of their country. . . . In short, of leading them in the study and practice of the exalted virtues of the Christian system. [116]

Although Samuel Adams and John Adams held divergent political views on the role of the federal government, John Adams wrote back to Samuel on October 18, 1790, telling him that on this issue, "You and I agree." [117] The plan for preserving America for future generations could not be clearer: education based on Christianity.

JOHN WITHERSPOON

John Witherspoon, in addition to signing the Declaration of Independence, was a member of the Continental Congress for six years, where he served on over 100 Congressional Committees. Earlier in this chapter, his influence on the nation was documented: while President of Princeton he trained scores of men for national positions, including those of President, Vice-President, Supreme Court Justices, Cabinet Members, U.S. Senators and Congressmen, not to mention a multitude of state and local officials. How did John Witherspoon feel about mixing politics and Christianity?

> It is in the man of piety and inward principle, that we may expect to find the uncorrupted patriot, the useful citizen, and the invincible soldier.—God grant that in America true religion and civil liberty may be inseparable and that the unjust attempts to destroy the one, may in the issue tend to the support and establishment of both. [118]

While this statement was strong, he made an even more forceful declaration:

What follows from this? That he is the best friend to American liberty, who is most sincere and active in promoting true and undefiled religion, and who sets himself with the greatest firmness to bear down profanity and immorality of every kind. Whoever is an avowed enemy of God, I scruple not [would not hesitate] to call him an enemy to his country. [119]

PATRICK HENRY

Patrick Henry, known for the fiery speech in which he declared, "Give me liberty, or give me death!", was active in American politics until his death. He was a member of the Continental Congress, Commander-in-Chief of Virginia's military, helped write the first constitution of Virginia, and served many years in Virginia's House of Burgesses and General Assembly. He also holds a distinction held by none other: he was elected Governor of Virginia for five terms and was so popular that, in spite of his *refusal* to run for re-election, the people elected him to the Governorship for a sixth term (which he refused to serve)! Additionally, even though he declined the offers, George Washington selected him as the nation's Secretary of State and as the first Chief Justice of the Supreme Court. He also declined appointments to the U.S. Senate and as Minister to France and Minister to Spain. Henry was largely responsible for the adoption of the first ten amendments to the Constitution, now known as the Bill of Rights. Since Patrick Henry was a driving force behind the First Amendment, did he see it as separating church and state? How did he feel about mixing public affairs with Christianity?

It cannot be emphasized too strongly or too often that this great nation was founded, not by religionists [pluralism], but by Christians; not on religions, but on the gospel of Jesus Christ! For this very reason peoples of other faiths have been afforded asylum, prosperity, and freedom of worship here. [120]

In assessment of Henry's life and work for America, his grandson, William Wirt Henry, said that Patrick Henry:

Looked to the restraining and elevating principles of Christianity as the hope of his country's institutions. [121]

Another of Henry's grandsons, Patrick Henry Fontaine, said that his grandfather had given himself to:

Earnest efforts to establish true Christianity in our country. [122]

On one occasion, not long before Henry's death, a friend found him engaged in reading the Bible. Henry held up the Bible and told his friend:

> Here is a book worth more than all the other books that were ever printed. [123]

JOHN JAY

John Jay was not only one of the three authors of *The Federalist Papers* and George Washington's selection as the first Chief Justice of the United States Supreme Court, he was also a member of the First and Second Continental Congresses and even served as its President.   Along with Ben Franklin and John Adams, he negotiated the final peace treaty with England. Jay was Governor of New York, helped author the New York Constitution of 1777, served as Secretary of Foreign Affairs under the Articles of Confederation, was Minister to Spain, and negotiated the 1794 treaty, now called the Jay Treaty, which kept the young nation from being pulled back into a war between England and France. Did he believe Christianity should be involved in public affairs?

> Providence has given to our people the choice of their rulers, and it is the duty as well as the privilege and interest of our Christian nation to select and prefer Christians for their rulers. [124]

Jay also served as President of the American Bible Society for several years before his death. On his deathbed, when asked if he had any final words for his children, he replied, "They have the Book." [125]

JAMES MADISON

James Madison, because of his efforts at the Convention, is known as "The Chief Architect of the Constitution." In addition to being one of the three authors of *The Federalist Papers,* he served eight years in Congress, eight years as Secretary of State, and eight years as President of the United States. While attending Princeton, he was trained by the Rev. John Witherspoon. The fact that Madison chose to attend a college which had declared, "Cursed be all learning that is contrary to the cross of Christ!" [126] is probably an adequate statement of the importance of Christianity in his life philosophy. These were Madison's strong tenets concerning the relationship between God and civil institutions:

> Before any man can be considered as a member of Civil Society, he must be considered as a subject of the Governour of the Universe. . . . Religion . . . [is] the basis and foundation of government. [127]

With his intimate knowledge of the Constitution, he would surely know if there was an intent to separate Christianity from the Constitution or from government. Yet, he declared:

> We have staked the whole future of American civilization, not upon the power of government, far from it. We have staked the future of all of our political institutions upon the capacity of mankind for self-government; upon the capacity of each and all of us to govern ourselves, to control ourselves, to sustain ourselves according to the Ten Commandments of God. [128]

Madison believed the future of America rested not on the Constitution, but on the ability of every individual to conduct himself according to the Ten Commandments! Yet, in *Stone* v. *Graham* in 1980, the Court ruled it unconstitutional for students to even see the Ten Commandments on school property. The "Chief Architect of the Constitution" states that the future of our institutions are built on keeping the Ten Commandments and the Court says it is unconstitutional for students even to see them. A reasonable question would be: "Who knows more about the intent of the Constitution, James Madison or the current Supreme Court?" (Additional statements and actions of both James Madison and Thomas Jefferson will be presented in Chapter 9).

GOUVERNEUR MORRIS

Gouverneur Morris was a Pennsylvania delegate to the Constitutional Convention. He was the most prolific member of the Convention, speaking 173 times on the Convention floor. As head of the Committee on Style, he was responsible for translating the rough ideas from the Convention floor onto paper; in a literal sense, he actually "wrote" the Constitution. Morris also served in the Continental Congress, helped write the New York State Constitution, and served as a U.S. Senator from New York.

Having been intimately involved with the formation of the new successful government in the United States, he offered some suggestions to the French in their efforts to establish their new government in his *Observations on Government, Applicable to the Political State of France* and *Notes on the Form of a Constitution for France.* What was his recommendation to France if they wanted a successful self-governing nation?

> Religion is the only solid basis of good morals; therefore education should teach the precepts of religion, and the duties of man towards God. [129]

The man who "wrote" the Constitution declared that for self-government to work, "*education* should teach the precepts of religion, and the duties of man towards God." The contemporary courts have taken the opposite view!

ROGER SHERMAN

Roger Sherman holds a unique and distinguished position among the Founding Fathers. He is the only Founder who signed the nation's four major documents: the Articles of Association in 1774, the Declaration of Independence in 1776, the Articles of Confederation in 1777, and the Constitution in 1787. At the Convention, it was Sherman who seconded Franklin's motion to commence each day with prayer. He also proposed the compromise between the larger and the smaller states whereby the representation in one house of Congress would be based on population and the other house would have equal votes for each state—our current system. He served in the U.S. House of Representatives, the U.S. Senate, and fourteen years as a judge in Connecticut. He believed strongly that Christianity had a place in government and he adhered to the Bible and Christianity as the foundation for governmental policy:

> Once [while in Congress] he objected to a War Committee report that would have permitted delinquents from the army to be given five hundred lashes by the courts-martial. His technically successful opposition was based on the principle laid down in Deuteronomy (xxv:3) that "Forty stripes he may give him, and not exceed: lest, if he should exceed, and beat him above these with many stripes, then thy brother should seem vile unto thee." [130]

In February 1776 [Sherman] was placed on a committee with Adams and George Wythe of Virginia to draw up instructions for an embassy going to Canada. . . . The instructions . . . included an interesting sentence: "You are further to declare that we hold sacred the rights of conscience, and may promise to the whole people, solemnly in our name, the free and undisturbed exercise of their religion." And . . . that all civil rights and the right to hold office were to be extended to persons of any *Christian* denomination. [131] (emphasis added)

Yet a further example of a Founding Father with strong opinions about basing governmental and public policy on Christianity!

JOHN ADAMS

It was John Adams who heartily recommended George Washington to the Congress to fill the role of Commander-in-chief and who later personally urged Thomas Jefferson to write the Declaration of Independence. Adams not only signed the Declaration, he also served in the Continental Congress, was the U.S. Minister to France, and, along with John Jay and Ben Franklin, negotiated the final treaty ending the war with Great Britain. Afterwards, while serving as the U.S. Minister to Britain, he wrote a three-volume work entitled *A Defense of the Constitutions of the Government of the United States,* urging the nation to ratify the Constitution. It is widely believed that this work was read by most of the delegates to the state ratifying conventions.

After 10 years of representing the United States abroad, he returned home to serve two terms as Vice-President under George Washington. He was elected the second President of the United States, succeeding George Washington, and was the first President to live in the White House. During his Presidency, the Department of the Navy was organized and the Library of Congress was established.

While Minister to France, Adams had worked closely with the French government. This provided him the opportunity to observe a government conducted without Christian principles which he later compared with the government in the United States that he had helped establish on Christian principles. Having been involved with both, Adams predicted that a republican form of government would not be successful in France, "a republic of thirty million atheists." [132] He further believed that not only atheism, but widespread immorality would keep the French from producing a lasting government. It was the two ingredients of religion and morality which made America distinctively different from France.

With his personal experiences in both styles of government, in a Presidential address to the military in October 1798, he was able to state with firm conviction that:

> We have no government armed with power capable of contending with human passions unbridled by morality and religion. Avarice, ambition, revenge, or gallantry, would break the strongest cords of our Constitution as a whale goes through a net. Our Constitution was made only for a moral and religious people. It is wholly inadequate to the government of any other. [133]

Notice other statements he made about the inclusion of Christianity in politics and public affairs:

> Statesmen, my dear sir, may plan and speculate for liberty, but it is religion and morality alone, which can establish the principles upon which freedom can securely stand. The only foundation of a free constitution is pure virtue. [134]

> The Christian religion is, above all the religions that ever prevailed or existed in ancient or modern times, the religion of wisdom, virtue, equity, and humanity. [135]

> Suppos [sic] a nation in some distant Region, should take the Bible for their only law Book, and every member should regulate his conduct by the precepts there exhibited. . . . What a Eutopa, What a Paradise would this region be. [136]

> Religion and virtue are the only foundations, not only of republicanism and of all free government, but of social felicity under all governments and in all the combinations of human society. [137]

There is no doubt that John Adams firmly believed Christianity to be the foundation for both politics and public affairs.

ALEXANDER HAMILTON

During the Revolution, Hamilton was a captain of a New York artillery unit and later became secretary and personal assistant to Commander-in-chief George Washington. As a member of Congress,

Hamilton called for the Constitutional Convention, served as a delegate to the Convention, and was responsible for almost two-thirds of the content of *The Federalist Papers*.   It was largely through Hamilton's efforts in *The Federalist Papers* that the nation understood the purpose of the new Constitution.   Following Washington's selection as the first President, he appointed Hamilton as the first Secretary of the Treasury.   Since Hamilton wrote much of Washington's Farewell Address, that address reveals Hamilton's beliefs as well as Washington's:

> Of all the dispositions and habits which lead to political prosperity, religion and morality are indispensable supports. In vain would that man claim the tribute of patriotism, who should labor to subvert these great pillars of human happiness. . . . The mere politician . . . ought to respect and cherish them. . . . Reason and experience both forbid us to expect that national morality can prevail in exclusion of religious principle. . . . Who that is a sincere friend to it can look with indifference upon attempts to shake the foundation of the fabric? [138]

In a letter to James Bayard in April 1802, Hamilton proposed the establishment of a "Christian Constitutional Society" to promote the two factors that had been most influential in America: "1st: The Support of the Christian Religion; 2nd: The Support of the Constitution of the United States." [139]

JOHN QUINCY ADAMS

John Quincy Adams received an early start in politics. In 1778, at the age of eleven, his mother, Abigail Adams, sent him to France to be with his father, John Adams, then serving as Minister to France. Within three years, at age fourteen, he had become so skilled that he received a Congressional appointment to a post in the Court of Catherine the Great of Russia. Later in his political career, Adams returned to Russia as Ambassador and also served as Ambassador to Britain and France.   While Ambassador in Russia, John Quincy Adams wrote a letter to his son, admonishing him:

> It is essential, my son . . . that you should form and adopt certain rules or principles. . . . It is in the Bible, you must learn them, and from the Bible how to practice them. [140]

John Quincy Adams was Secretary of State under James Monroe and was elected the sixth President of the United States. Following his Presidency, he served eighteen years in the House of Representatives. Having been in politics from his earliest years, having grown up during the Revolution as the son of a Patriot, and having served in some form of public office for almost seven decades, he held strong sentiments regarding the importance of Christian principles to civil government and saw no allowance for their separation from each other:

> [T]he birth-day of the nation is indissolubly linked with the birth-day of the Saviour [and] forms a leading event in the progress of the gospel dispensation. . . . [T]he Declaration of Independence first organized the social compact on the foundation of the Redeemer's mission upon earth [and] laid the corner stone of human government upon the first precepts of Christianity. [141]

NOAH WEBSTER

Although he is most frequently associated with the dictionary bearing his name, few realize that he was also a Founding Father. Webster was a soldier in the American Revolution, served nine terms in the Connecticut General Assembly, three terms in Massachusetts' Legislature, and four years as a judge. He was one of the first Founding Fathers to call for a Constitutional Convention and one of the most active in the ratification of the Constitution. Webster held unmistakable convictions regarding the relationship between Christianity and government:

> [T]he religion which has introduced civil liberty, is the religion of Christ and his apostles, which enjoins humility, piety and benevolence; which acknowledges in every person a brother, or a sister, and a citizen with equal rights. This is genuine Christianity, and to this we owe our free constitutions of government. [142]

> The moral principles and precepts contained in the Scriptures ought to form the basis of all our civil constitutions and laws. . . . All the miseries and evils which men suffer from vice, crime, ambition, injustice, oppression, slavery, and war, proceed from their despising or neglecting the precepts contained in the Bible. [143]

The Strengthening of Education

Following the Revolution, education, as did many other aspects of society, took on more of a national perspective. Although states continued to remain the highest authority, the new national consciousness caused common ideas and similar educational programs to be adopted among the individual states. Some of the pioneers of early education in the new nation included Noah Webster, Jedediah Morse, and William Holmes McGuffey. Their contributions to American education were immeasurable; their convictions undebatable.

NOAH WEBSTER

Noah Webster, for his extensive efforts in establishing sound education in America, has been titled "America's Schoolmaster." Webster authored textbooks and resource books for schools: dictionaries, spellers, catechisms, history books, and much more. While teaching school in New York in the 1780's he wrote his first speller—a speller that would change the entire nation. Eventually, millions were sold and they were used by virtually every educational group in America for 150 years after their introduction.

Prior to Webster's spellers, there was no objective standard in spelling—no right way or wrong way to spell a word! The same word might be spelled several different ways within the same document. It was through Webster's efforts that spelling and pronunciation were standardized throughout the nation.

Having helped establish the nation's successful constitutional government, Webster recognized that the principles which had given birth to the nation must be transmitted to future generations to ensure continued national success. Sound education was the guardian of true republican principles; the quality of our government would depend upon the quality of our education. Webster knew Christian principles must be inseparable from any sound educational system:

> In my view, the Christian religion is the most important and one of the first things in which all children, under a free government, ought to be instructed. . . . No truth is more evident to my mind than that the Christian religion must be the basis of any government intended to secure the rights and privileges of a free people. [144]

While in the Massachusetts Legislature, Webster worked to secure permanent funding for education. He wanted to see an educational system adopted that would:

> Discipline our youth in early life in sound maxims of moral, political, and religious duties. [145]

Webster's materials never divorced learning from Biblical principles. Notice these comments from some of his texts for schools:

> The brief exposition of the constitution of the United States will unfold to young persons the principles of republican government; and it is the sincere desire of the writer that our citizens should early understand that the genuine source of correct republican principles is the Bible, particularly the New Testament or the Christian religion. [146]

> It is extremely important to our nation, in a political as well as religious view, that all possible authority and influence should be given to the scriptures, for these furnish the best principles of civil liberty, and the most effectual support of republican government.   The principles of all genuine liberty, and of wise laws and administrations are to be drawn from the Bible and sustained by its authority.   The man therefore who weakens or destroys the divine authority of that book may be accessory to all the public disorders which society is doomed to suffer. [147]

An examination of his original *American Dictionary of the English Language* again illustrates his inclusion of Christianity in education. He regularly used Bible verses to clarify the context in which a word was used; here he established the individual connotations of the word "faith":

> Being justified by *faith*. Rom. v.
> Without *faith* it is impossible to please God. Heb. xi.
> For we walk by *faith*, not by sight. 2 Cor. v.
> With the *heart* man believeth to righteousness. Rom. x.
> They heard only, that he who persecuted us in times past, now preacheth the *faith* which once he destroyed. Gal. i.
> Shall their unbelief make the *faith* of God without effect? Rom. iii.
> Your *faith* is spoken of throughout the whole world. Rom. i.
> Hast thou *faith*? Have it to thyself before God. Rom. xiv.
> Children in whom is no *faith*. Deut. xxxii.

The same pattern held true throughout his dictionary; 27 percent of the examples he provided to clarify meanings were Bible verses. However, since its original publication in 1828 this dictionary has undergone extensive censorship to remove its Christian perspective. Although the most popular dictionary in America continues to bear Webster's name, it no longer reflects the spirit of the original.

JEDEDIAH MORSE

Dr. Jedediah Morse, while teaching school in the early 1780's in New Haven, became dissatisfied with the academic treatment of American geography in schools. He collected his own lectures and, in 1784, published them in *Geography Made Easy*. That book was a great success, as evidenced by the 25 successive reprints which followed. Morse continued his writing in American geography and history, authoring *The American Geography, Elements of Geography, The American Gazetteer, A New Gazetteer of the Eastern Continent, A Compendious History of New England,* and *Annals of the American Revolution.* His efforts deservingly earned him the title of "The Father of American Geography." This influential educator recognized the importance of Christianity to education:

> To the kindly influence of Christianity we owe that degree of civil freedom, and political and social happiness which mankind now enjoys. In proportion as the genuine effects of Christianity are diminished in any nation . . . in the same proportion will the people of that nation recede from the blessings of genuine freedom. . . . All efforts to destroy the foundations of our holy religion, ultimately tend to the subversion also of our political freedom and happiness. Whenever the pillars of Christianity shall be overthrown, our present republican forms of government, and all the blessings which flow from them, must fall with them. [148]

Notice that he said that if Christianity's effects are diminished then the blessings over the nation would recede. To confirm the truth of his statement, one need only observe what has happened since the effect of Christianity has been diminished in schools. Since the Court, in 1962, began disallowing Christianity in schools, achievement scores have plummeted, dropout rates have soared, violence and crime on school campuses have increased dramatically, suicides by school children have risen over 400 percent, pregnancies to schoolgirls have climbed over 500 percent, and the United States has become the industrial world's leader in illiteracy. Indeed, since the effect of Christianity has been diminished in education, the blessings over American education have unquestionably receded.

WILLIAM HOLMES McGUFFEY

Educator William Holmes McGuffey, best known for his *McGuffey Readers,* was professor and department chairman at Miami University of Ohio, formed the first teachers' association in that part of the nation, was President of Ohio University, and was a professor at the University of Virginia. His *Readers,* first printed in 1836, sold 122 million copies in only 75 years. His efforts in education have prompted many to title him "The Schoolmaster of the Nation."

McGuffey's *Readers* were compilations of the best available stories for students. With an abundance of quality sources and literary classics available for his selection, from which did he primarily draw? In the preface to his *Third Reader* he states:

> In making [my] selections, [I have] drawn from the purest fountains of English literature. . . . For the copious extracts made from the Sacred Scriptures, [I make] no apology. [149]

McGuffey even questioned whether he should have used more Scriptures:

> Indeed, upon a review of the work, [I am] not sure but an apology may be due for [my] not having still more liberally transferred to [my] pages the chaste simplicity, the thrilling pathos, the living descriptions, and the matchless sublimity of the sacred writings. [150]

In the Preface to his *Fourth Reader,* he was again clear in not only crediting his primary source, but in expressing what he felt to be an essential ingredient in education:

> From no source has the author drawn more copiously than from the Sacred Scriptures. For this [I] certainly apprehend[] no censure. In a Christian country, that man is to be pitied, who, at this day, can honestly object to imbuing the minds of youth with the language and spirit of the Word of God. [151]

The nation's three leading educators not only stressed the importance of Christianity to education, they also included it in their academic materials.

What Did the Fathers Say to Teach?

The prominent Founding Fathers also had delivered their own significant pronouncements concerning education in America. Recall this statement from Samuel Adams:

> Let divines and philosophers, statesmen and patriots, unite their endeavors to renovate the age by impressing the minds of men with the importance of educating their little boys and girls, of inculcating in the minds of youth the fear and love of the Deity and . . . the love of their country . . . in short, of leading them in the study and practice of the exalted virtues of the Christian system. [152]

Also recall that it was Gouverneur Morris, the Pennsylvania statesman so active in the formation of the Constitution, who had declared:

> Religion is the only solid basis of good morals; therefore education should teach the precepts of religion, and the duties of man towards God. [153]

Thomas Jefferson, while President of the United States, became the first president of the Washington D. C. public school board, which used the Bible and Watt's Hymnal as reading texts in the classroom. [154] Notice why Jefferson felt the Bible to be essential in any successful plan of education:

> I have always said, and always will say, that the studious perusal of the sacred volume will make us better citizens. [155]

The first Congress, too, had stressed the importance of Christianity to public education when, in 1789, it passed the "Northwest Ordinance" requiring religion, morality, and knowledge to be taught in schools and other means of education as a prerequisite for statehood in the United States. [156]

When Alexis de Tocqueville, the French observer of America, examined the role that ministers held in the nation in the 1830's, he commented that "almost all education is intrusted to the clergy." [157]

An 1854 report by the House Judiciary Committee further confirmed de Tocqueville's observation. After examining the historical role of chaplains in Congress and the military, the Committee referred to the Act of 1838 which stipulated that "chaplains . . . are to perform the double service of clergymen and schoolmasters." [158]

Not only was education not separated from Christianity, it was uniquely joined to Christian ministers!

An 1853 report by the Senate Judiciary Committee described the fundamental role of Christianity in American education:

> We are a Christian people . . . not because the law demands it, not to gain exclusive benefits or to avoid legal disabilities, but from choice and *education;* and in a land thus universally Christian, what is to be expected, what desired, but that we shall pay a due regard to Christianity? [159] (emphasis added)

Is there any indication that America's education system based on Christianity was successful?

> In the 1840 census, about 90 percent of white adults were listed as literate. [160]

That percentage, despite the difficult and demanding lifestyles facing Americans in the 1840's, is higher than the percentage recorded today. Project Literacy United States (PLUS) reports that the current *illiteracy* rate in America is higher than any other industrial nation in the world,[161] and according to the National Institute of Education, the pool of *additional* illiterates in America is growing at the rate of 2.3 million per year! [162]

So successful had been the American system of education that John Adams remarked as early as 1765:

> [A] native of America who cannot read or write is as rare as a comet or an earthquake. [163]

The success which resulted from including Christianity in all aspects of American life evinced this observation from de Tocqueville:

> There is no country in the whole world in which the Christian religion retains a greater influence over the souls of men than in America and there can be no greater proof of its utility, and of its conformity to human nature, than that its influence is most powerfully felt over the most enlightened and free nation on earth. [164]

It was no coincidence that the nation where Christianity had the greatest influence was also the world's most enlightened and free!

Congressional Investigations

There were those in America who did seek what the enlightenment had advocated: a total separation of church and state.   Since our Founders had made it clear that Christian principles were to be included in all aspects of public affairs, their attempts to use the courts to gain any semblance of a separation of Christianity from the government or public affairs had been completely unsuccessful (as evidenced in the previous chapter).

Having failed in the courts, they turned their efforts to a different arena: they petitioned Congress to separate church and state—to remove chaplains from the Congressional halls and from the military. These petitions were referred to the Judiciary Committees of Congress for consideration.   Those Committees, after conducting extensive investigations into historical records and laws to determine if it would be appropriate to separate church and state, released their final report:

> In the Senate of the United States, January 19, 1853, Mr. Badger made the following report: —
>
> The ground on which the petitioners found their prayer is, that the provisions of law . . . are in violation of the first amendment of the constitution of the United States, which declares that "Congress shall make no law respecting an establishment of religion, or prohibiting the free exercise thereof."
>
> It thus becomes necessary to inquire whether the position of the petitioners be correct.
>
> The clause speaks of "an establishment of religion." What is meant by that expression?   It referred, without doubt, to that establishment which existed in the mother-country, and its meaning is to be ascertained by ascertaining what that establishment was. It was the connection, with the state, of a particular religious society [denomination]. . . .
>
> *We are a Christian people* . . . not because the law demands it, not to gain exclusive benefits or to avoid legal disabilities, but from choice and education; *and in a land thus universally Christian, what is to be expected, what desired, but that we shall pay a due regard to Christianity . . . ?*
>
> The whole view of the petitioners seems founded upon mistaken conceptions of the meaning of the Constitution. . . . They intended, by this amendment, to prohibit "an establishment of religion" such as the English Church presented, or any thing like it. *But they had no fear or jealousy of*

religion itself, nor did they wish to see us an irreligious people . . . . *They did not intend to spread over all the public authorities and the whole public action of the nation the dead and revolting spectacle of atheistic apathy.* Not so had the battles of the Revolution been fought and the deliberations of the Revolutionary Congress been conducted. [165] (emphasis added)

March 27, 1854.   Mr. Meacham, from the [House] Committee on the Judiciary, made the following report:—

The Committee on the Judiciary . . . had the subject under consideration, and, after careful examination, are not prepared to come to the conclusion desired by the memorialists. Having made that decision, it is due that the reason should be given. . . .

At the adoption of the Constitution, we believe every State—certainly ten of the thirteen—provided as regularly for the support of the Church as for the support of the Government. . . . *Had the people, during the Revolution, had a suspicion of any attempt to war against Christianity, that Revolution would have been strangled in its cradle. At the time of the adoption of the Constitution and the amendments, the universal sentiment was that Christianity should be encouraged, not any one sect* [denomination]. . . .

It [Christianity] must be considered as the foundation on which the whole structure rests. Laws will not have permanence or power without the sanction of religious sentiment,—without a firm belief that there is a Power above us that will reward our virtues and punish our vices. *In this age there can be no substitute for Christianity:* that, in its general principles, is the great conservative element on which we must rely for the purity and permanence of free institutions. *That was the religion of the founders of the republic, and they expected it to remain the religion of their descendants.* There is a great and very prevalent error on this subject in the opinion that those who organized this Government did not legislate on religion. [166] (emphasis added)

Only two months later, the House passed a resolution declaring:

The great vital and conservative element in our system is the belief of our people in the pure doctrines and divine truths of the gospel of Jesus Christ. [167]

Those wanting to divorce God from government found no allies in either the courts or the Congress!

Outside Observers

Following behind those who had birthed and established the nation came many who made interesting observations on the relationship between Christianity and American government.   For example, Daniel Webster. Although Webster had no direct part in framing the Constitution, he was a member of government in the early years under the new Constitution, serving in the Senate and as Secretary of State for three different Presidents; his political career spanned almost four decades.

In December of 1820, while delivering a speech at Plymouth commemorating the arrival of the Pilgrims, he described the legacy they had left the nation:

> Cultivated mind was to act on uncultivated nature; and more than all, a government and a country were to commence, with the very first foundations laid under the divine light of the Christian religion. Happy auspices of a happy futurity! Who would wish that his country's existence had otherwise begun? [168]

What a rhetorical question! The overwhelming and resounding response from those then present would have been that no one could possibly have wished that the country had begun differently! They were proud that this country had been founded on the Christian religion! Webster concluded his address by summarizing the reasons the Pilgrims came to America:

> Our fathers were brought hither by their high veneration for the Christian religion. They journeyed by its light, and labored in its hope. They sought to incorporate its principles with the elements of their society, and to diffuse its influence through all their institutions, civil, political, or literary. [169]

Another observer with an interesting perspective on America was Alexis de Tocqueville. As noted earlier, he traveled throughout the nation in the early 1830's and published his observations in *Democracy in America*. His writings, unveiling what America was **really** like 50 years after its inception as an independent nation, make fascinating reading. Notice these excerpts:

Upon my arrival in the United States, the religious aspect of the country was the first thing that struck my attention; and the longer I stayed there, the more did I perceive the great political consequences resulting from this state of things, to which I was unaccustomed. In France I had almost always seen the spirit of religion and the spirit of freedom pursuing courses diametrically opposed to each other; but in America I found that they were intimately united, and that they reigned in common over the same country. [170]

The Americans combine the notions of Christianity and of liberty so intimately in their minds, that it is impossible to make them conceive the one without the other. [171]

Religion in America . . . must nevertheless be regarded as the foremost of the political institutions of that country. [172]

They brought with them . . . a form of Christianity, which I cannot better describe, than by styling it a democratic and republican religion. . . . From the earliest settlement of the emigrants, politics and religion contracted an alliance which has never been dissolved. [173]

I do not know whether all the Americans have a sincere faith in their religion; for who can search the human heart? but I am certain that they hold it to be indispensable to the maintenance of republican institutions. This opinion is not peculiar to a class of citizens or to a party, but it belongs to the whole nation, and to every rank of society. [174]

Christianity, therefore, reigns without any obstacle, by universal consent. [175]

It was obvious, even to a foreign observer fifty years *after* the Constitution, that Christianity continued to be the *first* of their *political* institutions! American historians from the same period reached identical conclusions and offered similar commentaries:

This is a Christian nation, first in name, and secondly because of the many and mighty elements of a pure Christianity which have given it character and shaped its destiny from the beginning. It is pre-eminently the land of the Bible, of the Christian Church, and of the Christian Sabbath. . . . The chief security and glory of the United States of America has been, is now, and will be forever, the prevalence and domination of the Christian Faith. [176] *B. F. Morris, 1864*

The government of the United States is acknowledged by the wise and good of other nations, to be the most free, impartial, and righteous government of the world; but all agree, that for such a government to be sustained for many years, the principles of truth and righteousness, taught in the Holy Scriptures, must be practiced. [177] *Emma Willard, 1843*

The North American Review, a magazine popular in 1867, stated:

The American government and Constitution is the most precious possession which the world holds, or which the future can inherit. This is true—true because the American system is the political expression of Christian ideas. [178]

The selections presented in this chapter represent only a minuscule portion of that which could be cited to establish why the 1892 Supreme Court declared:

This is a religious people. This is historically true. From the discovery of this continent to the present hour, there is a single voice making this affirmation. . . . These are not individual sayings, declarations of private persons: they are organic utterances; they speak the voice of the entire people. . . . These, and many other matters which might be noticed, add a volume of unofficial declarations to the mass of organic utterances that this is a Christian nation. [179]

No other conclusion is possible after an honest examination of America's history. Nonetheless, the contemporary courts, in their strong war against Christianity, have been forceful and effective both in ignoring history and in promoting their view on separation of church and state. Not only does the nation *not* realize that separation of church and state is **un**constitutional, many are not even aware that the privilege to exercise religious freedom *is* constitutional! A 1987 study showed that "only a third [of the nation's citizens] knew freedom of religion was guaranteed by the Constitution's First Amendment." [180] How did this nation's attitude toward Christianity and government get turned upside-down? How did we ever abandon our roots?

~6~
Protection from the Absurd

The departure from our Christian roots was initiated when contemporary courts refused to heed the warnings of earlier courts to rule by the intent of laws, not merely by their wording. When the intent for which a law has been framed is either discarded or ignored, that law can be applied in a manner that its sponsors would neither have imagined nor approved. The early courts diligently strived to ensure that the people were protected from the results of rulings based on absurd interpretations or applications of a law.

The *Holy Trinity* case is an excellent example. The U. S. Attorney had attempted to prosecute the church under a law which had been enacted for an entirely different purpose. Recall that in 1887, when the Church of the Holy Trinity in New York employed a clergyman from England as their pastor, they had technically violated the law which stated:

> It shall be unlawful for any . . . corporation, in any manner whatsoever . . . to . . . in any way assist or encourage the importation . . . of any alien or . . . foreigners, into the United States . . . to perform labor or service of any kind. [1]

The church argued that the law was never intended to affect ministers, but the prosecution contended that the church had violated the written, black-and-white wording of the statute. The Court searched for the law's intent and discovered, from the Congressional records, that the law was enacted only to correct a specific abuse in the domestic railway labor market by prohibiting the importation of slave-type labor.

Although the church's actions fell within the literal and technical wording of the law, they did not fall within the intent of that law. Therefore, the Court ruled that a prosecution of the church under that law would be an absurd application—a misuse—of that law. The Court commented on the principle which had guided its decision:

> It is a familiar rule that a thing may be within the letter of the statute and yet not within the statute, because not within its spirit, nor within the intention of its makers. . . . Frequently words of general meaning are used in a statute, words broad enough to include an act in question, and yet a consideration

of the whole legislation, or of the circumstances surrounding its enactment, or of the absurd results which follow from giving such broad meaning to the words, makes it unreasonable to believe that the legislator intended to include the particular act. [2]

The *Holy Trinity* Court cited a number of cases which, although proceeding from different laws, had arrived at similar conclusions:

> In the case of the *State* v. *Clark* . . . "The language of the act, if construed literally, evidently leads to an absurd result. If a literal construction of the words of a statute be absurd, the act must be so construed as to avoid the absurdity. . . . " In *United States* v. *Kirby* . . . "All laws should receive a sensible construction. General terms should be so limited in their application as not to lead to injustice, oppression or an absurd consequence. It will always, therefore, be presumed that the legislature intended exceptions to its language which would avoid results of this character. The reason of the law in such cases should prevail over its letter." [3]

The Court explained that to settle a dispute arising from under a law, it is necessary to first determine the spirit of that law by examining:

> The evil which was intended to be remedied, the circumstances surrounding the appeal to Congress, the reports of the committee of each house . . . [and] the intent of Congress. [4]

Legislators are unable to predict every circumstance that might arise under the enforcement of a law they enact. They believe that the law springing from their extensive discussions communicates more clearly than it actually does, for they vividly recall the context in which their legislation was framed. However, those called upon to enforce that law years later do not always see the intent that the legislators felt was so obvious.

Early courts understood this. Four times in the brief excerpt above from the *Holy Trinity* case, the Court specifically referred to the "absurd results" which can occur if a law is applied in a manner inconsistent with its original intent. Those early courts, evidentially unlike the contemporary ones, recognized the responsibility to interpret a law by its spirit and intent, even if their decision appeared to contradict the literal wording of the law.

Two of the fifteen cases the *Holy Trinity* Court cited in its discussion of "absurd" applications of laws are presented below to reinforce the importance of this principle.

The State *v.* Smith Clark, 1860

The offense is described from the case:

> The first count charges that the defendant [Smith Clark] did maliciously and willfully . . . break down . . . twenty panels of rail fence belonging to and in the possession of George Amwine. The section of the act upon which this indictment was found provides that if any person or persons shall willfully . . . break down . . . or destroy any fences . . . belonging to . . . any other person . . . [they] shall be deemed guilty of a misdemeanor. [5]

This is a very concise description of the law and of its violation by Smith Clark. Clark had intentionally destroyed George Amwine's fence; even common sense says it is wrong to go around destroying other people's fences. At this point, the defendant would be found guilty, for he has violated the law. However, there was more:

> The defendant [Smith Clark] offered to show, by way of defence, that at the several times when he broke down the fence[,] he had title to the land upon which it was built, and . . . that the fence which was destroyed was erected . . . upon [Smith Clark's] land. [6]

That puts a different light on it! The fence that Clark broke down was built by someone else on Clark's property—property to which Clark held clear legal title. Despite Clark's many "discussions" with his neighbor, George Amwine, Amwine had persisted in deliberately building his fences off his own property and on Smith Clark's property. Even though Smith Clark had literally violated the wording of the law, the law had not been designed to keep him from tearing down someone else's fences wrongly erected on his property. It was Amwine, not Clark, who was the real abuser of the law. The court recognized this case to be a violation of the "letter" of the law, but not of its "spirit":

> The language of the act, if construed literally, evidently leads to an absurd result. If a literal construction of the words of a

statute be absurd, the act must be so construed as to avoid the absurdity. . . . No one but a trespasser can be amenable to the provisions of the act. [7]

The legislature had not included the word "trespasser" in the law because it felt the intent of the law was obvious; it never could have imagined this attempt to misapply its law. Had the court applied the law solely by its wording and not according to its spirit, it would have created an injustice while supposedly administering "justice."

United States *v.* Kirby, 1868

The offense is described from the case:

The defendants were indicted for . . . wilfully obstructing . . . the passage of the mail and of a mail carrier. . . .
    The act of Congress . . . provides "that, if any person shall knowingly and wilfully obstruct or retard the passage of the mail, or of any driver or carrier . . . he shall, upon conviction, for every such offence, pay a fine not exceeding one hundred dollars. . . . "
    The indictment contained four counts, and charged the defendants with knowingly and wilfully obstructing the passage of the mail of the United States . . . and with knowingly and wilfully obstructing . . . the passage of one Farris, a carrier of the mail, while engaged in the performance of his duty; and with knowingly and wilfully retarding . . . the steamboat General Buell, which was then carrying the mail of the United States from the city of Louisville, in Kentucky, to the city of Cincinnati, in Ohio. [8]

The law stated that no one could interfere with a mail-carrier delivering mail and that no one could intentionally delay the delivery of the mail on a steamboat. Congress clearly intended that "the mail must go through!" According to testimony in the case, the defendant, Kirby, and the three with him, had admitted interferring with Farris—the mail-carrier—and with the steamboat. Under the law, these violations should be punished! However, there was more; the defendants pointed out that:

Two indictments were found by the grand jury of the county against the said Farris [the mail-carrier] for murder . . . and placed in the hands of Kirby . . . who was then sheriff of the county, commanding him to arrest the said Farris and bring him before the court to answer the indictments; that in obedience to these warrants [Kirby] arrested Farris, and was accompanied by other defendants as a posse, who were lawfully summoned to assist him in effecting the arrest; that they entered the steamboat Buell to make the arrest, and only used such force as was necessary to accomplish this end. [9]

That puts a different light on it! Kirby was the sheriff, and the three men were his posse. They did indeed interfere with the delivery of the mail by arresting Ferris, thus causing a delay for the steamship. Their actions indisputably constituted a literal violation of the wording of the law. But are we to believe that the law was intended to keep the Sheriff from arresting a mail-carrier with two murder indictments against him? As in the previous case, the Court recognized this as a violation of the "letter" of the law, but not of its "spirit":

All laws should receive a sensible construction. General terms should be so limited in their application as not to lead to injustice, oppression, or an absurd consequence. It will always, therefore, be presumed that the legislature intended exceptions to its language, which would avoid results of this character. The reason of the law in such cases should prevail over its letter.

The common sense of man approves the judgment mentioned by Puffendorf [a Christian philosopher quoted by several of the Founding Fathers], that the . . . law which enacted, "that whoever drew blood in the streets should be punished with the utmost severity," did not extend to the surgeon who opened the vein of a person that fell down in the street in a fit. The same common sense accepts the ruling . . . which enacts that a prisoner who breaks prison shall be guilty of felony does not extend to a prisoner who breaks out when the prison is on fire—"for he is not to be hanged because he would not stay to be burnt." And we think that a like common sense will sanction the ruling we make, that the act of Congress which punishes the obstruction or retarding of the passage of the mail, or of its carrier, does not apply to a case of temporary detention of the mail caused by the arrest of the carrier upon an indictment for murder. [10]

The *Holy Trinity* Court cited thirteen additional cases involving conflicts between the "letter" and the "spirit" of the law. While these will not be excerpted here, it is sufficient to note that the Court made thorough investigations to ensure that the intent of the law would always prevail over its literal construction. The Supreme Court summarized the responsibility resting on every court:

> The legislature used general terms . . . and thereafter, unexpectedly, it is developed that the general language thus employed is broad enough to reach cases and acts which the whole history and life of the country affirm could not have been intentionally legislated against. It is the duty of the courts, under those circumstances, to say that, however broad the language of the statute may be, the act, although within the letter, is not within the intention of the legislature, and therefore cannot be within the statute. [11]

When our Fathers enacted the First Amendment, the abuse they intended to avoid was that of having one, and only one, denomination of Christianity selected, protected, or promoted by the government. This was the evil they had experienced in England and planned to avoid in America.

Through their political writings and legal decisions they made clear their intent. They wanted to establish Christianity as the basis of government and public institutions, yet protect freedom of conscience to all individuals within the broad confines of basic Christian principles. As seen in chapter 4, the argument for freedom of conscience was not allowed to protect immorality, polygamy, blasphemy, the promotion of lewdness, etc.; freedom of conscience stopped where the violation of basic, orthodox Biblical principles of morality began. However, their laws prescribed nothing on baptism, the role of the Holy Spirit in a believer's life, the structure or organization of a church; these were denominational questions and not part of the basic principles of Christianity. Nor did the Founders or courts dictate where, how often, or even if a person chose to worship God. As stated in *Updegraph* v. *The Commonwealth, 1826:*

> "I would have it taken notice of, that we do not meddle with the difference of opinion, and that *we interfere only where the root of Christianity is struck at.* . . . The true principles of natural religion are part of the common law; the essential

principles of revealed religion are part of the common law; so that a person vilifying, subverting or ridiculing them may be prosecuted at common law; but temporal punishments ought not to be inflicted for mere opinions." Thus this wise legislature framed this great body of laws, for a Christian country and Christian people. [12] (emphasis added)

It was the basic principles of Christianity which were adopted by the governments and then expressed in the various state constitutions:

PENNSYLVANIA. Each [legislator] before he takes his seat, shall make and subscribe the following declaration, viz. "I do believe in one God, the creator and governour of the universe, the rewarder of the good and the punisher of the wicked. And I do acknowledge the scriptures of the Old and New Testament to be given by divine inspiration." [13]

DELAWARE. Every person, who shall be chosen a member of either house . . . shall . . . make and subscribe the following declaration, to wit: "I, _____, do profess faith in God the Father, and in Jesus Christ, His only Son, and in the Holy Ghost, one God, blessed for evermore; and I do acknowledge the holy scriptures of the Old and New Testament to be given by divine inspiration." [14]

NORTH CAROLINA. That no person who shall deny the being of God, or the truth of the [Christian] religion, or the divine authority either of the Old or New Testament . . . shall be capable of holding any office, or place of trust or profit in the civil department within this State. [15]

These were not declarations of denominational doctrine—these were declarations of Christian consensus. When a citizen was prosecuted under the laws of the nation, it was because of a violation of the civil laws (based on Christian principles); citizens were not prosecuted for spiritual reasons or to give spiritual correction.

Despite the well-documented intent of the Founders, it was not enough to deter the contemporary Court's absurd application of the First Amendment. Because the Framers did not actually include within the wording of the First Amendment that it pertained only to denominations within Christianity, and not to Christianity as compared to other beliefs (atheism, humanism, Islam, etc.), the Court has applied the letter of the law to circumvent its spirit and intent.   Our Fathers never envisioned that the First Amendment could be interpreted as it is now—a weapon used against the expansion of Christianity. As George Washington explained to the Baptists of Virginia on May 10, 1789:

> If I could have entertained the slightest apprehension that the Constitution framed by the Convention, where I had the honor to preside, might possibly endanger the religious rights of any ecclesiastical society, certainly I would never have placed my signature to it. [16]

And as Congress observed in 1854:

> Had the people, during the Revolution, had a suspicion of any attempt to war against Christianity, that Revolution would have been strangled in its cradle. At the time of the adoption of the Constitution and the amendments, the universal sentiment was that Christianity should be encouraged, not any one sect [denomination]. [17]

Since the courts have ignored the massive documentation from the Founders and have rejected the spirit of the First Amendment, we now find ourselves under the "absurd results" which inevitably proceed from ignoring original intent.

~7~
The Absurd Becomes Reality—
Dismantling the First Amendment

Since 1947, the Court's rulings on the First Amendment have completely opposed its spirit and intent, and have placed society under the absurd results forewarned by previous Courts. Eight contemporary cases are excerpted in this chapter, illustrating that the decisions now regularly reached by the courts qualify as "absurd," defying even common sense.

Engel *v.* Vitale, 1962
United States Supreme Court

This was the first case in which the Court applied its innovation of misapplied separation to overturn the longstanding tradition of school prayer. The controversy in this case was whether it was Constitutional for New York students' to offer this simple 22-word prayer:

> Almighty God, we acknowledge our dependence upon Thee, and we beg Thy blessings upon us, our parents, our teachers and our Country. [1]

The Court declared the use of this prayer unconstitutional. When the Court declares a matter unconstitutional, it is saying that the matter in question was against the will and design of the Founders as embodied through the Constitution. In other words, the Court, by declaring the use of this prayer unconstitutional, is saying that our Founders would have opposed it. This seems improbable, particularly when considering the details surrounding its use:

> The schools did not compel any pupil to join in the prayer over his or his parents' objection. [2]

Furthermore, not only was this prayer voluntary, it was non-denominational—a mere acknowledgment of God. A description of this "bland" prayer appeared eight years later in 1970, in *State Board of Educ.* v. *Board of Educ. of Netcong:*

> In Engel *v.* Vitale . . . this 22-word prayer, requiring less than ten seconds of reading time, is as innocuous, nonsec-

tarian and universal as could possibly be formulated. One commentator has described the prayer as a "to-whom-it-may-concern" prayer. [3]

This prayer, by being both voluntary and non-denominational, had fulfilled the Founders intent for the First Amendment. However, notice the Court's declaration about this "to-whom-it-may-concern" prayer:

> Neither the fact that the prayer may be denominationally neutral nor the fact that its observance on the part of the students is voluntary can serve to free it from the limitations of the [First Amendment]. . . . [It] ignores the essential nature of the program's constitutional defects. . . . Prayer in its public school system breaches the constitutional wall of separation between Church and State. [4]

However, the Court was not satisfied with merely declaring the use of this prayer unconstitutional—it felt a need to disperse more propaganda about *its* doctrine of separation:

> A union of government and religion tends to destroy government and to degrade religion. [5]

The Founders certainly did **not** agree that "a union of government and religion would destroy government and degrade religion":

> True religion affords to government its surest support. [6]
> *George Washington*

> Religion and virtue are the only foundations . . . of republicanism and of all free government. [7] *John Adams*

> Religion . . . [is] the basis and foundation of Government. [8]
> *James Madison*

> God grant that in America true religion and civil liberty may be inseparable and that the unjust attempts to destroy the one, may in the issue tend to the support and establishment of both. [9] *Dr. John Witherspoon*

> Our Constitution was made only for a moral and religious people. It is wholly inadequate to the government of any other. [10] *John Adams*

There is obvious conflict between our Founders and this Court!

The Court's contempt for the Founders is seen in this remark:

> It is true that New York's . . . prayer . . . does not amount to a total establishment of one particular religious sect to the exclusion of all others. . . . That prayer seems relatively insignificant when compared to the governmental encroachments upon religion which were commonplace 200 years ago. [11]

The Court claims that this prayer was only a minor violation of the Constitution when compared to the encroachment practiced by the Founders 200 years ago! This Court, by accusing the Founders of violating the principles of the Constitution, purports to understand the Constitution better than those who wrote it!

Court decisions always cite previous cases as precedents; citing precedent is the means by which the past is used to give credibility to the present; precedent serves as the foundation upon which current decisions are built. A significant legal note to this case is that *not one single precedent was cited by the Court in its removal of school prayer!* That the Court was able to overturn 340 years of educational history in America without citing a single precedent was an accomplishment of which it was proud, as evidenced by a comment made the following year in the *Abington* v. *Schempp* case:

> Finally, in *Engel* v. *Vitale,* only last year [1962], these principles were so universally recognized that the Court, *without the citation of a single case* . . . reaffirmed them. [12]
> (emphasis added)

Why did the Court fail to cite a precedent? The answer is simple and straightforward: there was none to support its decision in this case! The Court refused to cite the opinions of the Founders, Congress, and previous Courts on this issue because those opinions differed radically with the position the 1962 Court was now assuming. The *Engel* ruling was simply an unveiling of the Court's new policy, revealing the way it would now interpret the First Amendment.

Despite its failure to cite any precedent, the Court did employ a useful strategy to help create public acceptance of its new policy: the *appearance* of widespread support.

> These principles [of separation of church and state] were so *universally recognized* . . . [13] (emphasis added)

In other words, "*Everybody* knows this is right—the whole world!" Without history or legal precedents to aid them, the Court relied on purveying an image that its new policy had universal acceptance and support—a patent misrepresentation. Quite the contrary; state laws regarding prayer in schools, enacted in accordance with the views of the majority of each state's citizens, reflected a view exactly opposite to that of the Court. The Court had employed an effective marketing strategy, but not an honest one!

The question still remains: how could such an absurd decision occur—a decision which declared *voluntary* prayer unconstitutional? Perhaps the answer rests in the fact that of the 1962-63 Supreme Court Justices, eight of the nine had arrived on the Court with an extended history of *political* and *not* judicial experience.

For example, Chief Justice Earl Warren had been the Governor of California for ten years prior to his appointment to the Court; Justice Hugo Black had been a U.S. Senator for ten years preceding his appointment; Justice Felix Frankfurter had been an assistant to the Secretary of Labor and a founding member of the ACLU; Justice Arthur Goldberg had been the Secretary of Labor and Ambassador to the United Nations; Justice William Douglas was chairman of the Securities and Exchange Commission prior to his appointment; all the Justices except Potter Stewart had similar *political* backgrounds. [14]

Justice Potter Stewart, having been a *federal* judge for four years prior to his appointment, was the *only* member of the Court with extended federal Constitutional experience *before* his appointment. Interestingly, Justice Potter Stewart was also the only Justice who objected to the removal of prayer on the basis of precedent. He alone acted as a judge; the rest acted as politicians.

Despite the oath the Justices took upon entering office to uphold the Constitution, they did not intend to follow its original intent or plan. The Court determined to make the nation's policies reflect its own personal philosophical views. In a superficial attempt to justify the decision in this case, the Court quoted James Madison:

> "[A]ttempts to enforce . . . acts obnoxious to so great a proportion of Citizens tend to enervate the laws in general and to slacken the bands of Society." [15]

The Court was suggesting that students offering the 22-word prayer was an act so obnoxious to the nation's citizens that it would weaken "the bands of Society." However, the following year in the *Abington* v. *Schempp* case, the Court provided statistics which disproved its own suggestion.

Since the *Engel* prayer was merely a generic acknowledgment of God, was that really an "act obnoxious to so great a proportion of Citizens"? What percentage of the nation might object to such a simple acknowledgment of God? The Court revealed:

> Only last year [1962] an official survey of the country indicated that 64% of our people have church membership, while *less than 3% profess no religion whatever.* [16] (emphasis added)

Contrary to the Court's assertion, the use of that 22-word voluntary prayer was *not* an "act obnoxious to so great a proportion of Citizens"—it did not weaken society. The Court's dictum in the *Engel* case consisted of a series of poorly grounded arguments and ill-advised statements.

School District of Abington Township *v.* Schempp, 1963 United States Supreme Court

This case involved another voluntary activity by students: Bible reading. Occurring less than a year after the *Engel* case, it provided the Court further opportunity to solidify its new doctrine. At issue was a school policy which stated:

> Each school . . . shall be opened by the reading, without comment, of a chapter in the Holy Bible. . . . Participation in the opening exercises . . . is voluntary. The student reading the verses from the Bible may select the passages and read from any version he chooses. . . . There are no prefatory statements, no questions asked or solicited, no comments or explanations made and no interpretations given at or during the exercises. The students and parents are advised that the student may absent himself from the classroom or, should he elect to remain, not participate in the exercises. [17]

Like the prayer used in the previous case, this too seemed to be a relatively innocuous practice: it was voluntary; the Bible was read without comment by one of the students from a version of his choice; there was no instruction other than what was contained within the verses. Nonetheless, the Court produced "expert" testimony to prove that voluntary Bible reading was dangerous to the children:

> Dr. Solomon Grayzel testified that . . . if portions of the New Testament were read without explanation, they could be, and . . . had been, psychologically harmful to the child. [18]

This was a very unorthodox action by the High Court: it quoted from individual testimony. The Court cites individuals only if they are historically important, if they are Justices commenting from previous cases, or if they can help establish the "facts" in a case. In this case, since Dr. Solomon Grayzel was neither an historical personality nor a former Justice, the Court was utilizing his quote to establish a "fact": allowing children to read the New Testament could cause psychological damage. Compare the Court's feelings about the Bible with those of the Founders:

> I have always said, and always will say, that the studious perusal of the sacred volume will make us better citizens. [19]
> *Thomas Jefferson*

> It is impossible to rightly govern . . . without God and the Bible. [20] *George Washington*

> [The Bible] is a book worth more than all the other books that were ever printed. [21] *Patrick Henry*

> Suppos [sic] a nation in some distant Region, should take the Bible for their only law Book, and every member should regulate his conduct by the precepts there exhibited. . . . What a Eutopa, what a Paradise would this region be. [22] *John Adams*

> [T]he moral principles and precepts contained in the scriptures ought to form the basis of all our civil constitutions and laws. . . . All the miseries and evils which men suffer from vice, crime, ambition, injustice, oppression, slavery and war, proceed from their despising or neglecting the precepts contained in the Bible. [23] *Noah Webster*

These quotes illustrate the radical disagreement which exists between this Court and the Founders. However, the Court was not finished; after "establishing" the Bible's harmful effect on children, the Court proclaimed:

> The [First] Amendment's purpose was not to strike merely at the official establishment of a single sect. . . . It was to create a complete and permanent separation of the spheres of religious activity and civil authority. [24]

Again, contrast this statement by the Court with statements of the Founders and early Congresses:

[T]he birth-day of the nation is indissolubly linked with the birth-day of the Saviour [and] forms a leading event in the progress of the gospel dispensation. . . . [T]he Declaration of Independence first organized the social compact on the foundation of the Redeemer's mission upon earth [and] laid the corner stone of human government upon the first precepts of Christianity. [25] *John Quincy Adams*

Whoever shall introduce into public affairs the principles of primitive Christianity will change the face of the world. [26] *Benjamin Franklin*

Had the people, during the Revolution, had a suspicion of any attempt to war against Christianity, that Revolution would have been strangled in its cradle. At the time of the adoption of the Constitution and the amendments, the universal sentiment was that Christianity should be encouraged, not any one sect. . . . In this age there can be no substitute for Christianity: that, in its general principles, is the great conservative element on which we must rely for the purity and permanence of free institutions. [27] *House Judiciary Committee, 1854*

The *Abington* Court was attempting to create the appearance that it was making a rational and logical decision—a decision which would have been widely accepted by our Founders. Untrue on all counts! The Court's statement was not only historically inaccurate, it would have been almost universally rejected by the Founders. The Court's pronouncement is acceptable only for those who reject the original intent of the Constitution. The *Abington* Court continued:

Almost 20 years ago in *Everson [1947]* . . . the Court said " . . . [n]either a state nor the Federal Government . . . can pass laws which aid one religion, aid all religions, or prefer one religion over another." [28]

This statement is basis for a further conflict. The early court rulings, based on the acts and intents of the Founders, *did* prefer one religion above the others:

By our form of government, the Christian religion is the established religion; and all sects and denominations of Christians are placed upon the same equal footing. [29] *Runkel v. Winemiller, 1799*

Christianity, general Christianity, is and always has been part of the common law. . . . The laws and institutions . . . are built on the foundation of reverence for Christianity. [30] *Updegraph* v. *Commonwealth, 1826*

Providence has given to our people the choice of their rulers, and it is the duty, as well as the privilege and interest of our Christian nation to select and prefer Christians for their rulers. [31] *John Jay, First Chief Justice of the Supreme Court*

The *Abington* Court also stated:

It is true that religion has been closely identified with our history and government. As we said in *Engel* v. *Vitale,* "The history of man is inseparable from the history of religion." [32]

In this instance, the Court was correct: American history **cannot** be separated from religion. However, a Department of Education research project which investigated the portrayal of religion in students' textbooks did not substantiate that fact. The research revealed:

Not one of the . . . ten thousand pages [in the students' textbooks] had one *text* reference to a primary religious activity occurring in representative contemporary American life. [33]

To illustrate the absurdity of this finding, the following excerpt was one of many supplied by the researchers to indicate what was typical in high-school textbooks:

Of 642 listed events [listed in *A History of Our American People* by Laidlaw, 1981], only six refer to religion. . . . The following supposedly important dates in American history are listed in this book: 1893, Yale introduces ice hockey; 1897, first subway completed in Boston; 1920, United States wins first place in Olympic Games; 1930, Irish Sweepstakes becomes popular; 1960, Pittsburgh Pirates win World Series; 1962, Twist—a popular dance craze. The above categories make it clear that such trivia is given more emphasis than any aspect of religion. [34]

The Court, with the pressure it has placed on publishers through its rulings, has effectively censored textbooks. The rewriting and censorship of America's history never could have occurred without the anti-Christian sentiment promoted by the contemporary courts.

The absurdity of the Court's rulings in the *Engel* and *Abington* cases can be demonstrated by proposing a scenario. In legal cases, the Court allows groups or individuals who are not a direct party to the case to speak on behalf of one of the sides by written briefs of *amicus curiae*—friend-of-the-Court briefs. Imagine that George Washington, Benjamin Franklin, and Thomas Jefferson had each filed friend-of-the-Court briefs in the *Engel* and *Abington* cases in order to register their feelings with the Justices.

Begins George Washington: "Although I firmly believe the basis of our government is religion and morality, and despite saying I would never have signed the Constitution if I believed it would ever have encroached on the rights to publicly practice religious principles, and despite the fact that on August 7, 1789, as President I approved a bill requiring that religion be encouraged and promoted in all schools, I firmly support your efforts to rid our schools of voluntary prayer and voluntary Bible reading. Yes, you must prohibit prayer and Bible reading in schools and act to protect these young, impressionable students from the basis of our nation—religion. I urge you to disregard our history, our laws, and our traditions!"

"Let me add my support to what George has expressed," says Ben Franklin. "Despite the fact that I said that the principles of Christianity must be included in public affairs, and even though I called for prayer for each of our sessions at the Constitutional Convention, and although I declared that I didn't believe we could possibly succeed without God's aid and assistance, we definitely need to keep these students away from prayer and the Scriptures! Even though what I am now encouraging you to do is contradictory to everything I did during my long and extended years of public service, you must ignore what we did in the Constitutional Convention and in Congress; protect these students from the influence of religion!"

Thomas Jefferson echoes, "Yes! And please ignore the fact that this New York prayer came by the consent of the governed and that it was upheld by the New York legislature and New York courts. You must act! You must go against the consent of the governed; you must rule against the 97 percent in this nation who believe in God. Do not let these students pray to God, even if they want to!"

Obviously, we cannot picture our Founders making such appeals! Yet when the Court declares these actions unconstitutional, this is what it would have us believe!

Stone *v.* Graham, 1980
United States Supreme Court

This case occurred 17 years after voluntary Bible reading had been banned in schools. Nationwide, schools had succumbed to judicial legislation and had stopped the active use of the Bible. However, this case did not deal with its active use, but with its passive use: a copy of the Ten Commandments was hanging in the hallways of Kentucky schools. The question now to be answered was: Is it a violation of the Constitution for students to *see* a copy of the Ten Commandments while at school? After all, the Ten Commandments were *not* required reading for the students nor were they even in the classrooms; students looked at them only if they wanted to. Additionally, the Ten Commandments are not solely religious—they are the basis of the civil laws for the western world. When the Court was confronted with the argument that the Ten Commandments had secular importance, it erupted in an emotional outburst of religious prejudice:

> The pre-eminent purpose for posting the Ten Command-ments on schoolroom walls is plainly religious in nature. The Ten Commandments are undeniably a sacred text in the Jewish and Christian faiths, and no legislative recitation of a supposed secular purpose can blind us to that fact. [35]

The Court pointed out the problem with displaying the Ten Commandments:

> If the posted copies of the Ten Commandments are to have any effect at all, it will be to induce the schoolchildren to read, meditate upon, perhaps to venerate and obey, the Commandments. . . . This . . . is not a permissible state objective under the Establishment Clause. [36]

What a tragedy if students were somehow to read, meditate on, respect, or even obey the Ten Commandments! What if they were to respect their parents? Or not steal? Or perhaps even not murder someone? God forbid! If these children were to read and obey the Ten Commandments at school, it would be a violation of the First Amendment (so ruled the Court):

> The mere posting of the copies . . . the Establishment Clause [of the First Amendment] prohibits. [37]

A single quote by James Madison will demonstrate the absurdity of the Court's ruling. Madison, the "Chief Architect of the Constitution," engineered many of the essential elements of the First Amendment.   Certainly Madison would know what the First Amendment forbids.   Does it prohibit children from viewing the Ten Commandments?

> We have staked the whole future of American civilization, not upon the power of government, far from it. We have staked the future . . . upon the capacity of each and all of us to govern ourselves, to sustain ourselves, according to the Ten Commandments of God. [38]

Madison did not believe viewing the Ten Commandments was a violation of the Constitution; in fact, he believed that obeying them was its very basis! The Court declared unconstitutional the very tenet that the "Chief Architect of the Constitution" said was our basis.

State Board of Educ. *v.* Board of Educ. of Netcong, 1970
Supreme Court of New Jersey
Allowed to Stand by the United States Supreme Court

Despite the rulings in *Engel, Abington,* and several similar cases, many individuals still believed that surely there must be some program in which voluntary prayer and voluntary Bible reading could be constitutionally acceptable. After all, the First Amendment provides that the government may not "prohibit the free exercise [of religion]." With such a strong Constitutional guarantee, it should be possible to construct a statute which would be acceptable even to the contemporary courts. Notice this effort made by the Netcong, New Jersey, school board:

> On each school day before class instruction begins, a period of not more than five minutes shall be available to those teachers and students who may wish to participate voluntarily in the free exercise of religion as guaranteed by the United States Constitution. This freedom of religion shall not be expressed in any way which will interfere with another's rights. Participation may be total or partial, regular or occasional, or not at all. Non-participation shall not be considered evidence of non-religion, nor shall participation be considered evidence of or recognizing an establishment of religion. The purpose of this motion is not to favor one religion over another nor to favor religion over non-religion but rather to promote love of

neighbor, brotherhood, respect for the dignity of the individual, moral consciousness and civic responsibility, to contribute to the general welfare of the community and to preserve the values that constitute our American heritage. [39]

The plan was implemented in the following manner:

At 7:55 A.M. in the Netcong High School gymnasium, immediately prior to the formal opening of school, students who wish to join in the exercise either sit or stand in the bleachers.   A student volunteer reader, assigned by the principal on a first come, first serve basis, then comes forward and reads the "remarks" . . . of the chaplain [of the United States House or Senate] from the *Congressional Record.* . . . The selection of material to be read is made by the volunteer reader. . . . The volunteer reader is free to add remarks concerning such subjects as love of neighbor, brotherhood and civic responsibility.   At the conclusion of the reading the students are asked to meditate for a short period of time either on the material that has been read or upon anything else they desire. [40]

Even though this plan was constructed both on the wording of the First Amendment and according to the requirements given in the rulings of the contemporary courts, the New Jersey Supreme Court nevertheless found an ingenious way to declare the act unconstitutional—the court claimed that *it* owned the school children:

It is hereby declared to be a principle governing the law of this state that children under the jurisdiction of said court are wards of the state . . . which may intervene to safeguard them from neglect or injury. [41]

The court did *not* want *its* children exposed to religion; it intervened to protect "its" children from the "neglect or injury" that might be caused by allowing them to hear or offer a voluntarily prayer.   But the U.S. Government has chaplains; and it is legal for them to lead Congress in prayer; surely it can do no harm for students to hear the *same* prayers that our Congressmen hear. The court did not agree:

Public schools, unlike the halls of Congress, present a special case.   This audience is without the maturity to express independence. . . . What may be wholly permissible for adults therefore may not be so for children. [42]

But the prayers the students read were part of the *Congressional Record*—part of the *public* record published by the United States Government and available to *any* citizen!   The *Congressional Record* is simply a written transcript of every statement made on the floor of Congress.   Despite being a *public* record, the court prohibited students from reading it:

It is religious exercise to read from the *Congressional Record* "remarks" of the chaplain. . . . Reading from the *Congressional Record* may be an unconstitutional infringement upon the First Amendment. [43]

But this activity was *completely* voluntary; and it occurred *before* school! That made no difference to the court:

[A] School program for religious exercises is not saved from being unconstitutional establishment of religion by providing for permissive attendance . . . [a] "period for the free exercise of religion" . . . was unconstitutional establishment of religion, and not essential to free exercise of religion. [44]

The court explained that the "free exercise" of religion guaranteed to students in the First Amendment would be allowed *only* if it could be proven that the students would suffer harm by not being allowed to pray in the school gym. This case was further evidence that the courts were committed to thwarting *any* religious activity in schools! No matter how carefully worded or how thoughtfully constructed, the court could find a way to forbid it!

Walz *v.* Tax Commission of the City of New York, 1970 United States Supreme Court

This case centered on the constitutionality of tax exemptions for churches.   The Court, in reviewing the actions it had taken in previous cases on the First Amendment, complimented itself:

We have been able to chart a course that preserved the autonomy and freedom of religious bodies while avoiding any semblance of established religion. This is a "tight rope" and one we have successfully traversed. . . . The line we must draw between the permissible and the impermissible is one which accords with history and faithfully reflects the understanding of the Founding Fathers. [45]

It is incredible that the Court should claim that it had faithfully reflected the intent of the Founding Fathers, or that it had successfully walked the "tight rope" in the First Amendment! However, the Court's measure of its successes was based upon its own standards, not the standards of the Founders; by removing any acknowledgment of God from schools the Court reckoned itself successful. The Court then asserted:

> One of the mandates of the First Amendment is to promote a viable, pluralistic society and to keep government neutral, not only between sects, but also between believers and nonbelievers. [46]

A pluralistic society is one which acknowledges no one religion above any other. Our Founders certainly were not pluralistic:

> It cannot be emphasized too strongly or too often that this great nation was founded, not by religionists [pluralism], but by Christians; not on religions, but on the gospel of Jesus Christ! [47] *Patrick Henry*

> Let . . . statesmen and patriots, unite their endeavors to renovate the age by . . . educating their little boys and girls . . . [and] leading them in the study and practice of the exalted virtues of the Christian system. [48] *Samuel Adams*

> You do well to wish to learn our arts and ways of life, and above all, the religion of Jesus Christ . . . Congress will do every thing they can to assist you in this wise intention. [49] *George Washington to Delaware Indian Chiefs in 1779*

> [T]he religion which has introduced civil liberty, is the religion of Christ and his apostles. . . . This is genuine Christianity, and to this we owe our free constitutions of government. [50] *Noah Webster*

> In this age there can be no substitute for Christianity. . . . That was the religion of the founders of the republic, and they expected it to remain the religion of their descendants. [51] *House Judiciary Committee, 1854*

Much, much more could be quoted, but the inaccuracy of the Court's comment is obvious. The promotion of a religiously pluralistic society could not have been further from the intent of the First Amendment!

Wallace *v.* Jaffree, 1984
United States Supreme Court

In this case, the Court examined an Alabama law authorizing a one-minute period of silence in all Alabama public schools for the purpose of *silent* meditation or *silent* individual prayer. Not surprisingly, the Court declared the law unconstitutional; but the interesting part of this case is *why* the Court found it unconstitutional. Even though the Court conceded that a one-minute period of silence for meditation *was* constitutional, the Court struck down the law. Why?

It is not the activity itself that concerns us; it is the purpose of the activity that we shall scrutinize. [52]

In reviewing the statements of the legislator who authored the bill, the Court established that:

The "prime sponsor" of the bill . . . explained that the bill was an "effort to return voluntary prayer to our public schools . . . ". He intended to provide children the opportunity of sharing in their spiritual heritage of Alabama and of this country. [53]

Having established the legislator's intent when he authored the bill, and the intent of the people of Alabama and of the legislature by approving and passing the bill, the Court declared the statute:

Invalid because the sole purpose . . . was "an effort on the part of the State of Alabama to encourage a religious activity." [It] is a law respecting the establishment of religion within the meaning of the First Amendment. [54]

Even though the statute itself was constitutionally acceptable, it became unconstitutional because the sponsor's motive was "wrong"!

DeSpain *v.* DeKalb County Community School Dist., 1967
2nd Federal Court of Appeals
Allowed to Stand by the United States Supreme Court

A kindergarten teacher had her students recite this poem:

"We thank you for the flowers so sweet; We thank you for the food we eat; We thank you for the birds that sing; We thank you for everything." [55]

Even though the word "God" did not appear in this poem, and even though testimony by the teacher explained that she used this poem to teach the children to say "thank you," the court nonetheless ruled that it was unconstitutional for the children to recite it. A dissenting judge in this decision offered an insightful observation about the court's ruling:

> Despite the elimination of the word "God" from the children's recital of thanks, [DeSpain] maintain[s] . . . that that word is still there in the minds of the children. Thus we are asked as a court to prohibit, not only what these children are saying, but also what [DeSpain] *think[s]* the children are *thinking*. . . . One who seeks to convert a child's supposed thought into a violation of the constitution of the United States is placing a meaning on that historic doctrine which would have surprised the founding fathers. [56]

The dissenting judge was amazed that the court would conclude that it was unconstitutional for school children to think about God!

McCollum *v.* Board of Educ., 1948
United States Supreme Court

In this case, religious classes had been offered as school electives:

> In 1940 interested members of the Jewish, Roman Catholic, and a few of the Protestant faiths formed a voluntary association called the Champaign Council on Religious Education. They obtained permission from the Board of Education to offer classes in religious instruction to public school pupils in grades four to nine inclusive. Classes were made up of pupils whose parents signed printed cards requesting that their children be permitted to attend; they were held weekly, thirty minutes for the lower grades, forty-five minutes for the higher. The council employed the religious teachers at no expense to the school authorities, but the instructors were subject to the approval and supervision of the superintendent of schools. The classes were taught in three separate religious groups by Protestant teachers, Catholic priests, and a Jewish rabbi. [57]

Even though the classes were voluntary, and even though students must receive parents' written permission in order to attend the classes, the Court found these classes unacceptable:

As we said in the *Everson* case, the First Amendment has erected a wall between Church and State which must be kept high and impregnable. . . . Separation means separation, not something less. . . . It is the Court's duty to enforce this principle in its full integrity. . . . Illinois has here authorized the commingling of sectarian with secular instruction in the public schools. The Constitution of the United States forbids this. [58]

After ruling in favor of Mrs. Vashti McCollum, who brought the suit against the school program, the Court remanded the case back to the lower courts to implement its decision. A dissenting Justice argued that the Court had awarded McCollum too much by giving her the victory, for she had asked the Court to force the Illinois school board to:

Adopt and enforce rules and regulations prohibiting all instruction in and teaching of religious education in all public schools . . . in said district. [59]

The Justice explained why he thought the Court had gone too far:

The plaintiff, as she has every right to be, is an avowed atheist. What she has asked of the courts is that they not only end the "released time" plan but also ban every form of teaching which suggests or recognizes that there is a God. She would ban all teaching of the Scriptures. She especially mentions as an example of invasion of her rights "having pupils learn and recite such statements as, 'The Lord is my Shepherd, I shall not want.'" And she objects to teaching that the King James version of the Bible "is called the Christian's Guide Book, the Holy Writ and the Word of God," and many other similar matters. This Court is directing the Illinois courts generally to sustain plaintiff's complaint without exception of any of these grounds of complaint. [60]

The Court ruled in favor of a single atheist who was *not* involved in any of the voluntarily attended classes in question. She brought suit against the school district because she was *personally* offended by Christianity. She, a single individual, with the help of an eager Court, was able to "prohibit the free exercise [of religion]" in every school in the district! A concurring Justice in this decision commented that the Court was now assuming "the role of a super board of education for every school district in the nation." [61]

These are eight representative cases selected from among many to show how the First Amendment has been abused by the contemporary Court. The Court's current doctrine is diametrically opposed not only to our history, but to nearly two centuries of legal practice and precedent. The Court, by discarding both historical and legal precedent, has created its own new standards for the use of the First Amendment.

Recall the statue personifying Lady Justice? She is blindfolded, holding a balance in her hand. Why is she blindfolded? So that she cannot see the parties involved—so that she can administer justice impartially. The Court has now determined that she may no longer remain blindfolded. She must remove her blindfold to see if a Christian group or a Christian principle is involved in the case; if so, she must rule against it. The absurd has become reality!

~8~
The Absurd Becomes The Standard

No longer is there a reason to fear isolated instances of absurd decisions—they are now the bench mark of the Court. Rulings that our Founders never even imagined have become matter-of-fact.

Recall that when the Court first struck down school prayer in the *Engel* case, it was unable to cite a single precedent to justify the removal of that simple 22-word prayer. As illustrated by the following cases, a lack of precedent is no longer a hardship for the Court.

Wallace *v.* Jaffree, 1985 [1]
United States Supreme Court

This was the case in which the Court ruled that an Alabama statute authorizing a one-minute period of silence in schools for silent meditation or silent prayer was unconstitutional. When rendering this decision (22 years after *Engel* and 37 years after announcing its new doctrine of separation in *Everson),* the Court had no difficulty citing precedents; the Court made over 200 references to previous cases. Simply by the sheer quantity of their citations, the Court appeared to have more than a sufficient basis to justify their decision in *Wallace.*

An interesting question that might be posed would be: "What were the dates of those 200 citations? Were they older cases reflecting history, or were they recent cases?" Those 200 case citations can be grouped in the following chronological order: citations prior to 1947 (the year in which the Court had announced its new doctrine of separation) — 22; 1947-1950 — 10; the 1950's — 4; the 1960's — 44; the 1970's — 65; and the 1980's — 55. Only 22 of the 200 citations occurred before 1947; 178 occurred after the Court's 1947 declaration! Of those cited before 1947, many came from the 1940 case, *Cantwell* v. *Connecticut,* [2] in which the Court originally seized control of the First Amendment by its use of the Fourteenth Amendment (see Chapter 9). The other pre-1947 cases dealt with Court procedure, not school prayer.

Notice how the numbers increased as the years marched on: only 10 cases cited from the 1950's, but 65 from the 1970's. The 1980's appeared even more promising for this Court—only four years into the decade the Court already had accumulated 55 citations! The

Court no longer has difficulty providing precedents for a case—it has created its own pool to which it may refer. This pattern of citing only recent decisions occurs regularly in the Court's rulings.

Levitt *v.* Committee for Public Education, 1973 [3]
United States Supreme Court

New York law mandated that all schools within the state—public and non-public—keep certain administrative records. The record requirements were purely secular, relating only to testing, attendance, etc. This record-keeping was costly both in direct financial expenditures and in substantial outlay of staff time. The legislature appropriated money for the public schools to cover these expenses; it felt it should do the same for the non-public schools. After all, these were state requirements, and state tax money had been collected from *all* families in the state, not merely those attending public schools. Therefore, the legislature:

> Appropriated $28,000,000 for the purpose of reimbursing nonpublic schools throughout the State "for . . . the preparation and submission to the state of various other reports as provided for or required by law or regulation." [4]

Although the money was for non-religious activities, the Court ruled it unconstitutional because it went to religious groups. What precedents did the Court cite? **Pre-1947: 0; Post- 1947: 18.**

Committee for Public Education *v.* Nyquist, 1973 [5]
United States Supreme Court

To ensure that students had safe facilities in which to attend school, the New York legislature provided money designated solely for maintenance of physical school facilities. The funding was made available in large amounts for public schools and in token amounts for qualifying non-public schools. The money appropriated for the non-public schools was only for:

> "Maintenance and repair" of facilities and equipment to ensure the students' "health, welfare and safety." [6]

The Court declared the legislature's actions unconstitutional. On which precedents? **Pre-1947: 1; Post-1947: 99.**

Stone v. Graham, 1980 [7]
United States Supreme Court

This was the case in which the Court ruled it unconstitutional for students to view the Ten Commandments while at school. Only nine citations were used in this case. Six were from *Abington* v. *Schempp, 1963* (removal of school prayer and Bible reading), one referred to *Engel* v. *Vitale, 1962* (the first case on school prayer), and the other two were from *Lemon* v. *Kurtzman, 1971.* [8] *Lemon* v. *Kurtzman* established what the Court now calls "The Lemon Test," which declares that spiritual activities may be tolerated only if they have a predominately non-spiritual value—what the Court calls "secular legislative value." **Pre-1947: 0; Post-1947: 9.**

Marsh v. Chambers, 1982 [9]
United States Supreme Court

This case involved a challenge against the position of chaplain in the Nebraska legislature. The Court ruled one aspect of the chaplaincy to be constitutional and another portion to be unconstitutional. Where did it find its precedents? **Pre-1947: 1; Post-1947: 32.**

— — — • • • — — —

Many, many other cases can be cited; the results differ little. The Court has established its own reservoir of recent cases to which it may scurry to declare a public religious expression unconstitutional.

An examination of Court decisions relating to matters of religion and government since the ratification of the Constitution and the First Amendment identifies three discernible eras. The first and third eras are very distinct and easily identifiable; the second is less distinct and serves as a transition between the other two. The first era can be described as pro-Christian, the middle era as Christian-tolerant, and the last era as anti-Christian.

In the first era—the pro-Christian era—the Court describes America as "a Christian nation." This first era extends from the Court's earliest rulings through the 1931 decision in *Macintosh.* [10] In the second era, beginning after the *Macintosh* case, the Court began to drift away from describing the United States as "a Christian nation" and "a Christian people" and began to describe it in terms of "a religious people" *(Zorach* v. *Clauson, 1952).* [11] During this transition period, the Court moved away from the strong

Christian definition that had been applied since the founding to a more pluralistic interpretation. In the third era—the anti-Christian years—even the watery acknowledgment that we are a "religious people" is discarded. No overt religious recognition is allowed, as evidenced by the *Lemon* test declaring that a religious practice must have an underlying predominant "secular legislative value" to be tolerated in public *(Lemon v. Kurtzman, 1971)*.

In the pro-Christian era, the Court's citation of precedents was numerous and broad, often spanning two or more centuries. For example, in the *Holy Trinity* case the Court quoted over 60 different historical precedents, in addition to citing several early legal decisions, to rule that "No purpose of action against religion can be imputed to any legislation . . . because this is a religious people. . . . This is a Christian nation." [12] In the Christian-tolerant years, precedents span only a narrow band, being taken primarily from the decades immediately preceding the decisions. In the anti-Christian years, decisions prior to 1947 are virtually ignored (since they tend to disprove the Court's rulings).

In the pro-Christian years, the Court, relying heavily on the intent of laws, would methodically search historical records and frequently quote from a wide representation of Founders. In both the neutral and anti-Christian years, the only Founders quoted to show "intent" are James Madison and Thomas Jefferson, which is amazing when considering that Jefferson neither attended the Constitutional Convention nor participated in its framing or ratification. As noted earlier, had the enlightenment ideas in which Jefferson was tutored in France become part of our Constitution, we might have had the same results as France: seven different forms of government during the same period that we have had only one.

Since earlier history books identified nearly 250 Founders (56 who signed the Declaration, 55 who framed the Constitution, 90 in the first Congress which formed the First Amendment and the Bill of Rights, etc.), [13] it is quite a significant commentary on the historical shallowness of the contemporary Court's arguments that it cites only two Founding Fathers. Why not quote from other Founders to sustain what the Court calls its "universally recognized"[14] policy? Because most of the Founding Fathers never made a statement which could even be misconstrued into the policy which the Court upholds today!

~9~
The Court's Defense of Its Position

The Court has employed a carefully crafted series of historical misportrayals to shield itself from the attack and criticism arising from its misapplication of the First Amendment. This chapter will expose five of the Court's misportrayals: (1) its misuse of the Fourteenth Amendment, (2) its misuse of James Madison and his activities in Virginia, (3) its misuse of Thomas Jefferson, (4) its omission of major historical facts, and (5) its omission of important statements made by both Madison and Jefferson. The Court has become adept in its use of these five defenses, having refined them well over the past four decades. Nonetheless, these defenses have fatal flaws.

1. The Fourteenth Amendment

The Fourteenth Amendment was part of a quick succession of three Constitutional Amendments added at the conclusion of the Civil War: the Thirteenth, Fourteenth, and Fifteenth Amendments. All three Amendments, written by Congress and ratified by the states within the five-year period from 1865-1870, addressed a dominant issue in the conflict: slavery. The Thirteenth Amendment abolished slavery, the Fourteenth guaranteed civil rights for former slaves, and the Fifteenth provided former slaves with voting rights.

Following the abolition of slavery through the Thirteenth Amendment, some voices in the South erupted in bitter protest. Although conceding that the former slaves might now be technically free, they vowed that they would never allow former slaves to have any of the rights belonging to a citizen of that state; they would keep the former slaves isolated and suspended powerless in the state wherein they resided. Congress responded with the Fourteenth Amendment to guarantee that newly freed slaves would enjoy all the privileges and rights conveyed by being a citizen either of the state or of the nation. That the purpose of the Fourteenth Amendment was to secure civil rights for former slaves is a fact established in the records of the Congress which created the Fourteenth, and a fact widely understood by historians. Notice this explanation of the Fourteenth Amendment found in the *World Book Encyclopedia, 1986:*

> The principal purpose of this [Fourteenth] amendment was to make former slaves citizens of both the United States and the state in which they lived.

Despite the intent of the Fourteenth Amendment to provide civil rights for former slaves, in *Everson* v. *Board of Education, 1947*, the Court attached the Fourteenth Amendment to the First Amendment. The Court claimed that the Fourteenth Amendment now allowed it to apply the First Amendment against the states and not merely against the federal government, which had been the intent of the Founders.

In *Abington* v. *Schempp, 1963*, the Court discussed the impact from coupling these two Amendments:

> This Court has decisively settled that the First Amendment's mandate that "Congress shall make no law respecting an establishment of religion, or prohibiting the free exercise thereof" has been made wholly applicable to the States by the Fourteenth Amendment. . . . The First Amendment declares that Congress shall make no law respecting an establishment of religion or prohibiting the free exercise thereof. The Fourteenth Amendment has rendered the legislatures of the states as incompetent as Congress to enact such laws. [1]

In *Walz* v. *Tax Commission, 1970*, the Court reviewed the dramatic effects fomented in its twenty-three years of coupling these two Amendments:

> The Court largely overlooks the _revolution_ initiated by the adoption of the Fourteenth Amendment, _reversing the historic position_ that the foundations of those liberties rested largely in state law. The process of the "selective incorporation" of various provisions of the Bill of Rights into the Fourteenth Amendment . . . has been a steady one . . . The Establishment Clause was not incorporated in the Fourteenth Amendment until *Everson* v. *Board of Education* . . . was decided in 1947. . . . And so the _revolution_ occasioned by the Fourteenth Amendment has progressed as Article after Article in the Bill of Rights has been incorporated in it and made applicable to the States. [2] (emphasis added)

"The First Amendment made applicable to the states by the Fourteenth Amendment" is common phraseology today. Rarely, if ever, does a First Amendment case appear before the courts which does not contain this phrase.

Since the Fourteenth Amendment was designed and ratified to guarantee civil rights for recently emancipated slaves, how could the Court possibly attach it to the religious clauses of the First

Amendment? Because the Court used only the wording of the Fourteenth and rejected its intent. The Fourteenth specifically states:

All persons born or naturalized in the United States, and subject to the jurisdiction thereof, are citizens of the United States and of the state wherein they reside. No state shall make or enforce any law which shall abridge the privileges or immunities of citizens of the United States.

By taking the "letter" of the Fourteenth Amendment without regard to its "spirit" or intent, the Court was able to decide that the Constitutional Amendments which had previously pertained only to the federal government now also pertained to the states. This interpretation was diametrically opposed to the intent of the first ten Amendments (the Bill of Rights):

The Bill of Rights was intended to be a restriction on the national government, not the states. Chief Justice John Marshall in the 1833 decision of *Barron* v. *Baltimore* [3] emphasized that the Bill of Rights restricted only the national government. But since the 1940s, the Supreme Court has interpreted Section I of the Fourteenth Amendment . . . as incorporating the Bill of Rights, i.e., making it applicable to the states. The Supreme Court has thus achieved precisely the opposite of what was intended by the framers of the Bill of Rights: instead of being solely a restriction on the national government, the Bill of Rights is now a restriction on the states. [4]

Even the *Everson* Court conceded that the First Amendment had never before been applied to the states:

Prior to the adoption of the Fourteenth Amendment, the First Amendment did not apply as a restraint against the states. [5]

Did the Congress which created the Fourteenth Amendment intend that it should incorporate the First Amendment against the states? The answer, demonstrated through what is called the Blaine Amendment, is an emphatic and resounding "No!" The Blaine Amendment, submitted to Congress during the framing of the Fourteenth Amendment, was a specific attempt to do then what the Courts have done now—apply the First Amendment against the states. The Blaine Amendment, quoted by the 1948 *McCollum* Court stated:

No State shall make any law respecting an establishment of religion, or prohibiting the free exercise thereof ... No public property, and no public revenue ... shall be appropriated to ... the support of any school ... under the control of any religious or anti-religious sect, organization, or denomination. .... And no such particular creed or tenets shall be read or taught in any school or institution supported ... by such revenue. [6]

What happened to this proposed Amendment—an attempt to separate church and state in each state as now regularly done by the contemporary Courts? The Blaine Amendment, as well as five similar ones, were voted down! The *McCollum* Court explained:

The reason for the failure of these attempts seems to have been in part that the "provisions of the State constitutions are in almost all instances adequate on this subject, and no amendment is likely to be secured." *Id.* .... H. Res. 1, 44th Cong., 1st Sess. (1876). [7]

The Congress which formed the Fourteenth rejected *six* attempts to link it to the First Amendment. The contemporary Court, by using the Fourteenth Amendment to apply the First Amendment against the states, has embraced a purpose that Congress clearly opposed on six occasions!

The legislators who framed the Fourteenth Amendment never imagined that their repeated opposition to applying the First Amendment to the states would be ignored by later Courts. The Court's current use of the Fourteenth Amendment is not only an affront to the intent of the Amendment, it is even an insult to the Court's own hero, Thomas Jefferson, who instructed:

On every question of construction, carry ourselves back to the time when the Constitution was adopted, recollect the spirit manifested in the debates, and instead of trying what meaning may be squeezed out of the text, or invented against it, *conform to the probable one in which it was passed.* [8] (emphasis added)

For more than 70 years following the ratification of the Fourteenth Amendment, _no_ Court coupled the First and the Fourteenth. When the Court finally did couple the two Amendments, there was obviously no previous decisions on which it might rely for guidance;

it knew that it was charting new territory. For example, in *Murdock*
v. *Pennsylvania, 1943,* the Court revealed its uncertainty of how far
to advance its new interpretation:

> As a Court, we should determine what sort of liberty it is that
> the due process clause of the Fourteenth Amendment guaran-
> tees against state restrictions on speech and church. [9]

The Court, in effect, is saying, "Now, seventy-five years *ex post
facto,* we are going to determine exactly what they *should have said*
in the Fourteenth. No Court before us has enforced the Fourteenth
correctly, but we will!" This Court proceeded to do what Congress
had rejected on six occasions and what previous Courts had refused
to do for over 70 years! This was an obvious case of the Court
usurping the role of the legislators in the designing of laws.

The Court's description in *Walz* v. *Tax Commission, 1970,* of what
has happened since its "innovative" application of the Fourteenth is
indeed accurate—a "revolution" has been initiated. Unfortunately,
this revolution was entirely outside the control of the governed; it
was not by the people, but by the Courts. Justices now strike down
legislative laws they don't like and enact judicial laws they do.

2. The Efforts of James Madison and Thomas Jefferson in Virginia

A second ploy routinely utilized by the Court to give itself an
image of credibility is to invoke James Madison and Thomas
Jefferson. This excerpt from *Walz* v. *Tax Commission, 1970,* reveals
the Court's fixation with these two individuals:

> Thomas Jefferson was President . . . and James Madison sat
> in sessions of the Virginia General Assembly. . . . I have
> found no record of their personal views on the respective
> Acts. The absence of such a record is itself significant. . . .
> Both Jefferson and Madison wrote prolifically about issues
> they felt important, and their opinions were well known to
> contemporary chroniclers. [10]

When using these two, the Court typically focuses on their efforts
in Virginia prior to the Constitutional Convention, as illustrated by
these excerpts from *Everson* and *Engel:*

> This Court has previously recognized that the provisions of
> the First Amendment, in the drafting and adoption of which

Madison and Jefferson played such leading roles, had the same objective and were intended to provide the same protection against governmental intrusion on religious liberty as the Virginia statute. [11] *(Everson)*

In 1785-1786, those opposed to the established Church, led by James Madison and Thomas Jefferson . . . [who] opposed all religious establishments by law on grounds of principle, obtained the enactment of the famous "Virginia Bill for Religious Liberty" by which all religious groups were placed on an equal footing so far as the State was concerned. Similar though less far-reaching legislation was being considered and passed in other States. [12] *(Engel)*

The Court, relying heavily on these two Founders and their activities in Virginia prior to the Constitutional Convention, presents what was happening in Virginia as though it were standard throughout the nation. It was *not!*

The Church of England (the Anglican church) was the only legally established church in Virginia, even though the members of other Christian denominations (Baptists, Lutherans, Presbyterians, Quakers, etc.) were more numerous than the Anglicans. Therefore, Madison and Jefferson turned their efforts not toward opposing Christianity in public affairs as the Court now portrays, but toward assisting the other Christian denominations. Jefferson authored the "Virginia Bill for Religious Liberty" to place all Christian denominations in Virginia on an equal footing—already the case in the other states. Madison worked hard for the bill's passage and penned *Memorial and Remonstrance* to explain why the establishment of one Christian denomination above all others was wrong. When the vote on the bill was finally taken:

Thomas Jefferson was at his ambassadorial post in France, and James Madison was making one last eloquent plea on behalf of Jefferson's bill. Then the delegates began to vote. When the vote was counted, sixty-seven men had voted aye and twenty had voted no to disestablish the Church of England as the one legal state church, to end all taxation to support that church, and to grant religious freedom to the . . . settlers of Virginia. [13]

By reading the Court's portrayal, one would undoubtedly conclude that the situation in Virginia was typical of every state and that, somehow, Madison and Jefferson singlehandedly corrected the entire nation. Untrue. In fact, in the years immediately preceding the Constitutional Convention, Virginia was the *only* state that still had denominational-preference laws:

> For the first 163 years of Virginia history, the Church of England was Virginia's only legal church. By law, every plantation or settlement had a house or a room set apart for the worship of God. That worship was legally bound to follow the English Book of Common Prayer, and everyone— man, woman and child—was ordered to attend. [14]

What happened in Virginia was unusual; no other state had that practice. This was even reluctantly acknowledged by the Court in *Engel:* " . . . less far-reaching legislation was being considered . . . in other States." [15] That was because the other states had already eliminated what Virginia was still embracing. The report by the 1854 House Judiciary Committee reaffirmed this, stating that Virginia was the _only_ state which had a system of state-ordered tithes at the time of the Constitution. [16]

James Madison and Thomas Jefferson were **not** fighting against Christianity, they were fighting *for* its free expression! They were representing the Christians in Virginia—Baptists, Quakers, Presbyterians, etc.—and fighting *for* Christians when they made the statements which the Court now misportrays. When statements are removed from the context in which they were spoken, and examined without regard to the evil which they were intended to correct, they can be used to prove almost anything.

3. The Role of Thomas Jefferson

As noted from the Court's excerpts, Jefferson's name usually appears in conjunction with Madison's as an authority on the Constitution. The statement of the *Everson* Court bears repeating:

> This Court has previously recognized that the provisions of *the First Amendment, in the drafting and adoption of which Madison and Jefferson played such leading roles . . .* [17] (emphasis added)

As noted in Chapter 3, and contrary to the Court's statement above, Jefferson did _not_ play a leading role either in the First Amendment or the Constitution; he had been in Paris. In fact, during the

Congressional debate, it was Fisher Ames of Massachusetts [18] who proposed the wording of the First Amendment; and it was the conference committee of Senators Oliver Ellsworth, Charles Carroll, and William Paterson and Representatives Roger Sherman, John Vining, and James Madison which hammered out the final wording that the Congress subsequently approved and the states finally ratified;[19] Jefferson was not present.

Even though Jefferson did **_not_** participate in the framing of the First Amendment, he did have much to say about its intent (but evidently nothing the Court wants to cite):

> *Kentucky Resolutions of 1798:* No power over the freedom of religion . . . [is] delegated to the United States by the Constitution. [20]

> *Second Inaugural Address, 1805:* In matters of religion I have considered that its free exercise is placed by the Constitution independent of the powers of the General [federal] Government. [21]

> *Letter to Samuel Miller, 1808:* I consider the government of the United States as interdicted [prohibited] by the Constitution from intermeddling with religious institutions, their doctrines, discipline, or exercises. This results not only from the provision that no law shall be made respecting the establishment or free exercise of religion, but from that also which reserves to the States the powers not delegated to the United States [10th Amendment]. Certainly, no power to prescribe any religious exercise, or to assume authority in religious discipline, has been delegated to the General Government. It must then rest with the States, as far as it can be in any human authority. [22]

Even though Jefferson's statements on the First Amendment should not be considered "best evidence," if the Court is going to cite Jefferson, it should, as it requires of others, "tell the truth, the whole truth, and nothing but the truth."

4. Omission of Facts

The fourth maneuver effectively employed by the Court is that of omission. Not only does the Court regularly omit cases prior to 1947 from its discussions, equally absent are quotes from George Washington, Benjamin Franklin, John Adams, John Jay, Samuel Adams, Patrick Henry, John Hancock, Roger Sherman, or other prominent Founders. The Court's omission of these Founders implies that either they were not qualified to address First Amendment issues or that there exist no recorded statements from these Founders pertinent to the separation question. Since numerous writings of these Founders do exist on the relationship of religion to government and schools, one must conclude that the Court is unwilling to accept their testimony—even that of George Washington, the President of the Constitutional Convention and the President under whom the First Amendment was framed and ratified! Dr. Paul Vitz, who conducted the research previously presented on the treatment of religion in student textbooks, offered a profound observation:

> Over and over, we have seen that liberal and secular bias is primarily accomplished by exclusion, by leaving out the opposing position. Such a bias is much harder to observe than a positive vilification or direct criticism, but it is the essence of censorship. It is effective not only because it is hard to observe—it isn't *there*—and therefore hard to counteract, but also because it makes only the liberal, secular positions familiar and plausible. [23]

5. Some Words from Jefferson and Madison about Religion

The Court portrays Madison and Jefferson as being opposed *en toto* to permitting any religious influence on government or public affairs. However, such is not the case, as shown by Jefferson's actions:

> While serving in the Virginia General Assembly he was the one who personally introduced a resolution for a Day of Fasting and Prayer in 1774. . . . When he established the University of Virginia, he encouraged the teaching of religion and set apart space in the Rotunda for chapel services. He also praised the use of the local courthouse in his home town for religious services. [24]

Additionally, while President of the United States, Jefferson also became the first president of the Washington D. C. public school board, which used the Bible and Watt's Hymnal as reading texts in the classroom[25]—well subsequent to the adoption of the First Amendment. According to Jefferson:

> I have always said, and always will say, that the studious perusal of the sacred volume will make us better citizens. [26]

Notice other actions Jefferson took while in government:

> In 1803 President Jefferson recommended that Congress
> pass a treaty with the Kaskaskia Indians which provided,
> among other things, a stipend of $100 annually for seven
> years from the Federal treasury for the support of a
> Catholic priest to minister to the Kaskaskia Indians. This
> and two similar treaties were enacted during Jefferson's
> administration—one with the Wyandotte Indians and other
> tribes in 1806, and one with the Cherokees in 1807. In
> 1787, another act of Congress ordained special lands "for
> the sole use of Christian Indians" and reserved lands for the
> Moravian Brethren "for civilizing the Indians and
> promoting Christianity" . . . Congress extended this act
> three times during Jefferson's administration and each time
> [Jefferson] signed the extension into law. [27]

Jefferson understood the important relationship between religion
and government. He stated that religion is "deemed in other
countries incompatible with good government and yet proved by our
experience to be its best support." [28] In his "Notes on the State of
Virginia," Jefferson declared:

> And can the liberties of a nation be thought secure when we
> have removed their only firm basis, a conviction in the
> minds of the people that these liberties are of the gift of
> God? That they are not to be violated but with His wrath?
> Indeed I tremble for my country when I reflect that God is
> just; that his justice cannot sleep forever. [29]

And now the Court, supposedly on Jefferson's authority,
absolutely prohibits students from being exposed to the concept that
liberties are the gift of God. The Court prohibits the very activities
that Jefferson promoted and enacted while President (i.e., Bible
reading in schools). History shows that the man allegedly responsible for today's separation doctrine didn't practice what the
contemporary Court says he preached, which clearly implies he
didn't preach what the Court claims.

James Madison also said much about the importance of religious
principles to public affairs:

> Before any man can be considered as a member of Civil
> Society, he must be considered as a subject of the Governor
> of the Universe. [30]

It is the mutual **_duty_** of **_all_** to practice **_Christian_** forbearance, love, and charity toward each other. [31] (emphasis added)

Further recall that it was Madison who had declared that the success of our government and political institutions was based on keeping the Ten Commandments.

6. Some Words from Jefferson and Madison about the Court

Madison and Jefferson not only had much to say about the importance of religion to public affairs, they also had much to say about the proper role of the Court. However, since the Court omits their important quotes on religion, it is not surprising that their quotations about the Court should also be expunged. If the Court sincerely believes Madison and Jefferson to be Constitutional experts, then it should heed the following statements. In a letter written to Abigail Adams on September 11, 1804, Jefferson said:

> Nothing in the Constitution has given them [the federal judges] a right to decide for the Executive, more than to the Executive to decide for them. . . . But the opinion which gives to the judges the right to decide what laws are constitutional, and what not, not only for themselves in their own sphere of action, but for the legislature and executive also, in their spheres, would make the judiciary a despotic branch. [32]

Jefferson wrote to William Jarvis on September 28, 1820:

> You seem . . . to consider the judges as the ultimate arbiters of all constitutional questions; a very dangerous doctrine indeed, and one which would place us under the despotism of an oligarchy. Our judges are as honest as other men, and not more so. . . . and their power [is] the more dangerous as they are in office for life, and not responsible, as the other functionaries are, to the elective control. The Constitution has erected no such single tribunal. [33]

And in a letter to Charles Hammond on August 18, 1821, Jefferson declared:

> The germ of dissolution of our federal government is in . . . the federal judiciary; an irresponsible body, (for impeachment is scarcely a scare-crow,) working like gravity by night and by day, gaining a little to-day and a little to-morrow, and advancing its noiseless step like a thief, over the field of jurisdiction, until all shall be usurped from the States. [34]

Madison had much to say about judges not becoming lawmakers:

> The preservation of a free Government requires not merely, that the metes and bounds which separate each department of power be invariably maintained; but more especially that neither of them be suffered to overleap the great Barrier which defends the rights of the people. The Rulers who are guilty of such an encroachment, exceed the commission from which they derive their authority, and are Tyrants. The People who submit to it are governed by laws made neither by themselves nor by an authority derived from them, and are slaves. [35]

We are now ruled by laws "neither made by [the people] nor by an authority derived from them." In 1788, Madison warned:

> As the courts are generally the last in making the decision [on laws], it results to them, by refusing or not refusing to execute a law, to stamp it with its final character. This makes the Judiciary dept paramount in fact to the Legislature, which was never intended, and can never be proper. [36]

History reveals that the defenses on which the Court so heavily relies to justify separation are really no defense at all!

~10~
Dilemmas for the Court

Not only have the current courts discarded the documented beliefs, intents, and laws of the Founders, they have also repudiated the rulings of their predecessors. While the Constitution has been the same, the rulings of the contemporary courts have been diametrically opposed to those of the earlier courts. This chapter will highlight some of the conflicts which are typical.

ON PROFANITY

Notice the position of the current Court on profanity:

> Appellant was . . . wearing a jacket bearing the words "Fuck the Draft" in a corridor of the Los Angeles Courthouse. *Held:* . . . the State may not . . . make the simple public display of this single four-letter expletive a[n] . . . offense. . . . The [California statute prohibiting such use of words] infringed his rights to freedom of expression guaranteed by the First and Fourteenth Amendments of the Federal Constitution. . . . This is not . . . an obscenity case. . . . That the air may at times seem filled with verbal cacophony is, in this sense not a sign of weakness but of strength. [1] *Cohen* v. *California, 1971*

The rulings of previous courts differed significantly:

> Nothing could be more offensive to the virtuous part of the community, or more injurious to the tender morals of the young, than to declare such profanity lawful . . . and shall we form an exception in these particulars to the rest of the civilized world? [2] *The People* v. *Ruggles, 1811*

Quite a difference of opinion! The current Court says protecting profanity like "f— the draft" shows the strength of our society; earlier courts said that such language injured the morals of youth and weakened the community.

ON LEWDNESS AND INDECENCY

In *Erznoznik* v. *City of Jacksonville, 1975,* the city sought to restrict indecent movies shown in a public drive-in theater because:

The screen . . . is visible from two adjacent public streets and a nearby church parking lot. [3]

Jacksonville attempted to protect its children and citizens from this open lewdness and nudity by passing this ordinance:

It shall be unlawful . . . for any . . . drive-in theater in the City to exhibit . . . any motion picture . . . in which the human male or female bare buttocks, human female bare breasts, or human bare pubic areas are shown, if . . . visible from any public street or public place. [4]

The Supreme Court ruled this ordinance:

Invalid . . . [as] an infringement of First Amendment rights. . . . Nor can the ordinance be justified as an exercise of the [city] . . . for the protection of children. [5]

This decision by the current Court was markedly different from earlier rulings:

The destruction of morality renders the power of the government invalid. . . . The corruption of the public mind, in general, and debauching the manners of youth, in particular, by lewd and obscene pictures exhibited to view, must necessarily be attended with the most injurious consequences. . . . No man is permitted to corrupt the morals of the people. [6]
The Commonwealth v. *Sharpless, 1815*

ON BLASPHEMY

In *Grove* v. *Mead School District, 1985,* Cassie Grove, a high school sophomore, had been required to read *A Learning Tree* for her English Literature class.   She filed suit to have that book removed from the curriculum because she objected to several portions, including those:

Declaring Jesus Christ to be a "poor white trash God," or "a long-legged white son-of-a-bitch." [7]

The court refused to rule in her favor or to remove the book from the school's required curriculum—all students taking that class would continue to use that book. This ruling again conflicted with those of previous courts:

"Jesus Christ was a bastard, and his mother must be a whore"
. . . . Such words . . . were an offense at common law. . . . It
tends to corrupt the morals of the people, and to destroy good
order. Such offenses . . . are treated as affecting the essential
interests of civil society. [8] *The People* v. *Ruggles, 1811*

ON DETERRING NO RELIGIOUS BELIEF

In *Walz* v. *Tax Commission, 1970,* the Court stated, as it frequently
does, that all religious beliefs were to be tolerated:

> The fullest realization of true religious liberty requires that
> government . . . effect no favoritism among sects or between
> religion and nonreligion, and *that it work deterrence of no
> religious belief.* [9] (emphasis added)

Earlier Courts had declared that there were numerous religious
beliefs which would *never* be tolerated in the United States:

> There have been sects which denied as a part of their relig-
> ious tenets that there should be any marriage tie, and
> advocated promiscuous intercourse of the sexes as prompted
> by the passions of its members. . . . Should a sect of [these]
> kinds ever find its way into this country, swift punishment
> would follow the carrying into effect of its doctrines, and no
> heed would be given to the pretence that . . . their supporters
> could be protected in their exercise by the Constitution of the
> United States. Probably never before in the history of this
> country has it been seriously contended that the whole
> punitive power of the government for acts, recognized by the
> general consent of the Christian world . . . must be suspended
> in order that the tenets of a religious sect . . . may be carried
> out without hindrance. [10] *Davis* v. *Beason, 1889*

> Every person who has a husband or wife living . . . and
> marries another . . . is guilty of polygamy, and shall be
> punished . . . no legislation can be . . . more wholesome and
> necessary . . . than that which seeks to establish it on the basis
> of the idea of the family as consisting in and springing from
> the union for life of one man and one woman in the holy estate
> of matrimony; the sure foundation of all that is stable and
> noble in our civilization. [11] *Murphy* v. *Ramsey, 1885*

ON ATHEISM

The First Amendment's guarantee for free exercise of religion was always understood to exclude atheism, since atheism was not a religion. However, in *Theriault* v. *Silber, 1978*,[12] the court determined that the First Amendment was too narrow. It decided that the meaning of the First Amendment's religious clause should be expanded to cover those who have no religious beliefs. Consequently:

Atheism may be a religion under the establishment clause. [13] *Malnak* v. *Yogi, 1977*

Secular humanism may be a religion for purposes of First Amendment. [14] *Grove* v. *Mead School Dist., 1985*

Contrast these rulings with previous ones:

[The First Amendment] embraces all who believe in the existence of God, as well ... as Christians of every denomination. . . . This provision does not extend to atheists, because they do not believe in God or religion; and therefore ... their sentiments and professions, whatever they may be, cannot be called *religious* sentiments and professions. [15] *Commonwealth* v. *Abner Kneeland, 1838*

The Founders knew what the word "religion" meant; atheism did not qualify as a religion. Their understanding of the word "religion" at the time of the First Amendment is revealed from Webster's original dictionary:

RELIGION. Includes a belief in the being and perfections of God, in the revelation of his will to man, and in man's obligation to obey his commands, in a state of reward and punishment, and in man's accountableness to God; and also true godliness or piety of life, with the practice of all moral duties. . . . The practice of moral duties without a belief in a divine lawgiver, and without reference to his will or commands, is not religion. [16]

What is it that was *not* a religion, and therefore *not* subject to the protection of the First Amendment?

The practice of moral duties *without a belief in a divine lawgiver* and without reference to his will or his commands *is not religion.* [17] (emphasis added)

Neither atheism nor secular humanism qualified as "religions" in earlier decisions on the First Amendment.

ON SUNDAY LAWS

Notice the contemporary courts' view of Sunday:

> Laws setting aside Sunday as a day of rest are upheld, *not from any right of the government to legislate for the promotion of religious observances,* but from its right to protect all persons from the physical and moral debasement which comes from uninterrupted labor. [18]   *McGowan* v. *Maryland, 1960* (emphasis added)

> Sunday closing laws upheld as establishing uniform day-of-rest and recreation with *only remote or incidental religious benefit.* [19]   *Florey* v. *Sioux Falls School District, 1979* (emphasis added)

Contrast these declarations with previous ones:

> The Lord's day, the day of the Resurrection, is to us, who are called Christians, the day of rest after finishing a new creation. It is the day of the first visible triumph over death, hell and the grave! It was the birth day of the believer in Christ, to whom and through whom it opened up the way which, by repentance and faith, leads unto everlasting life and eternal happiness! On that day we rest, and to us it is the Sabbath of the Lord—its decent observance, in a Christian community, is that which ought to be expected. [20]   *City of Charleston* v. *S. A. Benjamin, 1846*

Another emphatic pronouncement concerning Sundays came from the 1853 Senate Judiciary Committee:

> Sunday, the Christian Sabbath, is recognized and respected by all the departments of the Government. . . . Here is a recognition by law, and by universal usage, not only of *a* Sabbath, but of the *Christian* sabbath, in exclusion of the Jewish or Mohammedan Sabbath. [21]

Conclusions

By repudiating the stands of earlier courts, the current courts have created some interesting dilemmas for themselves. For example, consider the difficulty created by declaring atheism and secular humanism to be religions and still trying to maintain a position of neutrality between religions.

First, the Court has been very emphatic in its position that no preference can be given between religion and non-religion:

> The First Amendment mandates governmental neutrality between religion and religion, and between religion and nonreligion. [22] *Epperson* v. *Arkansas, 1968*

> The fullest realization of true religious liberty requires that government . . . effect no favoritism among sects or between religion and nonreligion. [23] *Walz* v. *Tax Commission, 1970*

Second, the Court has defined the religious practice of atheists as that of having *no* religious practice.

Combine these two positions (neutrality between religion & non-religion + and atheism as a religion) and try to apply them practically in schools. The Court has prohibited the inclusion of *any* religious activities in schools; however, if God and religious activities are excluded, then the Court has then installed non-religion, which is the religious practice of atheism; the Court, by being non-religious has become religious and has violated its own position of neutrality. It is impossible to practically and equitably apply the Court's rulings!

A further dilemma the Court has created for itself regards the principle articulated by the 1892 Court:

> No purpose of action against religion can be imputed to any legislation, state or national. [24]

This principle is understood and widely accepted. For example, if Congress were to pass a law prohibiting youth below the age of 18 from praying, it immediately would be declared unconstitutional in any court. If a legislature should make it illegal for an adolescent to read the Bible, it would also be declared unconstitutional. These types of laws would never be tolerated.

However, the Court now prohibits the very acts impossible to prohibit by law. Laws and legislators cannot ban voluntary Bible reading by youth; the Court can. Laws and legislators cannot prohibit adolescents from seeing and reading the Ten Commandments; the Court can. Laws and legislators cannot prohibit the free exercise of Christianity; however, the Court can. A Congress, constitutionally elected by the people and responsible to them—the heart and soul of a democratic-republic—cannot do these things; the Court, in an insult to our Constitutional form of government, *has* done it. The Court routinely enacts "legislation" that would be unconstitutional for the people's representatives even to consider!

~11~
Double Standards

Not only do current court decisions clash both with the Founders and earlier courts, they even contradict themselves. The fluctuating standards from current courts have created an uncertainty for society; in effect, a set of double standards. The following examples of double standards within the judiciary are illustrative of the many now existing.

ON CHAPLAINS

On one hand, the prayers of the Congressional Chaplains are constitutional:

> The legislature by majority vote invites a clergyman to give a prayer; neither the inviting nor the giving nor the hearing of the prayer is making a law. On this basis alone . . . the saying of prayers, per se, in the legislative halls at the opening session is not prohibited by the First and Fourteenth Amendments. [1] *Chambers* v. *Marsh, 1982*

However, hearing the prayers of the Chaplains is unconstitutional:

> Students . . . would listen to reading of "remarks" of the chaplain read from the *Congressional Record*. . . . [This] was unconstitutional establishment of religion. [2] *State Bd. of Educ.* v. *Bd. of Educ. of Netcong, 1970*

It is constitutional for Chaplains to pray prayers, but unconstitutional for students to hear those prayers.

ON THE TEN COMMANDMENTS

On the one hand, to display the Ten Commandments on public property is constitutional:

> The exact origin of the Ten Commandments is uncertain, but . . . a large portion of our population believes they are Bible based. Even so . . . it also has substantial secular attributes. . . . The Ten Commandments is an affirmation of at least a precedent legal code . . . .

But this creed does not include any element of coercion concerning these beliefs, unless one considers it coercive to look upon the Ten Commandments. Although they are in plain view, no one is required to read or recite them.

It does not seem reasonable to require removal of a passive monument, involving no compulsion, because its accepted precepts, as a foundation for law, reflect the religious nature of an ancient era. [3] *Anderson* v. *Salt Lake City Corp., 1973*

However, on the other hand, to display the Ten Commandments on public property is unconstitutional:

The posting of a copy of the Ten Commandments . . . on the wall of each public school classroom . . . has no secular legislative purpose, and therefore is unconstitutional as violating the Establishment Clause of the First Amendment. While the state legislature required the notation in small print at the bottom of each display that "[t]he secular application of the Ten Commandments is clearly seen in its adoption as the fundamental legal code of Western Civilization and the Common Law of the United States," such an "avowed" secular purpose is not sufficient to avoid conflict with the First Amendment. . . . Nor is it significant that the Ten Commandments are merely posted rather than read aloud. [4] *Stone* v. *Graham, 1980*

While both cases involve the passive use of the Ten Commandments, the rulings are contradictory.

ON INVOCATIONS

On the one hand, invocations are constitutional:

[The case] *Bogen* v. *Doty* [5] . . . involved a county board's practice of opening each of its public meetings with a prayer offered by a local member of the clergy. . . . This Court upheld that practice, finding that it advanced a clearly secular purpose of "establishing a solemn atmosphere and serious tone for the board meetings" . . . "establishing solemnity is the primary effect of all invocations at gatherings of persons with differing views on religion." [6] *Chambers* v. *Marsh, 1982*

On the other hand, invocations are unconstitutional:

> School district's inclusion of religious invocation and religious benediction as part of its graduation ceremonies violated establishment clause of First Amendment. [7] *Graham* v. *Central Community School Dist., 1985*

> Religious invocation . . . included in high school commencement exercise conveyed message that district had given its endorsement to prayer and religion, so that school district was properly [prohibited] from including invocation in commencement exercise. [8] *Kay* v. *Douglas School Dist., 1986*

ON CHRISTMAS AND NATIVITY SCENES

On the one hand, it is constitutional to depict the origins of Christmas:

> The city of Pawtucket, R. I., annually erects a Christmas display in a park. . . . The creche [nativity] display is sponsored by the city to celebrate the Holiday recognized by Congress and national tradition and to depict the origins of that Holiday; these are legitimate secular purposes. . . . The créche . . . is no more an advancement or endorsement of religion than the congressional and executive recognition of the origins of Christmas. . . . It would be ironic if . . . the créche in the display, as part of a celebration of an event acknowledged in the Western World for 20 centuries, and in this country by the people, the Executive Branch, Congress, and the courts for 2 centuries, would so "taint" the exhibition as to render it violative of the Establishment Clause. To forbid the use of this one passive symbol . . . would be an overreaction contrary to this Nation's history. [9] *Lynch* v. *Donnelly, 1985*

On the other hand, it is unconstitutional to depict the origins of Christmas:

> The display of a creche—a representation of the nativity of Jesus . . . conveys an endorsement of religion, in violation of the establishment of religion clause of the Federal Constitution's First Amendment and therefore must be permanently enjoined. [10] *County of Allegheny* v. *ACLU, 1989*

Further, it is even unconstitutional for students to ask questions about the origins of Christmas, even if those questions are historically based:

> A variety of Christmas assemblies has been presented in the Sioux Falls public schools for a number of years. During the Christmas season of 1977, two Sioux Falls kindergarten classes rehearsed, memorized and then performed for parents a Christmas assembly . . . including a responsive discourse between the teacher and the class entitled, "The Beginners Christmas Quiz." The "Quiz" consisted of the following:
>
> > TEACHER: Of whom did heav'nly angels sing,
> > And news about His birthday bring?
> > CLASS: Jesus.
> > TEACHER: Now, can you name the little town where they the Baby Jesus found?
> > CLASS: Bethlehem.
> > TEACHER: Where had they made a little bed for Christ, the blessed Savior's head?
> > CLASS: In a manger in a cattle stall.
> > TEACHER: What is the day we celebrate as birthday of this One so great?
> > CLASS: Christmas. . . .
>
> The kindergarten program presented in 1977 . . . exceeded the boundaries of what is constitutionally permissible under the Establishment Clause. [11] *Florey* v. *Sioux Falls Sch. Dist., 1979*

Additionally, if there is to be a nativity scene at a school, it must be at a time when students will not see it:

> The Supreme Court . . . held that where [a] Nativity Scene was not erected or displayed while school was in session . . . [it] was not unconstitutional as violating doctrine of separation of church and state. [12] *Baer* v. *Kolmorgen, 1958*

While Christmas is a holiday created and endorsed by the government, it is unconstitutional for students to view or ask questions about those origins, even if the questions *are* historical and *do* relate to the reason that Congress established the holiday.

ON PERSONAL APPEARANCE

On the one hand, the freedom to govern one's personal appearance is a fundamental constitutional right:

> The Founding Fathers wrote an amendment for speech and assembly; even they did not deem it necessary to write an amendment for personal appearance. . . . The Constitution guarantees rights other than those specifically enumerated, and . . . the right to govern one's personal appearance is one of those guaranteed rights. [13] *Bishop* v. *Colaw, 1971*

> No right is held more sacred, or is more carefully guarded, by the common law, than the right of every individual to the possession and control of his own person, free from all restraint or interference of others. . . . As well said by Judge Cooley [in *Union Pacific Railway Co.* v. *Botsford]* [14]: "The right to one's person may be said to be a right of complete immunity; to be let alone." [15] *Wallace* v. *Ford, 1972*

On the other hand, the right to govern one's personal appearance is not a fundamental constitutional right:

> A public schoolteacher, while teaching, may not wear distinctly religious garb. [16] *Finot* v. *Pasadena City Board of Education, 1967*

ON FREEDOM OF SPEECH

Free speech is protected by the Constitution, including the right to use the word "God" in a derogatory or vulgar manner. Recall that in *Cohen* v. *California, 1971*, the Court declared it to be a sign of our society's strength to permit the air to be filled with profanity [17] and in *Grove* v. *Mead, 1985*, the court defended the right of the school to use a textbook describing Jesus as a "poor white trash God" and "a . . . white s.o.b." [18] With Court protection for such language, it would appear that nearly any expression is constitutionally protected.

Although there is protection for free speech and the use of the word "God" is constitutional as long as it is hyphenated with other profanity, that constitutional protection does not include the right to use the word "God" in a respectful manner:

> To include reference to God . . . in State Board of Education minimum standards relating to operation of schools would

violate establishment clause of First Amendment. [19] *The State of Ohio* v. *Whisner, 1976*

Furthermore, it is even improper to provide opportunity to express respect for God:

> During the regular school day . . . no themes will be assigned on such topics as "Why I believe . . . in religious devotions." [20] *Reed* v. *van Hoven, 1965*

Not only is it improper for school officials and students to use the word "God" in a respectful manner, recall from *DeSpain* v. *DeKalb, 1967*, that it is also improper for students to think about God. [21]

On the one hand, it is constitutional to express contempt for God; on the other hand, it is unconstitutional to express respect for Him.

ON FREE EXERCISE

On the one hand, free exercise of religion cannot be interfered with unless its exercise creates a paramount danger to the public:

> The scales are always weighed in favor of free exercise of religion, and the State's interest must be compelling, it must be substantial, and the danger must be clear and present and so grave as to endanger paramount public interests before the state can interfere with the free exercise of religion. [22] *Swann* v. *Pack, 1975*

However, on the other hand, the "period for the free exercise of religion" in which students voluntarily met together before school to read the remarks of the Chaplain from the *Congressional Record* was evidently a "clear and present" danger to the community, since it was prohibited by the court in *State Board of Educ.* v. *Board of Educ. of Netcong, 1970.* [23]

ON THE OWNERSHIP OF CHILDREN

On the one hand, children are not wards of the state:

> The fundamental theory of liberty upon which all governments in this Union repose excludes any general power of the state to standardize its children. . . . The child is not the mere creature of the state. *Pierce* v. *Society of Sisters;* [24] *Reed* v. *van Hoven, 1965* [25]

On the other hand, children are wards of the state:

> The courts for many years have held: Children are the wards of the State. [26] *State Bd. of Ed.* v. *Bd. of Ed. of Netcong, 1970*

ON PROTECTION OF CHILDREN

On the one hand, the court intervened in *State Board of Educ.* v. *Board of Educ. of Netcong, 1970,* to protect children from voluntary prayer. [27]   On the other hand, the Court would not intervene in *Erznoznik* v. *City of Jacksonville, 1975,* to protect children from public lewdness and nudity. [28] Evidently the court considers prayer harmful to children but not promiscuous public nudity.

ON LONGSTANDING PRACTICES

On the one hand, the Court pointed out in *Walz* v. *Tax Commission, 1970,* that the fact that tax exemptions for churches had existed for 200 years was a strong factor in declaring them constitutional:

> In resolving such questions of interpretation "a page of history is worth a volume of logic." *New York Trust Co.* v. *Eisner* [29]
> . . . . The more longstanding and widely accepted a practice, the greater its impact upon constitutional interpretation. [30]

On the other hand, as pointed out by a dissenting Justice in the same case, the fact that school prayer had existed for 340 years had **no** effect in protecting it from being declared unconstitutional. [31]

CONCLUSION

Notice the pattern that has emerged in many of these double standards? The general public may hear the prayers of the Congressional Chaplain, students may not; the general public may view the Ten Commandments, students may not. Why does the Court so zealously prohibit religious principles and activities from students? It is not merely coincidence that so many of the Court's double standards involve students; as Abraham Lincoln observed:

> The philosophy of the schoolroom in one generation will be the philosophy of government in the next. [32]

~12~
Toward A New Constitution?

Every government in history has been the product of a specific political theory. Each government embraces a philosophy which, at least in its own eyes, justifies its existence and manner of conducting affairs. In short, people have distinct reasons for establishing the governments they do; our Founders were no exception. The Declaration of Independence and Constitution were well-devised plans for government which reflected our Founders' specific political philosophy.

As Ben Franklin noted in his speech at the Constitutional Convention, there has never been a shortage of philosophies on which to base a government; numerous and widely differing types have long abounded:

> We have gone back to ancient history for models of Government, and examined the different forms of those Republics which having been formed.... And we have viewed Modern States all round Europe. [1]

Our wise Founders investigated many differing philosophies in their own quest for a prosperous, successful government. How can we determine which philosophy they finally selected?

> One way is to read what they wrote, and check the sources they cited. . . . Two professors, Donald S. Lutz and Charles S. Hyneman, have reviewed an estimated 15,000 items, and closely read 2,200 books, pamphlets, newspaper articles, and monographs with explicitly political content printed between 1760 and 1805. . . . From these items, Lutz and Hyneman identified [the philosophers quoted most frequently by our Founders]. . . . Baron Charles Montesquieu . . . followed closely by Sir William Blackstone . . . and John Locke. [2]

What did Montesquieu, Blackstone, and Locke think, believe, and articulate that caused them to be the three most quoted men during America's founding era?

The Baron Montesquieu of France (Charles Louis Joseph de Secondat, 1689-1755) lived in France and taught in French universities. His writing, *The Spirit of Laws (1748),* greatly influenced our own Founders and thus, our Constitution.   Montesquieu believed that certain unchanging laws underlay all things:

> Society, notwithstanding all its revolutions, must repose on principles that do not change. [3]

It was man's responsibility to discover and apply these laws. What did Montesquieu believe to be the source of these unchanging principles?

> The Christian religion, which ordains that men should love each other, would, without doubt, have every nation blest with the best civil, the best political laws; because these, next to this religion, are the greatest good that these men can give and receive. [4]

Montesquieu believed that Christianity fostered good laws and good government. His Biblically-based philosophy of governing as well as many of his specific applications were adopted by the Founders. For example, the Founders incorporated Montesquieu's belief that the powers of government should be separate and distinct to allow power to check power. The separation of powers doctrine is found in two Biblical concepts: Isaiah 33:22 which identified three branches of government, and Jeremiah 17:9 which taught that man did not naturally tend toward good.   Since man, when left unchecked, moved toward moral and civil degradation, society would be much safer if all power did not repose in the same authority.   The three branches of government would provide a perfect means to separate the power and provide protection for society, because hopefully not all three branches would ever become corrupt at the same time and could therefore place outside safeguards and checks on each other. Separation of powers, as were many of the Founder's political innovations, was a Biblically based idea.

While Montesquieu provided the concept of separation of powers, Blackstone contributed the superstructure for the natural law philosophy utilized by the Founders.   Blackstone, the second most frequently quoted man by our Founders, was an English judge, professor, and author. His *Commentaries on the Laws of England (1765-69)* were the basis of legal education in America. Evidence that he was widely accepted by Americans was provided by Edmund Burke in remarks delivered before Parliament:

> I hear that they have sold nearly as many of Blackstone's *Commentaries* in America as in England. [5]

James Madison, the "Chief Architect" of our own Constitution, heartily endorsed Blackstone:

I very cheerfully express my approbation of the proposed edition of Blackstone's *Commentaries.* [6]

Blackstone influenced many great founding Americans:

It was from Blackstone that most Americans, including John Marshall, acquired their knowledge of natural law. . . . Blackstone remained the standard manual of law until the publication of the *Commentaries on American Law (1826-1830)* of Chancellor James Kent of New York. [7]

Blackstone, like Montesquieu, was very explicit concerning the source of good laws and good government:

Man, considered as a creature, must necessarily be subject to the laws of his creator, for he is entirely a dependent being. . . . And consequently, as man depends absolutely upon his maker for every thing, it is necessary that he should in all points conform to his maker's will. This will of his maker is called the law of nature. [8]

That phrase, the "law of nature," not only was a key term identifying the natural law philosophy, it was a very revealing term in our founding documents. According to Blackstone, the natural law—or law of nature—was made up of two components: (1) the *physical* laws of nature, and (2) the *revealed* or Divine law of the Scriptures:

This law of nature . . . dictated by God himself, is of course superior in obligation to any other. . . . No human laws are of any validity, if contrary to this; . . . . The revealed or divine law . . . found only in the holy scriptures . . . are found upon comparison to be really a part of the original law of nature. [9]

How important were these two elements of the law of nature?

Upon these two foundations, the law of nature and the law of revelation, depend all human laws; that is to say, *no human laws should be suffered to contradict these.* [10] (emphasis added)

In Blackstone's natural law philosophy, civil laws could not be allowed to contradict either the laws of God which had been revealed through nature or the laws of God which were revealed through the

Bible. However, in the areas where neither natural laws nor Divine laws provided guidance, men were free to determine their own laws. Blackstone provided examples of such an occasion:

> To instance in the case of murder: this is expressly forbidden by the divine, and demonstrably by the natural law; and, from these prohibitions, arises the true unlawfulness of this crime. . . . If any human law should allow or enjoin us to commit it, we are bound to transgress that human law, or else we must offend both the natural and the divine. But, with regard to matters that are . . . not commanded or forbidden by [the Scriptures]—such, for instance, as exporting of wool into foreign countries,—here the . . . legislature [of men] has scope and opportunity to interpose, and to make that action unlawful which before was not so. [11]

John Locke, the third most cited man in early American political thought, was a British philosopher and author. He had been strongly influenced by the writings of Richard Hooker:

> Hooker argued that where the Scripture is clear, Scripture alone must govern. Where Scripture is unclear . . . tradition may be employed to help interpret it; and where both Scripture and . . . tradition are unclear, or where new circumstances arise, reason may also be employed to apprehend God's truth. [12]

John Locke, like Montesquieu, Blackstone, and Hooker, was a strong advocate of the natural law philosophy. Locke's writings, particularly his *Two Treatises of Government, 1690,* strongly influenced Jefferson. When Jefferson wrote the Declaration of Independence, he quoted directly from the phraseology of John Locke.

In addition to utilizing Locke's natural law beliefs, the Founders also adopted his theory of social compact. Social compact is defined as:

> The idea that men in a state of nature realize their rights are insecure, and compact together to establish a government and cede to that government certain power so that government may use that power to secure the rest of their rights. [13]

Under the social compact theory, the power that is given to the government is:

> Only the power God and/or people delegate. This is the cornerstone of limited government. It finds expression in the

Tenth Amendment to the Constitution and in the Declaration of Independence which states that governments exist to secure human rights and "derive their just powers from the consent of the governed." [14]

Natural law; social compact; limited government; the consent of the governed—Locke's concepts were incorporated throughout the government established by our Founders. Locke had relied heavily on the Bible when developing his political views:

> In his first treatise on government he cited the Bible eighty times. . . . Twenty-two biblical citations appear in his second treatise. . . . His basic doctrines of parental authority, private property, and social compact were based on the historical existence of Adam and Noah. [15]

Notice some of Locke's statements on laws and government:

> Thus the Law of Nature stands as an eternal rule to all men, legislators as well as others. The rules that they make for other men's actions, must . . . be conformable to the Law of Nature, *i.e.* to the will of God . . . no human sanction can be good, or valid against it. [16]

> Laws human must be made according to the general laws of Nature, and without contradiction to any positive law of Scripture, otherwise they are ill made. [17]

In addition to these three men, there were others whose philosophies the Founders found quite agreeable to their own. Alexander Hamilton, another influential Constitutional thinker, recommended:

> Apply yourself, without delay, to the study of the law of nature. I would recommend to your perusal, Grotius, Puffendorf, Locke, Montesquieu. [18]

Grotius and Pufendorf, like Locke and Montesquieu, maintained natural law as the basis of their philosophies:

> Hugo Grotius (1583-1645), [was a] famous Dutch lawyer, theologian, statesman. . . . In his writings on law and government Grotius attempted to apply Christian principles to politics. He emphasized, perhaps more clearly than any other writer, that "What God has shown to be his will that is law." [19]

Samuel de Pufendorf (1632-1694). . . . held diplomatic posts in Germany and Sweden and was Professor of the Law of Nature, first at the University of Heidelberg (1661-1668) and then at the University of Lund in Sweden. He became the royal historian for Sweden. . . . Pufendorf, influenced by Grotius, helped to establish the law of nature as the basis for international law. [20]

Pufendorf was widely respected by many of the Founders:

Alexander Hamilton, Benjamin Franklin, James Wilson, Samuel Adams and other founding fathers paid tribute to Pufendorf, acknowledged his influence on their thinking, and recommended his writings to others. [21]

The philosophers embraced by the Founders all expounded a similar theme: the importance of natural law and the Bible as the foundation for any government established by men. Natural law and the Bible formed the heart of our Founder's political theories and was incorporated as part of their new government:

George Mason, author of the Virginia's Bill of Rights in its Constitution, stated before the General Court of Virginia: "The laws of nature are the laws of God, whose authority can be superseded by no power on earth." It was in this context that the phrase, "the laws of nature and nature's God," was subsequently incorporated in the Declaration of Independence. [22]

The natural law belief is not only evident in the Declaration of Independence, it is also apparent in the Constitution:

The Constitution is not a neutral document but presupposes a belief in a *transcendent, unchanging order,* and the cause behind that order: God. It is founded on the conviction that rights do not derive from government but from God. Indeed, governments are instituted to secure the inalienable rights endowed by the Creator. The Constitution in short, is not a positivistic document but presupposes and is deeply rooted in *theism.* This is only natural for the men who framed the Constitution were all theists—mostly Christians, some deists. [23]

America was unquestionably a nation established on natural law; God's laws revealed through both nature and the Bible were the basis of government. This is even further established by re-examining the results of the research into the Founders' writings conducted by the political science professors cited earlier in this chapter. Recall that the three men quoted most often by the Founders were Montesquieu, Blackstone, and Locke. Yet, there was a source the Founders cited _four_ times more often than either Montesquieu or Blackstone, and _twelve_ times more often than Locke. What was that source? The Bible! The Bible accounted for 34 percent of all the Founders' quotes. [24] Another 60 percent of their quotes was drawn from authors who had derived their ideas from the Bible. Therefore, it can be shown that 94 percent of their quotes are based either directly or indirectly on the Bible. [25] Even major news magazines have conceded that "historians are discovering that the Bible, perhaps even more than the Constitution is our Founding document." [26] The fact that the Founders quoted the Bible _four times_ more frequently than any other source is an impressive testimony to its importance in the foundation of our government!

The natural law philosophies on which this nation was birthed and established remained the unquestioned basis of law and governmental practices until the early 1900's, at which time an opposing philosophy began gaining strength among the nation's leading educators and judges. By the 1940's, strong signals began appearing in Supreme Court decisions which indicated that a philosophy known as legal positivism was being embraced. The widespread acceptance and application of legal positivism within the judiciary led to the repudiation and discarding of the natural law theories which had long been the foundation of our government.

The Court's current application of legal positivism was derived from the philosophy of relativism (later called pragmatism) which had been promoted by the American philosophers Charles S. Pierce, William James, and John Dewey. Pierce had advanced the basic tenets of relativism; James made them practical and understandable; and Dewey applied them to key areas of life. The central theme of their relativism was:

The belief that truth cannot be immutable, that there are no abiding, timeless truths or absolute moral norms, because reality is judged to be in a constant state of flux. "Truth" . . . is whatever "works" in a given situation. [27]

This encyclopedia excerpt describes the basic tenets of relativism:

> RELATIVISM. [V]iews are to be evaluated relative to the
> societies or cultures in which they appear and are not to be
> judged true or false, or good or bad, based on some overall
> criterion but are to be assessed within the context in which
> they occur. Thus, what is right or good or true to one person
> or group may not be considered so by others . . . there [are]
> no absolute standards. . . . "Man is the measure of all
> things," and . . . each man could be his own measure. . . .
> Cannibalism, incest, and other practices considered taboo are
> just variant kinds of behavior, to be appreciated as accept-
> able in some cultures and not in others. . . . [Relativism]
> urges suspension of judgment about right or wrong. [28]

Relativism originally was embraced only by a few individuals in
isolated groups. For example, when the Supreme Court began to
apply relativism in its decisions in the 1940's, the majority of
Americans were still strong natural law adherents. After relativism
had become the stalwart of judicial policy, the philosophy was then
expanded to other arenas and by the 1970's entire curriculums based
on relativism were being used in public schools. These courses were
first identified as "situation ethics" and later as "values clarification."

In these courses, students were taught that everything was relative.
Nothing was, of itself, right or wrong; right and wrong was determined only by the "circumstances." "Dilemmas" were posed to the
students who then had to decide the "right" course of action for the
specific situation. The following "dilemma" is typical of those
proposed to students under relativism:

> A young girl finds herself interned by an oppressive govern-
> ment in a prison where "unpleasant" things frequently happen.
> While confined, the girl discovers that there is a law which
> states that anyone pregnant cannot be held in the prison.
> However, this girl is very "traditional" and holds "traditional"
> views on marriage and pre-marital sexual relations. She now
> faces a "dilemma": she can seduce a guard, have sex with him
> regularly until she becomes pregnant, and then be released
> from prison—but only by violating the standards which she
> has been taught constitute right and wrong. She ends up
> seducing the guard and does eventually become pregnant.
> The question is now posed to the students: "Was what she did

right or wrong?" The answer? Since what she did helped achieve her release from prison, it was not wrong (according to the philosophy of relativism).

Students were conditioned to reject absolutes—*anything* can, in the "proper" situation, be right (incest, cannibalism, murder, adultery, lying, etc.) since right and wrong are determined only by how something "turns out." Acts absolutely wrong under natural law can be right under relativism, where the end *always* justifies the means.

Those who embrace relativism (also called pragmatism) typically hold the Founders and their natural law beliefs in disdain. The founding beliefs of natural law were viewed as an enemy by proponents of relativism as evidenced by this statement from John Dewey:

> The belief in political fixity, of the sanctity of some form of state consecrated by the efforts of our fathers and hallowed by tradition, is one of the stumbling-blocks in the way of orderly and directed change. [29]

Justices who agreed with Pierce, James, and Dewey, rejected the beliefs of the Founders, instead believing that:

> The natural law and natural rights principles which [earlier Justices] had also been reading into the Constitution . . . were not applicable to a society that was in a constant state of flux and change. . . . But in the process, the idea of transcendent rights would be discarded, and there would be no appeal from the edicts of the true law-giver—the Court. Government would become the sole source of rights. [30]

Relativism, when applied through the courts, is called legal positivism and easily can be identified by its major tenets:

(1) There are no objective, God-given standards of law, or if there are, they are irrelevant to the modern legal system.

(2) Since God is not the author of law, the author of law must be man; it is law simply because the highest human authority, the state, has said it is law and is able to back it up.

(3) Since man and society evolve, law must evolve as well.

(4) Judges, through their decisions, guide the evolution of law.

(5) To study law, get at the original sources of law—the decisions of judges; hence most law schools today use the "case law" method of teaching law. [31]

Justice Oliver Wendell Holmes (who served on the Court from 1902-1932), Justice Benjamin Cardozo (from 1932-1938), and legal educator Roscoe Pound (active in the 1920's and '30's) helped pioneer the trail of legal positivism which enabled the Court to repudiate the philosophy of the Founders. Justice Holmes openly rejected the beliefs of the Founders:

> Every one instinctively recognizes that in these days the justi- fication of a law for us cannot be found in the fact that our fathers always have followed it. It must be found in some help which the law brings toward reaching a social end. [32]

Holmes believed that decisions were not to be based upon natural law and fixed standards, but upon:

> The felt necessities of the time, the prevalent moral and political theories, . . . even the prejudices which judges share with their fellow-men, have had a good deal more to do than the syllogism in determining the rules by which men should be governed. [33]

Justice Cardozo, as a strong relativist, also rejected fixed standards and rights and wrongs:

> If there is any law which is back of the sovereignty of the state, and superior thereto, it is not law in such a sense as to concern the judge or lawyer, however much it concerns the statesman or moralist. [34]

According to Justice Cardozo, the judge is not to "concern" himself with natural law. Numerous other Justices followed in the footsteps of these pioneers in relativism. Chief Justice Earl Warren, who served on the Court from 1953-1969, wrote about the Constitution in *Trop* v. *Dulles,* explaining that the Constitution:

> Must draw its meaning from the evolving standards of decency that mark the progress of a maturing society. [35]

Cardozo not only rejected natural law, he also advocated usurping the traditional separation of powers under which legislators had always been the lawmakers:

> I take *judge-made law* as one of the existing realities of life. [36]
> (emphasis added)

The Court first disregarded and then eradicated the use of the philosophy which had formed the foundation of the nation and its legal decisions for 150 years. The Court now has:

> Liberated itself from what the Declaration of Independence called "the Laws of Nature and of Nature's God." [37]

Is it significant that the basis and the intent of the Constitution and Declaration of Independence have been discarded?

> If a judge can interpret the Constitution or laws to mean something obviously not intended by the original makers . . . then the nation's Constitution and laws are meaningless. [38]

As Chief Justice Charles Evan Hughes said:

> The Constitution is what the judges say it is. [39]

~13~
Even A Child . . .

There now have been two distinctly differing philosophies under which the Constitution has been interpreted: first, the philosophy of natural and Divine law (introduced by the Founders), and second, the philosophy of legal relativism and positivism (introduced by contemporary Courts). The primary tenet of each philosophy has been articulated by two Supreme Court Justices, one from each school of thought. Justice Felix Frankfurter declared:

> The ultimate touchstone of constitutionality is the Constitution itself and not what we have said about it. [1]

New York Governor Charles Evans Hughes, who later became Chief Justice of the Supreme Court, declared:

> We are under a Constitution, but the Constitution is what the judges say it is. [2]

These two differing approaches to the Constitution are reflected in the academic degree plans of law schools—some emphasize the study of constitutional law and some the study of case law. While the focus of constitutional law is the study of the *Constitution* itself, the focus of case law is the study of the *written opinions of Justices* handed down concerning the Constitution. Under the study of case law it is possible to obtain a law degree without ever having read the Constitution. The primary difference between these two approaches was summed up by the United States Attorney General in a speech given before the American Bar Association in 1985:

> Under the old system the question was *how* to read the Constitution; under the new approach, the question is *whether* to read the Constitution. [3]

There are avid proponents of each system; does it really make any difference which one is followed? Did the Court's rejection of Divine and natural law actually affect our lifestyles? That question can be answered by an ancient proverb:

> A child is known by his doings, whether his work . . . be right.
> PROVERBS 10:11

In other words, simply check the results. The measured outworkings of each philosophy will speak far more authoritatively than any words of conjecture or debate.

Even though many of the Justices had individually rejected Divine law standards prior to the 1960's, the 1962-63 rulings marked the first decisions in which they collectively—as a Court—rejected Divine law. For example, in *Abington* v. *Schempp, 1963,* the Court *openly* repudiated the Bible and its teachings—the heart of Divine and natural law. Scores of cases quickly followed which systematically overturned long-standing practices stemming from Divine law. Those decisions have caused dramatic policy changes on morality, education, families, and society in general.

Data is available in numerous categories which records the difference in the statistical measurements during the years of the application of Divine and natural law and the years under the application of relativism and legal positivism. If the change in legal philosophy made any significant difference, it should be apparent statistically. The following charts represent several areas which might have been affected by the Court's "new" rulings. Each chart accentuates the year in which the Court openly rejected Divine law in applying their decisions; the charts demonstrate the stark results of that rejection.

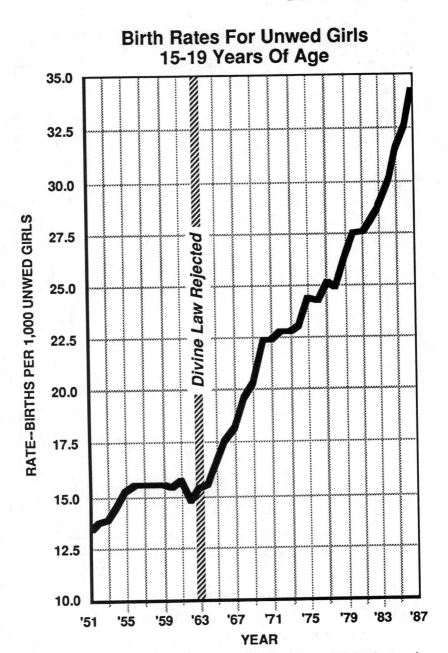

**Birth Rates For Unwed Girls
15-19 Years Of Age**

Basic data from Department of Health and Human Services and
Statistical Abstracts of the United States.

Violent Crime: Number Of Offenses

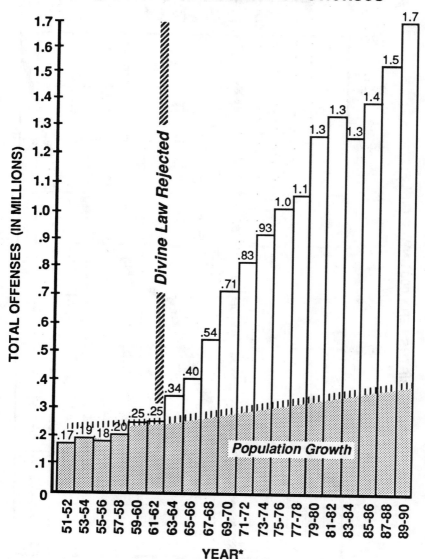

IIIIIIIIIII Indicates population growth profile.

* Groupings represent average rate per year over the two-year period.

Basic data from *Statistical Abstracts of the United States,*
and the Department of Commerce, Census Bureau.

Sexually Transmitted Diseases
Gonorrhea: Age Group 15-19

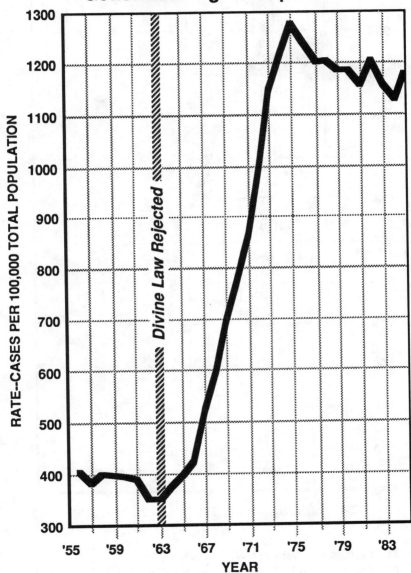

Basic data from the Center for Disease Control and
Department of Health and Human Resources.

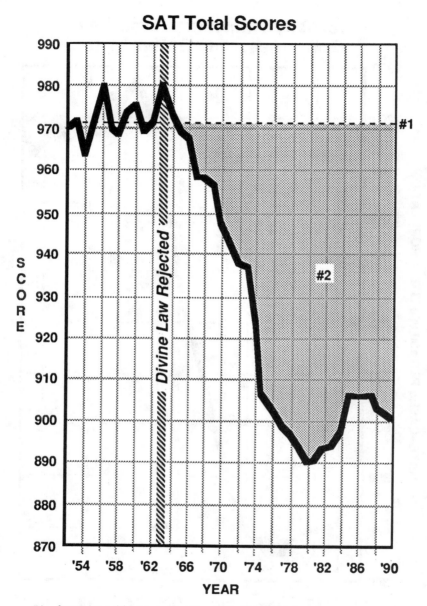

SAT Total Scores

#1 - Average achievement level prior to the rejection

#2 - Amount of reduced academic achievement since the rejection

Basic data from the College Entrance Exam Board.

Pregnancies To Unwed Girls
Under 15 Years of Age

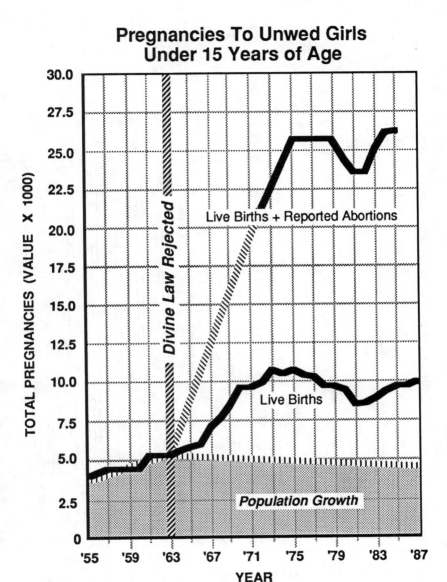

IIIIIIIIIIIIIII Indicates population growth.
ᗰᗰᗰᗰᗰᗰᗰ Indicates interpolated data.

Basic data from Department of Health and Human Services,
Statistical Abstracts of the United States, the Center for Disease Control,
and the Department of Commerce, Census Bureau.

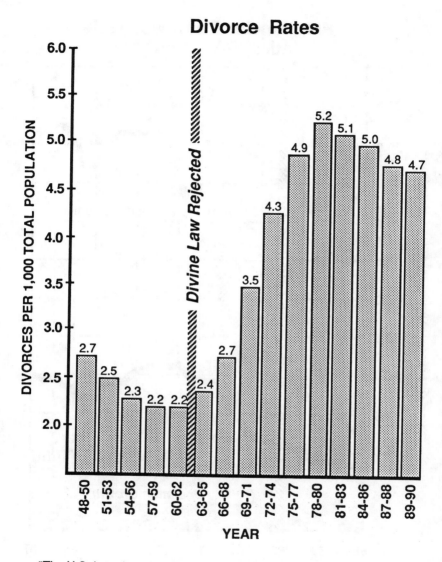

Divorce Rates

"The U.S. is at the top of the world's divorce charts on marital breakups."
U.S. News and World Report, June 8, 1987, pp. 68-69.

"The number of divorces tripled each year between 1962 and 1981."
Time, July 13, 1987, p. 21.

Basic data from the U. S. National Center for Health Statistics,
Vital Statistics of the United States, annual.

Cases Of Sexually Transmitted Diseases

Includes: Gonorrhea, Syphilis, Chancroid, Granuloma Inguinale, Lymphogranuloma Venereum, and AIDS

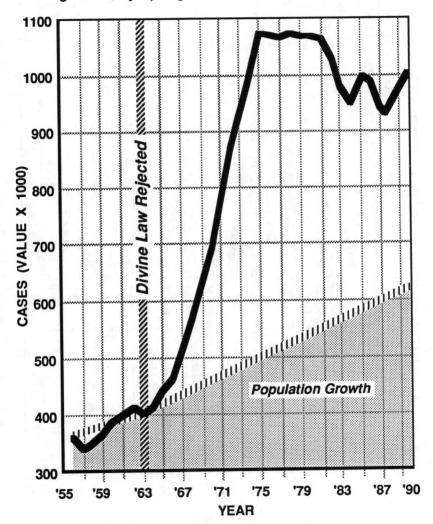

IIIIIIIIII Indicates population growth profile.

Basic data from Department of Health and Human Services, the Center for Disease Control, and the Department of Commerce, Census Bureau.

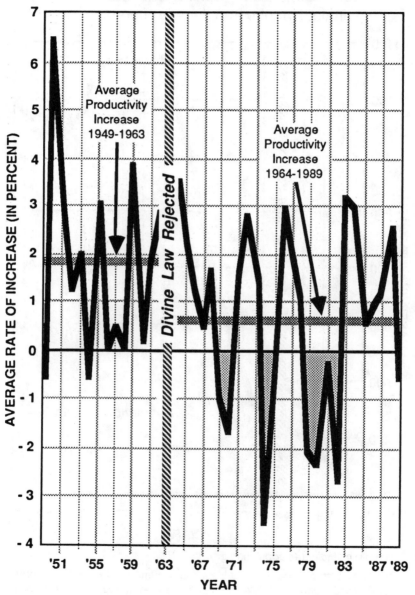

Multi-Factor Productivity:
Non-Farm Business

Basic data from Department of Labor, Bureau of Labor Statistics.

These are but a few examples of the many dramatic upheavals which have occurred since 1962-1963 (for a complete statistical examination of the results of this rejection, see an earlier work by David Barton: *America: To Pray or Not To Pray?*). Following the judicial rejection of natural law and the embracing of relativism, the United States has become number one in the *world* in violent crime, divorce, and illegal drug use; number one in the western world in teenage pregnancies; and number one in the industrial world in illiteracy. While America has always been a world leader, since 1962-63 it has been leading in many of the wrong categories. Relativism and positivism have not produced national betterment or prosperity, but rather their opposites! By removing Divine law, the Court removed the source of our previous national stability.

At the time of the Founders, politicians were required, by their state constitutions, to express their belief in future punishments and rewards. By so doing, they were individually recognizing and personally accepting responsibility for any effects from their actions, decisions, or laws. These politicians not only acknowledged that their actions would have consequence, either for good or bad, but that they would answer for them, whether in this life or in the next.

The Founders, however, not only recognized that God required individual accountability, they perceived that God also required a national accountability. Yet a nation, unlike an individual, does not have an afterlife in which to answer for its actions; the only time it can be recompensed for its actions, whether good or bad, is at present. George Mason, a Virginia delegate at the Constitutional Convention, explained the principle:

> As nations can not be rewarded or punished in the next world they must be in this. By an inevitable chain of causes & effects providence punishes national sins, by national calamities. [4]

Ben Franklin knew the same to be true; at the Continental Convention, he declared:

> I have lived, Sir, a long time, and the longer I live, the more convincing proofs I see of this truth—*that God governs in the affairs of men*. . . . We have been assured, Sir, in the sacred writings, that "except the Lord build the house they labour in vain that build it." I firmly believe this; and I also believe that *without his concurring aid we shall succeed in this political building no better, than the builders of Babel:*

> We shall be divided by our little partial local interests; our projects will be confounded, and we ourselves shall become a reproach. [5] (emphasis added)

The previous charts tend to validate what was predicted by Mason, Franklin, and many other Founders. Since the rejection of His "concurring aid," the nation clearly has experienced "an inevitable chain of causes and effects." The rejection of Divine law indeed had national repercussions.

When the contemporary Courts rejected Divine and natural law, they not only used poor judgment, they acted illegally. They rejected the standards which had been established in the Declaration of Independence: "the laws of nature and of nature's God." Many people erroneously consider the Constitution to be a higher document than the Declaration. However, under our form of government, the Constitution is _not_ superior to the Declaration of Independence; a violation of the Declaration is just as serious as a breech of the Constitution:

> The role of the Declaration of Independence in American law is often misconstrued. Some believe the Declaration is simply a statement of ideas that has no legal force whatsoever today. Nothing could be further from the truth. The Declaration has been repeatedly cited by U.S. Supreme Court as part of the fundamental law of the United States of America [at least 10 cases].
>
> The *United States Code Annotated* includes the Declaration of Independence under the heading "The Organic Laws of the United States of America" along with the Articles of Confederation, the Constitution, and the Northwest Ordinance. Enabling acts frequently require states to adhere to the principles of the Declaration; in the Enabling Act of June 16, 1906, Congress authorized Oklahoma Territory to take steps to become a state. Section 3 provides that the Oklahoma Constitution "shall not be repugnant to the Constitution of the United States and the principles of the Declaration of Independence." [6]

The Declaration of Independence, and consequently "the laws of nature and of nature's God," holds an important legal position in our form of government:

> The Declaration of the United States is our Charter. It is the legal document that made us a nation like all the other

nations of the world. It doesn't tell us how we are going to run our country—that is what our Constitution does. In a corporation, the Charter is higher than the By-laws and the By-laws must be interpreted to be in agreement with the Charter. Therefore, the Constitution of the United States must be in agreement with the Declaration of the United States (more commonly known as the Declaration of Independence). The most important statement in our Declaration is that we want to operate under the laws of God.

Why is all of this so important? Because today, when the courts are deciding what the Constitution means, they should remember our Charter—the Declaration of the United States. The Constitution doesn't specifically mention God, but then it doesn't have to because the Declaration is a higher document.

The Declaration says that we are a nation under God's laws. Therefore, all other laws of our country should be consistent with the law of God or they violate our national charter. [7]

Today, some lament that the Founders did not place explicit value declarations of right and wrong in the Constitution. However, the Founders knew that they did not need to; the Constitution was derived from a document which had already announced the values to be used in American government: "the laws of nature and of nature's God."

The United States Constitution is not a source of fundamental values. It is an instrument whereby fundamental values can be protected. . . . But the Constitution itself cannot give that content. In the early days, no one supposed that it would. There was a sufficiently clear value-consensus among Americans so that . . . there was little doubt as to the fundamental nature of good and evil, of virtue and vice. . . . Today, if there is disagreement or ignorance—as increasingly there is—fundamental values cannot be found in the Constitution. They simply are not there. [8]

Contemporary Americans simply do not realize the magnitude of the statement "the laws of nature and of nature's God." That eight-word phrase, commonly used and well-understood at the time of the founding, encompasses an entire legal and political system. Today, however, most of those in the legal profession would be hard-pressed to offer an acceptable definition of Divine or natural law; it simply is missing from current legal training! Why is it important to understand natural law today? Because:

The American Republic was founded upon the natural law. . . .
From natural law flow basic human rights, such as the right to
life, liberty, and property, which are ultimately derived from
God and which are antecedent to all government. Natural law
was thus perceived by the Founders to be unchanging because
it was grounded in the constancy of human nature. [9]

Natural law-natural rights was . . . a body of moral law
superior to human law. . . . [The Founders intended that]
Each department of the government be composed of men
imbued with natural law-natural rights principles. [10]

The Constitution cannot be properly interpreted or applied apart from
the natural law principles presented in the Declaration. The two
documents must be used together to understand either one individually:

The Declaration of Independence. . . . stated clearly the
purpose of the government of this nation, which was to
preserve and protect certain God-given rights for every
citizen. . . . eleven years later . . . the Constitution of the United
States. . . . stated the plan by which government would carry
out its purpose. . . . The Declaration of Independence and the
Constitution must be seen as one. Each is incomplete without
the other. This nation stands strong and free today, two
hundred years later, because one foot stands on the
Declaration of Independence; the other, on the Constitution.
Remove either document and the nation will not stand at all. [11]

This was well understood at the time of our founding, and it was
President John Adams who linked the value system of the
Declaration to the Constitution:

Our Constitution was made only for a moral and religious people. It is wholly inadequate to the government
of any other. [12]

To protect the foundation upon which the Founders formed this
nation is essential not only to this form of government, but to the
continued existence of this nation:

The French historian, Francois Guizot, asked James Russell
Lowell: "How long will the American Republic endure?"
Lowell replied, "As long as the ideas of the men who
founded it continue dominant." [13]

~14~
... Government of the People,
By the People, For the People ...

Not only did the Founders clearly define the value system by which the government was to be operated, they also defined the function of each of its three branches. However, just as the Court rejected the Founders' value system, it has also rejected many of the restrictions the Founders placed on the judiciary.

A prime contributor to the Court's success in its massacre of the Constitution is that most individuals have never read the Constitution for themselves. In current education, little exposure is given to the content of the Constitution or of the Declaration of Independence. Instruction received by students typically emphasizes what others have said about the Constitution, not what the Constitution itself says. Such a practice instills in the students any prejudices that exist in a commentator's personal interpretation (or misinterpretation) of the Constitution. Since the Constitution is perhaps the single most important document of our entire government—certainly it is one of the two most important documents—it should be read and reread by _every_ individual.

As in many documents, the Constitution lists the most important aspects first, progressing to those of lesser consequence; following the preamble, Article I describes the Congress, Article II the Presidency, and Article III the Judiciary. Not only does the order of listing reveal their relative position of importance, the amount of detail provided about each branch also reflects its relative importance. The Legislature (Article I) received 255 lines of print while the Presidency (Article II) required only 114 lines. The Judiciary (Article III) merited a mere 44 lines! [1]

The fact that Congress was presented first and that 255 of the 413 lines (62 percent) described its responsibilities indicates that our Founders felt it to be the most important aspect of the new government. The primary emphasis the Founders placed on Congress in the Constitution is obvious to those who read it. As former Presidential candidate Pat Robertson stated:

> I have read and reread the Constitution. It doesn't take many
> readings to see that the responsibilities of Congress are most

carefully and specifically stated. They should be. Congress makes the laws. The president executes the laws, and the courts interpret them; but Congress is the branch given responsibility to make them in the first place. [2]

The Founders never intended nor imagined that the Court would become as powerful as it has today. It currently wields power greater than that of the Congress or the President—it strikes down their acts and determines which will survive and which will be condemned to oblivion. Further, if Congress does not address the "proper" issues, courts decree their own policies (prison reform, educational reform, business policies, etc.)—policies made without input from the people or their representatives. The Founders would be stunned by both the position and the power of today's Supreme Court:

> Indeed, the designers of the National Capitol neglected to provide even a chamber for the Court, and the Court's first home when the government was transferred to Washington was in "a humble apartment in the basement beneath the Senate Chamber." [3]

> An idle passerby might wander in and find two or three onlookers and a court clerk and several men who had given up trying to find work and felt grateful for a warm place to sit on a cold day. . . . One could not tell he had entered the highest courtroom in the land. [4]

Even the Founding Fathers who served as members of the early Supreme Court realized that it was never destined for great power, as reflected in the comments of its first Chief Justice, who had been appointed by George Washington:

> When John Jay refused to resume the chief justiceship in 1801, he told President Adams that he had no faith the Court could acquire enough "energy, weight and dignity" to play a salient part in the nation's affairs. [5]

And John Jay was one of the men most influential in the construction of our government and in the division of its powers! The meager emphasis placed on the judiciary had been recommended by the philosophers from which the Founders most frequently quoted, for example, Montesquieu:

Of the three powers above mentioned [executive, legislative, judiciary], the judiciary is in some measure, next to nothing. [6]

Things are certainly different now! Since the role of judges was well known and understood during our founding—documented both by court practices and writings—the Constitution did not specifically delineate all the prohibitions on the Court's power; it did not need to:

Following the ancient traditions of biblical and common law, the framers assumed that judges would know their limits. The judges are asked to judge, no more. They hear all sides in disputes about the law under the Constitution of the United States. They discover and decide the meaning of the laws. They apply the laws. They judge between the parties who disagree about the laws. But they do not *make* laws. . . . And those judicial judgments are not laws but only opinions about the law. [7]

Blackstone, another favorite of the Founders, described the essence of judicial misconduct:

If [the legislature] will positively enact a thing to be done, the judges are not at liberty to reject it, for that were to set the judicial power above that of the legislature, which would be subversive of all government. [8]

Like Montesquieu and Blackstone, the Founders were very clear about the proper role of the judiciary. For example, James Madison opposed the assertion that the courts should have the final say on laws. He contended that allowing the courts the position of:

Refusing or not refusing to execute a law, to stamp it with its final character . . . makes the judiciary department paramount in fact to the legislature, which was never intended and can never be proper. [9]

Thomas Jefferson expressed similar sentiments in a letter in 1820:

You seem . . . to consider the judges as the ultimate arbiters of all constitutional questions; a very dangerous doctrine indeed, and one which would place us under the despotism of an oligarchy. . . . The Constitution has erected no such single tribunal. [10]

Alexander Hamilton, writing in *Federalist 81* of *The Federalist Papers,* confirmed that under the Constitutional plan, the courts would *not* be given the power to strike down laws:

> In the first place, there is not a syllable in the plan under consideration which directly empowers the national courts to construe the laws according to the spirit of the Constitution.

Congress, not the courts, was to judge laws against the spirit of the Constitution. Congress was to build its laws on the intent of the Constitution, and the courts were to interpret the laws according to the intent of Congress.

During the debates at the Constitutional Convention, a Council of Revision was proposed. This council, to be composed of members from the executive and judicial branches, would rule on the constitutionality of proposed legislation *before* it became law; however, the decision of this council would not be binding—it could be overridden by the legislature. Even though limited to an *advisory* capacity, delegate Elbridge Gerry of Massachusetts argued that:

> [The Council of Revision] was making Statesmen of the judges; and setting them up as guardians of the Rights of the people. It was making the [judges into] Legislators, *which ought never to be done.* [11] (emphasis added)

As the discussion at the Convention progressed, and the role of each branch further defined, the Court was given very limited spheres of jurisdiction under the law. However, delegate William Johnson of Connecticut, wanting to broaden the Court's power, moved "that the judicial power ought to extend to equity as well as law." [12] But "Mr. [James] Madison doubted whether it was not going too far to extend the jurisdiction of the Court. . . . The right of expounding the Constitution in cases not of this nature ought not to be given to [the judiciary]." [13]

The Council of Revision was *not* approved. When the final draft of the Constitution was ratified, the right for the judiciary to impose its opinion of constitutionality on the other branches was not found:

> Read Article III, looking for the line or phrase that gives the Supreme Court power to make laws or to discard laws that the Congress or state and local legislatures have made. You will not find it. [14]

Luther Martin, one of Maryland's delegates to the Convention, explained why the roles had been defined as they were:

> A knowledge of Mankind, and of Legislative affairs cannot be presumed to belong in a higher degree to the Judges than to the Legislature. . . . It is necessary that the Supreme Judiciary should have the confidence of the people. This will soon be lost, if they are employed in the task of remonstrating agst popular measures of the Legislature. [15]

Even the judicial branch understood that it was not to be the focus of power. The source of power was to remain the people themselves, and the legislature was the one branch closest and most responsive to the people. In *Federalist 49*, Madison explained why the legislative branch was the most important in a republican form of government:

> The members of the legislative department are numerous. They are distributed and dwell among the people at large. Their connections of blood, of friendship, and of acquaintance embrace a great proportion of the most influential part of the society. . . . they are more immediately the confidential guardians of the rights and liberties of the people.

Since the legislature is the branch closest to the people, it most accurately reflects their will. If changes and reforms were to occur, it was to be through the legislature, not the courts. The judiciary expressed its keen understanding of its own role in *Commonwealth v. Kneeland, 1846*:

> The Court, therefore, from its respect for the legislature, the immediate representation of that sovereign power whose will created and can at pleasure change the constitution itself, will ever strive to sustain and not annul [the legislature's] expressed determination. . . . And whenever the people become dissatisfied with [the legislature's] operation, they have only to will its abrogation or modification and let their voice be heard through the legitimate channel, and it will be done. But until they wish it, *let no branch of the government, and least of all the judiciary, undertake to interfere with it.* [16] (emphasis added)

The courts had always accepted their designated role in the government, and in this case, 60 years after its ratification, they were still
adhering to the intent of the Constitution.   The Founders _never_
intended the judiciary to be the chief branch. In *Federalist 51*, James
Madison identified the primary branch:

> In republican government, the legislative authority neces-
> sarily predominates.

John Locke had similarly stated:

> The first and fundamental positive law of all common-
> wealths is the establishing of the legislative power. [17]

But if the legislative is the predominant branch, what is the check
or balance on that branch? Congressman John Randolph of Roanoke
identified it when he stated that the:

> Proper restraint upon Congress . . . was not found in a
> pretended power of the Judiciary to veto legislation, but in
> the people themselves, who at the ballot box could "apply
> the Constitutional corrective. That is the true check; every
> other is at variance with the principle that a free people are
> capable of self government." [18]

The check on Congress is the people, not the Supreme Court. If
any branch was to have the power of review, it would be the legislative branch, not the judicial. As Montesquieu had explained:

> And, as [the three branches] have need of a regulating power
> to temper them, the part of the legislative body . . . is
> extremely proper for this very purpose. . . . It has a right, and
> ought to have the means of examining in what manner its
> laws have been executed. [19]

Logic demands that those making the laws hold a more important
position than those interpreting them:

> It is of the very essence of law in a republican form of
> government that the legislative power has primacy over the
> judicial, the power to make laws is antecedent to the power
> to interpret them. The judicial power, passive in nature, is
> attendant upon legislative initiative. To invert this order
> would be subversive of republican government. [20]

For this form of government to be successful, each branch must refrain from encroaching into the designated responsibilities of the other branches. George Washington warned that the three branches must:

> Confine themselves within their respective constitutional spheres, avoiding in the exercise of the powers of one department to encroach upon another. The spirit of encroachment tends to consolidate the powers of all the departments in one, and this to create . . . a real despotism. . . . Let there be no change by usurpation . . . it is the customary weapon by which free governments are destroyed. [21]

James Madison similarly cautioned:

> The preservation of a free government requires not merely, that the metes and bounds which separate each department of power be invariably maintained. . . . The Rulers who are guilty of such an encroachment, exceed the commission from which they derive their authority, and are Tyrants. The People who submit to it are governed by laws made neither by themselves nor by an authority derived from them, and are slaves. [22]

The warnings by Washington and Madison echoed Montesquieu's:

> Again there is no liberty, if the power of judging be not separated from the legislative and executive powers. Were it [the power of judging] joined with the legislative, the life and liberty of the subject would be exposed to arbitrary control; for the judge would then be the legislator. Were it joined to the executive power, the judge might behave with all the violence of an oppressor. There would be an end of every thing were the same man, or the same body . . . to exercise those three powers. [23]

Our national charter and by-laws (the Declaration and Constitution) use phrases such as: "government of the people, by the people, and for the people" and "the consent of the governed" It is incontrovertible that our Founders intended that the power of this government reside solely in the hands of the people. Congressman Robert K. Dornan, in his book *Judicial Supremacy,* accurately summarized the beliefs of the Founders when he stated:

The representatives are chosen by the people, act in place of the people for the people's welfare, are accountable to the people, and have superior resources with which to determine and provide for the welfare of the people. The aloofness and unaccountability of the judicial branch creates around it an atmosphere in which it is all too easy for the judiciary to substitute its own idea of the general welfare for that of the people. . . . Furthermore, the resources available to the judiciary for determining the general welfare are in no way superior to those of the national legislature. [24]

Laws are to reflect the general public consensus, not the desires of a few individuals or of a small group such as the Court. Samuel Adams summarized the basic tenet of a republic when he declared:

"Laws they are not, which the public approbation hath not made so." This seems to be the language of nature and common sense; for if the public are bound to yield obedience to laws to which they cannot give their approbation, they are slaves to those who make such laws and enforce them. [25]

~15~
Judicial Supremacy—
The Three Percent Majority

Although today we are accustomed to hearing that we are a democracy, such was never the intent. The form of government entrusted to us by our Founders was a republic, not a democracy (remember: we pledge allegiance to a republic, not a democracy); there *is* a definite difference between the two.

A democracy operates by direct majority vote, or what the Founders and early historians described as "mobocracy." [1] When an issue is to be decided, the entire population votes on it and the majority wins and rules. A democracy is a series of referendum votes based on the predominant popular opinion at the time.

A republic differs in that the general population elects representatives who then pass laws to govern the nation. In a republic, although a majority vote of the elected representatives will determine a policy, the minority can have influence on the majority decision; compromises are worked out whereby the majority rules with consideration given to minority feelings. Democracy is rule by majority feelings; a republic is rule by law.

Our form of government contains some elements of democracy. There are occasions when the people do have referendum or direct votes on certain state or national issues and the people do select, by simple majority vote, their chief executive and their representatives, who then act in accordance with fixed laws. For this we might be termed a democratic-republic, but not a democracy.

The Founders were no strangers to democracies, and they made it clear that America was *not* a democracy—it was a republic, a fact made apparent by a verbal exchange following the Constitutional Convention. Having concluded their work on the Constitution, Benjamin Franklin walked outside and seated himself on a public bench. A woman approached him and inquired, "Well, Dr. Franklin, what have you done for us?" Franklin quickly responded, "My dear lady, we have given to you a republic—if you can keep it; if you can keep it." [2]

Benjamin Rush of Pennsylvania, a Founding Father and a signer of the Declaration of Independence, articulated how many of the Founders viewed a democracy:

A simple democracy has been very aptly compared by Mr. [Fisher] Ames of Massachusetts [the Founder who proposed the wording of the First Amendment and two year terms for Congressmen], to a volcano that contained within its bowels the fiery materials of its own destruction. A citizen of one of the cantons of Switzerland, in the year 1776, refused in my presence to drink "the commonwealth of America" as a toast, and gave as a reason for it, "that the simple democracy was the devil's own government." [3]

Benjamin Rush, having rejected the concept of democracy, described the essential element of the preferred government (a republic): a government whose laws were based on fixed principles:

Where there is no law, there is no liberty; and nothing deserves the name of law but that which is *certain*, and universal in its operation, upon all the members of the community. [4] (emphasis added)

A republic, unlike a democracy, could never become a "mobocracy," for it reposed, as Montesquieu had explained, "on principles that do not change." [5] Those principles were the principles of natural law, described in the Declaration as "the laws of nature and of nature's God." Since they were unchanging, they were therefore not subject to the rapidly fluctuating feelings and emotions of the people.

A republic is the highest form of human government, but also requires the greatest amount of care and maintenance. If a republic is neglected, it can deteriorate into one of several inferior forms of government: a democracy, an anarchy, an oligarchy, or a dictatorship. A democracy, as mentioned above, is government conducted by direct vote of the people and by popular referendum; in an anarchy, every person is his own final authority, determining his own rules and standards; an oligarchy is a government run by a small council or group of elite individuals; and a dictatorship is rule by a single individual.

In both a republic and a democracy, numbers are important. When a majority—either by the representatives in a republic or by the people themselves in the democracy—has expressed itself on an issue, that expression is significant and becomes policy. However, since oligarchies and dictatorships are based on minority rule, numbers are not important; policies may be enacted by a small group or by a single individual, even if contrary to the will of the majority of the population.

Our founding documents make it clear that in our form of government numbers *are* important. Our government is to function with "the consent of the governed," and the percentages given in the Constitution define what constitutes that consent: usually a simple majority vote, or on occasion, a two-thirds or three-fourths vote. At no time do our founding documents allow a nationwide policy to be enacted by a minority group over the objection of the majority. The minority does have the right to attempt to persuade the majority to its point of view, or to persuade the majority to include portions of the minority's views in its decisions; however, the minority is *not* the equivalent of the majority and is *never* to exercise strength over the majority.

Although this was the Founder's original plan, it has now been thwarted, particularly in domestic areas. In some fundamental ways which seriously distort constitutional checks and balances, our nation is no longer a republic, or even a democratic-republic—it has become an oligarchy. A simple majority of a council of nine individuals is able to make final, irreversible determinations on what will and will not become domestic policy in the land. A mere five Justices can now overturn any law of the land, even if that law was legitimately enacted by the people through their elected representatives. The Supreme Court—composed of unelected officials not answerable to the people—has become the most powerful ruling body in the nation.

In many areas, with the willing assistance of the Court, the minority belief has become the "majority" view—the law of the land. An example is the removal of school prayer. The Court's own records reveal that only 3 percent of the nation had no religious ties of any type—no belief in God. [6] Nonetheless, the Supreme Court aligned itself with the 3 percent and declared that, in opposition to the beliefs of the 97 percent, the acknowledgment of God and non-denominational prayer to Him would be prohibited in schools. That national policy was enacted by a three percent "majority"! The percentages given by the Court in the *Abington* case in 1963 have changed little in recent years:

A recent Gallup Poll [1986] shows that 95% of the American public reports a belief in God (a figure that has remained unchanged since 1944 when Gallup first asked the question). [7]

The following numbers were provided by the court, and then ignored, in *State Board of Educ.* v. *Board of Educ. of Netcong, 1970:*

> Public opinion polls, such as the Gallup, Harris, and Good Housekeeping polls . . . shows that 82% of the public favors prayer in public schools. [8]

Further, a Gallup poll published in *Emerging Trends* in March 1985, showed that 87 percent of Americans pray to God, down only 3 percent from the 90 percent mark in 1948. Well over 90 percent of the nation continues to believe in God, almost 90 percent of the nation prays to God, and over 80 percent of both students and citizens desire that prayer be returned to schools. Such percentages clearly fulfill the requirement of being the majority in a democracy, or even the two-thirds or three-fourths sometimes required in a republic; nevertheless, that majority, despite extensive effort, has been absolutely powerless to overturn the decisions of the minority.

It is obvious that the 80-plus percent is *not* in power; unelected judges are in power. Such a form of rulership is identified by the term "judicial supremacy":

> According to the doctrine of judicial supremacy, the judiciary has the sole right to place an authoritative interpretation on the Constitution, an interpretation that is, moreover, binding on the executive and legislative branches of the government. The only recourse for those who disagree with the Supreme Court is to the formal amendment procedures of Article V of the Constitution. Thus, a Supreme Court decision has acquired the same status as a fixed provision of the Constitution itself! . . . The one respect in which a Supreme Court decision differs from a fixed provision is that it has acquired that status not through the endorsement of a clear national consensus (three-fourths of the states), as required by Article V, but through the certification of a mere five-man majority! Moreover, if the interpretation of the Constitution of one coordinate department is final and binding upon the other coordinate departments, then obviously this department is no longer "coordinate," but "supreme." Thus, the Supreme Court has in fact become the supreme branch of a supposedly republican form of government. [9]

The Court portrays itself as supreme and allows neither discussion of nor recourse from its decisions. In *Wallace* v. *Jaffree (1984)*, the Court issued a stiff rebuke to any lower court who might attempt to "read" the Constitution for itself:

> Federal district courts and circuit courts are bound to adhere to the controlling decisions of the Supreme Court. . . . A precedent of this Court must be followed by the lower federal courts no matter how misguided the judges of those courts may think it to be. . . . Only this Court may overrule one of its precedents. [10]

A similar warning was also delivered in *State Board of Educ.* v. *Board of Educ. of Netcong, 1970:*

> [A] Trial court cannot claim right to independent interpretation of United States Constitution, and is obliged to apply law as last pronounced by superior judicial authority. [11]

The Court has appointed itself as the sole custodian and interpreter of the Constitution. As Charles Evan Hughes, a Chief Justice of the United States Supreme Court, explained:

> The Constitution is what the judges say it is. [12]

Such statements disclose the underlying contempt which the judiciary holds for the legislature, the presidency, and especially the people. The Court considers itself the only branch able to determine the meaning of the Constitution. That belief, and the statements proceeding from that belief, are diametrically opposed to the form of government designed by our Founders:

> The spectacle of even *one* unelected judge . . . successfully thwarting the will of a majority of the duly elected representatives of an entire nation, representatives who have sworn to uphold the Constitution, reveals the very essence of judicial supremacy. . . . It is government by judiciary in place of government of, by, and for the people. [13]

When Thomas Jefferson observed and then commented on what some judges were attempting to accomplish during his term of office, he accurately described what has now happened in America:

> They have retired into the judiciary as a stronghold. . . . and from that battery, all the works of republicanism are to be beaten down and erased. [14]

The Court has gradually usurped more and more power, moving further and further away from its intended role. Jefferson had foreseen this tendency on the part of the judiciary:

> The germ of dissolution of our federal government is in . . . the federal judiciary; an irresponsible body, (for impeachment is scarcely a scare-crow,) working like gravity by night and by day, gaining a little to-day and a little to-morrow, and advancing its noiseless step like a thief, over the field of jurisdiction, until all shall be usurped from the States. [15]

With the position the Court now holds, it wields incredible power:

> At one bold stroke the federal judiciary is able to by-pass the legislative process . . . and by judicial fiat . . . impose its own values on an entire nation. [16]

The Supreme Court in its first eighty years, acting in accord with Constitutional intent, rarely declared laws unconstitutional; furthermore, its decisions were not binding on the other branches. However, in recent years the Court has not only declared hundreds of laws unconstitutional, it has imposed its decisions upon legislatures and the presidency. The Court has now passed far beyond its designated role of settling disputes under the law (not to the law) and has moved into actual legislation and policy-making from the bench— solely the responsibility of elected representatives:

> Judicial usurpation of legislative power has become so common and so complete that the Supreme Court has become our most powerful . . . instrument of government in terms of determining the nature and quality of American life. Questions literally of life and death (abortion and capital punishment), of public morality (control of pornography, prayer in the schools, and government aid to religious schools), and of public safety (criminal procedure and street demonstrations), are all, now, in the hands of judges in the guise of questions of constitutional law. The fact that the Constitution says nothing of, say, abortion, and indeed, explicitly and repeatedly recognizes the capital punishment the Court has come close to prohibiting, has made no difference. The result is that the central truth of constitutional law today is that it has nothing to do with the Constitution. . . .

Constitutional law has become a fraud, a cover for a system of government by the majority vote of a nine-person committee of lawyers, unelected and holding office for life. [17]

The following is a graphic example of the type of case now routinely handled by the courts—a case having nothing at all to do with any law or any violation of a law. The court's ruling in the following case is clearly a social engineering decision, the type of decision to be handled by the legitimate policy-makers—the legislature:

The case started when a group of radical activists, mostly white, sued the school system on behalf of a group of black families. They claimed that the poor academic progress of the blacks was due to the fact that their native language was black English while standard English was used in the schools. The solution was for teachers to be trained to use and respect black English. . . . To those on the scene the proposed position seemed frivolous. For example, there was no evidence that black children spoke black English exclusively, or that they couldn't understand standard English. After all, these black children watched television daily and talked easily with their white classmates. Those who really knew these children reported "that black English is a variant dialect that can be turned on and off depending on the circumstances, in much the same way that many middle class Southern children learn to speak both standard English and 'country.' " . . . However, a federal judge decided to hear the case. To the community's astonishment, he decided that black English was a factor in these children's poor performance. The remedy ordered was to require teachers to attend lectures on black English. Subsequent tests showed that this remedial program for teachers made no difference in the children's performance.

What should trouble us most about this case is the ease with which a judge has intruded himself into the heart of the educator's domain, into what is to be taught, how it is to be taught, and how teachers are to be trained to teach it. What qualifies the judge to do so? What qualifies him to pronounce on the linguistics of English dialects? What qualifies him to pronounce on the causes of scholastic achievement, and the means needed to enhance it? The answer is-nothing at all. [18]

Courts amend and change the meaning of the Constitution at will to reflect their own predispositions:

> The problem is that . . . where the Supreme Court's interpretation of the Constitution is considered final and binding upon all other authorities, the philosophical predilections of the Justices become, in effect, part of the Constitution. This allows the Supreme Court to act as somewhat of a continuous constitutional convention, continually amending the written document by interpretation, so that the Constitution means whatever five members of the Supreme Court decide it should mean. [19]

As Jefferson so aptly described it:

> The Constitution . . . is a mere thing of wax in the hands of the judiciary, which they may twist and shape into any form they please. [20]

The following piercing statements about the courts are worthy of contemplation:

> The President, who exercises a limited power, may err without causing great mischief in the state. Congress may decide amiss without destroying the Union. . . . But if the supreme court is ever composed of imprudent men or bad citizens, the Union may be plunged into anarchy or civil war. [21]

> When the ultra-liberals lose elections, they fight all the more desperately for control of our third branch, the courts. Why? Because the courts control the Constitution and the Constitution is the "trump card" in politics. That's why this war is crucial. Now, there are only two sides really in this struggle. Either the Constitution controls the judges, or the judges rewrite the Constitution. [22]

> Government of, by, and for the people has become government of and by judges and lawyers for the people. [23]

> How long can public respect for the Court, on which its power ultimately depends, survive if the people become aware that the tribunal which condemns the acts of others as unconstitutional is itself acting unconstitutionally? [24]

~16~
When Three Percent Was A Minority

The Court has worked diligently to amass the power it now possesses. It even refuses to allow itself to be called into question, as evidenced by the remarks of Justice Felix Frankfurter in *American Federation of Labor* v. *American Sash & Door Co., 1949:*

> Our right to pass on the validity of legislation is now too much part of our constitutional system to be brought into question. [1]

Nonetheless, the Court's power must be called into question! We must reclaim from the courts our right to be a republic, returning the judicial branch to its proper position—the least of three co-sovereign branches. The people of the nation, not its courts, must control its destiny. Any national reforms which occur must be guided by the people, not by the social engineering of an elite few.

Alexis de Tocqueville, a visitor to America in the 1830's, admired the American system, what he called "the most enlightened and free . . . on earth." [2] Yet he observed what he considered to be a weakness in our structure: the supposed right of the courts to determine the constitutionality of a law. He commented on what would happen in his homeland France if the courts ever were given such a right:

> If in France the tribunals were authorized to disobey the laws on the ground of their being opposed to the constitution, the supreme power would in fact be placed in their hands, since they alone would have the right of interpreting a constitution. . . . They would, therefore, take the place of the nation, and exercise as absolute a sway over society as the inherent weakness of judicial power would allow them to do. [3]

What he feared and foresaw a century-and-a-half ago has become a reality today. Yet this was not always the case. In our early years, Courts periodically did attempt what de Tocqueville had predicted. However, whenever that occurred, the Founders quickly rose up and dramatically forced the Court back to its proper constitutional function. The example provided by our Founders of how to respond to the Court's attempts to extend itself beyond its designated function is worthy of emulation today.

The first occasion in which the Supreme Court attempted to flex and enlarge its judicial "muscle" was during the presidency of Thomas Jefferson. In the final days of President John Adams— immediately before Jefferson took office—Adams made several Federalist appointments of federal justices-of-the-peace to positions in the District of Columbia.

Since Jefferson, an Anti-Federalist, had been voted to office over John Adams, the Federalist candidate, Jefferson felt that his election was a clear mandate that the people did not want the Federalist philosophy further extended or strengthened. Consequently, when he took office, the appointments had not yet been delivered and they therefore fell into his possession; he refused to deliver them.

William Marbury, one of the thwarted appointees—along with three others who did not receive their commissions—sued James Madison, Jefferson's Secretary of State, to receive the appointments. That suit, *Marbury* v. *Madison*,[4] went before the Supreme Court.

The Court first determined that it did not have any authority over the case, but explained that if it had had the authority, it would have ordered the delivery of the appointments. In a letter to Judge William Johnson, Thomas Jefferson recounted the *Marbury* decision and gave his opinion of the Court's actions:

> The Court determined at once, that being an original process, they had no cognizance of it [no authority over the case]; and therefore the question before them was ended. But the Chief Justice went on to lay down what the law would be, had they jurisdiction of the case, to wit: that they should command the delivery. . . . Besides the impropriety of this gratuitous interference, could anything exceed the perversion of law? [5]

Further, the Court digressed from the issue of the appointments and used the case as an opportunity to declare unconstitutional a portion of the 1789 Judiciary Act. This action by the Court was its first attempt to strike down a law passed by the "people," in this case the "people" being the Founding Fathers of the 1789 legislature!

This action was astonishing: one group of Founding Fathers was striking down a law passed by another group of Founding Fathers! It not only seemed ironic, but moreover dangerous that an unelected Court should declare a law passed in the legislature (passed by the men who had personally created the government and the Constitution, and therefore intimately understood their intent) to be "unconstitutional."

The Court had not only ruled and delivered its opinion, it was now striking down a law and ordering the other branches to submit to its decision. This was an overt action by the Court to gain more power by attempting to force its own opinion on another branch of government. What would be the response?

Jefferson and Madison completely ignored the Court's decision in *Marbury* v. *Madison*. Their response was *not* greeted with outrage from the public, Congress, or even the Court; their action was normal under this form of government.

Shortly after this incident, in a letter to Mrs. John Adams, Jefferson expounded his belief on the proper role of the judiciary:

> Nothing in the Constitution has given to them a right to decide for the Executive, more than to the Executive to decide for them. . . . [T]he opinion which gives to the judges the right to decide what laws are constitutional, and what not . . . for the legislature and the executive . . . would make the judiciary a despotic branch. [6]

Jefferson asserted that each branch not only had the ability, but indeed the sworn responsibility to interpret the Constitution for itself. If this were not true, America could never rightfully be called a republic with three co-sovereign branches.

James Madison, the defendant in the case, was neither a constitutional neophyte nor a "lightweight." As "Chief Architect of the Constitution," Madison, too, knew the proper role for each of the three branches. His statements explaining the Court's constitutional responsibilities reveal why he was neither impressed with nor intimidated by the Court's order:

> [Some contend] that wherever [the Constitution's] meaning is doubtful, you must leave it to take its course, until the judiciary is called upon to declare its meaning. . . . But I beg to know upon what principle it can be contended that any one department draws from the Constitution greater powers than another. . . . I do not see that any one of these independent departments has more right than another to declare their sentiments on that point. [7]

The attempt by the Court to impose its view on the other branches either overlooked or ignored a basic principle: President Jefferson and Secretary of State James Madison—like the Justices—had taken an oath to uphold the Constitution. The Court's attempt to force its view of the Constitution upon the President and Secretary of State—two prominent Founders—implied:

> Only the judges *really* understand [the Constitution] and truly uphold it. . . . Lesser mortals must allegedly defer to the "enlightened" views of a few, and this in a republican form of government! In a word, the Justices avow themselves to be superior in mental and moral faculties to their colleagues in the other supposedly coordinate branches of the government. [8]

The *Marbury* v. *Madison* case was not the only incident in which Jefferson refused to become a servant of the Court; although commanded by the Court to appear at the Aaron Burr conspiracy trial, Jefferson refused:

> Jefferson saw quite clearly that any acquiescence to assertions of judicial supremacy would result in the Court becoming the final judge of its own authority. [9]

If the other two branches capitulate to the Court's decisions and accept them as binding and final, then no checks and balances remain over the power of the Court.

The need to keep the Court's power in check was widely understood by the Founders. In fact, many of them did more than merely ignore the Court when it began to declare the acts of Congress unconstitutional. On the floor of the Senate, William Giles of Virginia declared:

> If . . . the Judges of the Supreme Court should dare . . . to declare the acts of Congress unconstitutional . . . it was the undoubted right of the House to impeach them, and of the Senate to remove them. [10]

Although alien to current thinking, in early America it was customary for the legislature to reverse the judiciary, not vice versa:

> In 1787 judicial interpretation of the law was often not final even in the decision of cases, it being common practice for the legislature . . . to reverse decisions of the ordinary courts, to order cases retried or appeals granted. [11]

The legislative reversal of judicial decisions was not a practice limited solely to the early years of the nation; Abraham Lincoln confirmed this to be the policy in his day.

Lincoln had been adamantly opposed to the *Dred Scott* [12] decision in which the Supreme Court had declared that, according to their interpretation of the Constitution, blacks could not become citizens and Congress could not prohibit slavery. The Court's radical ruling did not particularly panic Lincoln, for he knew that the Court was **_not_** the final authority in constitutional issues. As he pointed out in the famous Lincoln-Douglas debates:

> A [Supreme Court] decision . . . has always needed confirmation before the lawyers regarded it as settled law. [13]

How was a Supreme Court decision confirmed so that it could then be recognized by the legal profession? By the approval of the legislature! Without a legislative confirmation, there would be no check over the power of the judiciary; judges would be able to strike down laws or impose their own personal interpretations upon the nation.

Even though Congress could overturn judicial decisions, Congress was not supreme over the nation. The check and balance over Congress was the people themselves. If the people felt their representatives were acting improperly, they would replace them. As John Randolph of Virginia had explained in Congress:

> The proper restraint [was] in the people themselves, who at the ballot box could "apply the Constitutional corrective." [14]

Jefferson's and Madison's flat refusal to allow the Court to have the final word and to assume a power not rightfully theirs has provided a valuable precedent—a precedent followed by other prominent Americans. For example, while Andrew Jackson was President, the Court, speaking through its Chief Justice in the *Cherokee Indian* cases (1831-1832),[15] ruled that Jackson was to take certain actions. In reply to the Court's decision, Jackson retorted:

> [The Chief Justice] has made his decision: *now let **_him_** enforce it!* [16] (emphasis added)

As Presidents before him, Jackson refused to be ordered about by the Court. Jackson's retort disclosed his strong beliefs regarding three *distinct* branches of government, beliefs he explained to Congress in a message on July 10, 1832:

> Each public officer who takes an oath to support the Constitution swears that he will support it as he understands

it, and not as it is understood by others. . . . The opinion of the judges has no more authority over the Congress than the opinion of Congress has over the judges, and on that point the President is independent of both. The authority of the Supreme Court must not, therefore, be permitted to control the Congress or the Executive. [17]

Jackson's beliefs wisely replicated those of the Founders before him. For example, it was Madison who announced the same principle:

Nothing has yet been offered to invalidate the doctrine that the meaning of the Constitution may as well be ascertained by the legislature as by the judicial authority. [18]

Another occasion when President Jackson refused to allow the Court to govern the nation was related by Abraham Lincoln:

Do not gentlemen here remember the case of that same Supreme Court . . . deciding that a national bank was constitutional? [19] . . . [Jackson] denied the constitutionality of the bank that the Supreme Court had decided was constitutional . . . [saying] that the Supreme Court had no right to lay down a rule to govern a co-ordinate branch of the Government, the members of which had sworn to support the Constitution— that each member had sworn to support that Constitution as he understood it. [20]

Abraham Lincoln, like his predecessors, also refused to allow the Court to be the guide for the nation. In his first Inaugural Address he explained the philosophy behind such a denial:

I do not forget the position assumed by some that constitutional questions are to be decided by the Supreme Court. . . . At the same time, the candid citizen must confess that if the policy of the Government upon vital questions affecting the whole people is to be irrevocably fixed by decisions of the Supreme Court, the instant they are made . . . the people will have ceased to be their own rulers, having . . . resigned their Government into the hands of that eminent tribunal. [21]

Recall that in the *Dred Scott* decision of 1857, the Supreme Court had declared that Congress could not prohibit slavery and that slaves were only property, not persons eligible to receive any rights of a citizen. President Lincoln disregarded that decision and declared freedom for the slaves in the Emancipation Proclamation; Congress, too, rejected the Court's ruling when it *prohibited* the extension of slavery into the free territories on June 9, 1862. [22] Had Lincoln allowed the Court's ruling to be binding upon the executive branch—had he not been guided by his own understanding of the Constitution—he could not have declared freedom for slaves.

A foreign observer of this nation today likely would conclude that the President and Congress had taken oaths not to uphold the Constitution, but to uphold the *Court's opinion* of the Constitution. By allowing themselves to be governed by the Court, both the President and Congress are required to relinquish the responsibilities for which they were elected:

> Congress and the President are vested not only with the power but with the *duty* to read the Constitution for *themselves*. . . . They are entitled to consult the opinions of the Court. . . . [But] They are *not* entitled to abdicate their own official function of independent judgment. [23] (emphasis added)

Based on the examples and writings of our nation's heroes, the antidote for judicial supremacy is simply to refuse to allow the courts to rule the nation.

In 1871, Charles Hodge, President of Princeton, provided a compelling argument that this constitutional republic should remain on the same foundation upon which it had been built, not the foundation on which some philosophical minorities wanted to place it:

> The proposition that the United States of America [is] a Christian . . . nation, is . . . the statement of a fact. That fact is not simply that the great majority of the people are Christians . . . but that the organic life, the institutions, laws, and official action of the government, whether that action be legislative, judicial, or executive, is . . . in accordance with the principles of . . . Christianity. . . .
>
> If a man goes to China, he expects to find the government administered according to the religion of the country. If he goes to Turkey, he expects to find the Koran supreme and regulating all public action. If he goes to a [Christian] country, he has no right to complain, should he find the Bible in the ascendancy and exerting its benign influence not only on the people, but also on the government. . . .

In the process of time thousands have come among us, who are [not] Christians. Some are . . . Jews, some infidels, and some atheists. All are welcomed; all are admitted to equal rights and privileges. All are allowed to acquire property, and to vote in every election. . . . All are allowed to worship as they please, or not to worship at all. . . . No man is molested for his religion or for his want of religion. No man is required to profess any form of faith, or to join any religious association. More than this cannot reasonably be demanded. More, however, is demanded. The infidel demands that the government should be conducted on the principle that Christianity is false. The atheist demands that it should be conducted on the assumption that there is no God. . . . The sufficient answer to all this is, that it cannot possibly be done. [24]

Despite the fact that, as Charles Hodge asserted, "it cannot possibly be done," it has been done; however, not by the people, but by the courts! Government now is conducted on the assumptions that "Christianity is false" and that "there is no God." It should never have happened:

Judicial supremacy was never intended because it was not a republican remedy. . . . The indictment against judicial supremacy is that it is unconstitutional. The bitter irony is that the Justices acting in the name of the Constitution are often acting unconstitutionally. . . . The members of Congress and the Executive branch [should] return to the meaning of the Constitution that was intended by the framers and so ably expounded by such great men as Madison, Jefferson, Jackson, and Lincoln. Two of the grandest and most resplendent monuments in our capital are dedicated to Thomas Jefferson and Abraham Lincoln, yet we do not heed their words regarding the meaning of the Constitution. [25]

~17~
The Potential Downfall of the Republic

Not only did the Founders hold strong beliefs on what constituted a good government, they held equally strong beliefs about what would cause its downfall. Their warnings are numerous and convey the same message: government stability is grounded in the morality of its citizens, and citizen morality is grounded in religion. When the importance of religion is diminished, so is the effectiveness of government. Notice their overwhelming consensus on the belief that religion and morality are inseparable from good government:

> Of all the dispositions and habits which lead to political prosperity, religion and morality are indispensable supports. . . . The mere politician, equally with the pious man, ought to respect and to cherish them. . . . Whatever may be conceded to the influence of refined education . . . reason and experience both forbid us to expect that national morality can prevail in exclusion of religious principle. [1]
> *George Washington*

> Statesmen . . . may plan and speculate for liberty, but it is religion and morality alone, which can establish the principles upon which freedom can securely stand. The only foundation of a free constitution is pure virtue. [2] *John Adams*

> The principles of all genuine liberty, and of wise laws and administrations are to be drawn from the Bible and sustained by its authority. The man therefore who weakens or destroys the divine authority of that book may be accessory to all the public disorders which society is doomed to suffer. [3] *Noah Webster*

> The only assurance of our nation's safety is to lay our foundation in morality and religion. [4] *Abraham Lincoln*

> God grant that in America true religion and civil liberty may be inseparable and that the unjust attempts to destroy the one, may in the issue tend to the support and establishment of both. [5] *John Witherspoon*

> We have staked the whole future of American civilization, not upon the power of government, far from it. We have

staked the future of all of our political institutions . . . upon the capacity of each and all of us to govern ourselves, to control ourselves, to sustain ourselves according to the Ten Commandments of God. [6] *James Madison*

The state must rest upon the basis of religion, and it must preserve this basis, or itself must fall. But the support which religion gives to the state will obviously cease the moment religion loses its hold upon the popular mind. [7] *B. F. Morris*

And can the liberties of a nation be thought secure when we have removed their only firm basis, a conviction in the minds of the people that these liberties are of the gift of God? That they are not to be violated but with His wrath? Indeed I tremble for my country when I reflect that God is just; that his justice cannot sleep forever. [8] *Thomas Jefferson*

Religion is the only solid basis of good morals; therefore education should teach the precepts of religion, and the duties of man towards God. [9] *Gouverneur Morris*

[N]either the wisest constitution nor the wisest laws will secure the liberty and happiness of a people whose manners are universally corrupt. [10] *Samuel Adams*

The safeguard of morality is religion, and morality is the best security of law as well as the surest pledge of freedom. [11] *Alexis de Tocqueville*

Where there is no religion, there is no morality. . . . With the loss of Religion . . . the ultimate foundation of confidence is blown up; and the security of life, liberty, and property buried in the ruins. [12] *Timothy Dwight*

Republican government loses half of its value, where the moral and social duties are . . . negligently practiced. To exterminate our popular vices is a work of far more importance to the character and happiness of our citizens, than any other improvements in our system of education. [13] *Noah Webster*

True religion affords to government its surest support. [14] *George Washington*

A general dissolution of principles and manners will more surely overthrow the liberties of America than the whole force of the common enemy. While the people are virtuous they cannot be subdued; but when once they lose their virtue they will be ready to surrender their liberties to the first external or internal invader. [15] *Samuel Adams*

[O]nly a virtuous people are capable of freedom. As nations become corrupt and vicious, they have more need of masters. [16] *Benjamin Franklin*

We have no government armed with power capable of contending with human passions unbridled by morality and religion. . . . Our Constitution was made only for a moral and religious people. It is wholly inadequate to the government of any other. [17] *John Adams*

At what point then is the approach of danger to be expected? I answer, if it ever reach us, it must spring up amongst us; it cannot come from abroad. If destruction be our lot we must ourselves be its author and finisher. As a nation of freemen we must live through all time, or die by suicide. [18] *Abraham Lincoln*

[This] Form of Government . . . is productive of every Thing which is great and excellent among Men. But its Principles are as easily destroyed, as human nature is corrupted. . . . A Government is only to be supported by pure Religion or Austere Morals. Private, and public Virtue is the only Foundation of Republics. [19] *John Adams*

The cultivation of the religious sentiment represses licentiousness . . . inspires respect for law and order, and gives strength to the whole social fabric. [20] *Daniel Webster*

What follows from this? That he is the best friend to American liberty, who is most sincere and active in promoting true and undefiled religion, and who sets himself with the greatest firmness to bear down profanity and immorality of every kind. Whoever is an avowed enemy of God, I scruple not [would not hesitate] to call him an enemy to his country. [21] *John Witherspoon*

The happiness of a people and the good order and preservation of civil government essentially depend upon piety, religion and morality. [22] *United States Supreme Court, 1892*

Religion and morality . . . are the foundations of all governments. Without these restraints no free government could long exist. [23] *Pennsylvania Supreme Court, 1824*

Offenses against religion and morality . . . strike at the root of moral obligation, and weaken the security of the social ties. . . . This [First Amendment] declaration . . . never meant to withdraw religion . . . and with it the best sanctions of moral and social obligation from all consideration and notice of the law. [24] *Supreme Court of New York, 1811*

Religion, morality, and knowledge [are] necessary to good government, the preservation of liberty, and the happiness of mankind. [25] *United States Supreme Court, 1892*

The destruction of morality renders the power of the government invalid. [26] *Pennsylvania Supreme Court, 1815*

Governments, like clocks, go from the motion men give them; and as governments are made and moved by men, so by them they are ruined too. Wherefore governments rather depend upon men, than men upon governments. Let men be good, and the government cannot be bad. [27] *William Penn*

In vain are Schools, Accademies, and Universities instituted, if loose Principles and licentious habits are impressed upon Children in their earliest years . . . . The Vices and Examples of the Parents cannot be concealed from the Children. How is it possible that Children can have any just Sense of the sacred Obligations of Morality or Religion if, from their earliest Infancy, they learn that their Mothers live in habitual Infidelity to their fathers, and their fathers in as constant Infidelity to their Mothers? [28] *John Adams*

It yet remains a problem to be solved in human affairs whether any free government can be permanent where the public worship of God, and the support of religion, constitute no part of the policy or duty of the state in any assignable shape. [29] *Supreme Court Justice Joseph Story*

It is impossible to rightly govern the world without God and the Bible. [30] *George Washington*

[T]he moral principles and precepts contained in the scriptures ought to form the basis of all our civil constitutions and laws. . . . All the miseries and evils which men suffer from vice, crime, ambition, injustice, oppression, slavery and war, proceed from their despising or neglecting the precepts contained in the Bible. [31] *Noah Webster*

Suppos [sic] a nation in some distant region, should take the Bible for their only law book, and every member should regulate his conduct by the precepts there exhibited. . . . What a Eutopa, What a Paradise would this region be! [32] *John Adams*

A patriot without religion . . . is as great a paradox, as an honest Man without the fear of God. . . . The Scriptures tell us righteousness exalteth a Nation. [33] *Abigail Adams*

The foundations of our society and our government rest so much on the teachings of the Bible that it would be difficult to support them if faith in these teachings would cease to be practically universal in our country. [34] *President Calvin Coolidge*

Without God there is not virtue because there is no prompting of the conscience . . . without God there is a coarsening of the society; without God democracy will not and cannot long endure. . . . If we ever forget that we are One Nation Under God, then we will be a Nation gone under. [35] *President Ronald Reagan*

Without an humble imitation of the characteristics of the Divine Author of our blessed religion . . . we can never hope to be a happy nation. [36] *George Washington*

Moral habits . . . cannot safely be trusted on any other foundation than religious principle, nor any government be secure which is not supported by moral habits. . . . Whatever makes men good Christians, makes them good citizens. [37] *Daniel Webster*

He who shall introduce into public affairs the principles of primitive Christianity will change the face of the world. [38] *Benjamin Franklin*

To the kindly influence of Christianity we owe that degree of civil freedom, and political and social happiness which mankind now enjoys. In proportion as the genuine effects of Christianity are diminished in any nation . . . in the same proportion will the people of that nation recede from the blessings of genuine freedom. . . . Whenever the pillars of Christianity shall be overthrown, our present republican forms of government, and all the blessings which flow from them, must fall with them. [39] *Jedediah Morse*

Why may not the Bible, and especially the New Testament . . . be read and taught as a divine revelation in the [school]? . . . Where can the purest principles of morality be learned so clearly or so perfectly as from the New Testament? [40] *United States Supreme Court, 1844*

The morality of the country is deeply engrafted on Christianity. [41] *Pennsylvania Supreme Court, 1824*

The morality of the country is deeply ingrafted upon Christianity, and not upon the doctrines or worship of [other religions]. . . . [In] people whose manners are refined, and whose morals have been elevated and inspired with a more enlarged benevolence, [it is] by means of the Christian religion. [42] *Supreme Court of New York, 1811*

The morality of the country is deeply ingrafted upon Christianity, and not upon the doctrines or worship of [other religions]. [43] *United States Supreme Court, 1892*

Christianity has reference to the principles of right and wrong; . . . it is the foundation of those morals and manners upon which our society is formed; it is their basis. Remove this and they would fall. . . . [Morality] has grown upon the basis of Christianity. [44] *Supreme Court of South Carolina, 1846*

What constitutes the standard of good morals? Is it not Christianity? There certainly is none other. Say that cannot be appealed to, and . . . what would be good morals? The day of moral virtue in which we live would, in an instant, if that standard were abolished, lapse into the dark and murky night of pagan immorality. [45] *Supreme Court of South Carolina, 1846*

A malicious intention . . . to vilify the Christian religion and the scriptures . . . would prove a nursery of vice, a school of preparation to qualify young men for the gallows, and young women for the brothel, and there is not a skeptic of decent manners and good morals, who would not consider such . . . a common nuisance and disgrace. [46] *Pennsylvania Supreme Court, 1824*

Whatever strikes at the root of Christianity tends manifestly to the dissolution of civil government . . . because it tends to corrupt the morals of the people, and to destroy good order. [47] *Supreme Court of New York, 1811*

Religion . . . must be considered as the foundation on which the whole structure rests. . . . In this age there can be no substitute for Christianity; . . . the great conservative element on which we must rely for the purity and permanence of free institutions. [48] *House Judiciary Committee, 1854*

The Christian religion is the most important and one of the first things in which all children, under a free government, ought to be instructed. . . . No truth is more evident . . . than that the Christian religion must be the basis of any government intended to secure the rights and privileges of a free people. [49] *Noah Webster*

No free government now exists in the world, unless where Christianity is acknowledged, and is the religion of the country. . . . Christianity is part of the common law. . . . Its foundations are broad and strong, and deep. . . . It is the purest system of morality . . . and only stable support of all human laws. [50] *Pennsylvania Supreme Court, 1824*

The great vital and conservative element in our system is the belief of our people in the pure doctrines and divine truths of the gospel of Jesus Christ. [51] *House Judiciary Committee, 1854*

Our Founders believed intensely that religion—specifically Christianity—produced public morality, and that government simply could not survive without public morality. On this basis, they neither created nor tolerated legislation diminishing Christianity's effect. To do so would invite the demise of good government, and no intelligent government would intentionally commit suicide by destroying its very foundation! Religion, which produces morality, must be publicly encouraged and supported for the sake of the future of this nation which we love and respect.

Advocates of natural law believe, as did the Founders, that there are fixed standards for right and wrong. Proponents of relativism believe that the only thing absolutely wrong is having fixed standards of right and wrong. Those who resent restraints and discipline proclaim, "You can't legislate morality!" That is not true. Relativists fail to realize that morality is *always* legislated—it is simply a matter of *whose* morality is being legislated:

> "Morality". . . . pits right against wrong. To "legislate" means to make a law. . . . What law has ever been enacted by any government in the history of mankind that has not named something wrong and its opposite right? [52]

Even those who argue against the legislation of morality cling to their own standards of morality. The debate, therefore, is not really over legislating morality; it is over whose standards should be used:

> What today's critics are saying is, "We don't want God to have anything to do with today's morality. We want to determine what is right and wrong without God. . . . "
>
> It is no accident that America has moved from George Washington's "It is impossible to rightly govern the world without God and the Bible," to today's humanistic view that insists "you can't legislate morality." . . . What is happening is that America has become the battleground between the world's two oldest religions. The first religion to appear in the history of mankind worships God. The second worships man. In America, the first is expressed primarily by Christianity. The second by humanism. . . .
>
> Check out the latest law enacted or the most recent Supreme Court decision. God was either recognized as the Creator or ignored; man was either recognized as the created or deified.
>
> And it is not a question of whether politics and religion will be mixed. It is a question of which religion will be mixed with American politics. Will it be a religion that worships God, or a religion that worships man? It is a question of which religious guidelines will undergird the legislation: religious guidelines that deify God, or religious guidelines that deify man? [53]

For the Founders, the only standards of morality which could withstand the scrutiny applied under the "laws of nature and of nature's God" were Christian principles.

However, excluding all "religious" reasons for including Christian principles in government, there are pragmatic rewards for basing civil laws on Christian principles. Consider murder as an example. Since civil law prohibits murder, how can Christianity contribute anything more? Because Christianity, unlike purely civil statutes, attempts to deal with murder before it occurs—while it is still only a thought:

> You have heard that it was said . . . "Do not murder". . . . But I tell you that anyone who is angry with his brother will be subject to judgment. *Matthew 5:22-23*

Civil laws can address only externalized crimes; Christianity, however, can address and help prevent crimes while they are still internalized. In the case of murder, Christianity can deal with it before it occurs; the civil laws can do nothing until after the fact. Civil laws do not deal with the heart, which is the actual source of violence, crime, drug abuse, etc. Without the aid from religion, government utilizes extensive manpower and expends massive sums attempting to restrain behavior which is the external manifestation of internal sins. The moral teachings of Christianity provide a basis for civil stability which allows a government to perform its primary function: serving, not restraining.

To deal effectively with internal sin is to prevent external crime. Hate is not a crime, it is a sin; yet it often leads to a crime (assault, murder, perjury, slander, etc.). To covet is not a crime, it is a sin; yet it often leads to a crime (theft, burglary, embezzlement, etc.). Only religion can effectively deal with hate, covetousness, etc.—the real source of crime. It was because of Christianity's vital contributions to good government that the Founders emphasized its importance. They understood that:

> A Christian society is capable of having its individuals self-govern themselves under God. . . . A Christian society asks its citizens to deal with their heart condition. . . . A [non-Christian] society is turbulent and riotous because there isn't any prescription or medicine for the sinful inward man. [54]

Thomas Jefferson, in explaining why the teachings of Christianity were so valuable, stated:

The precepts of philosophy, and of the Hebrew code, laid hold of actions only. [Jesus] pushed his scrutinies into the heart of man, erected his tribunal in the region of his thoughts, and purified the waters at the fountain head. [55]

Man must be controlled by either the internal restraints provided through religion or by the threat of force and punishment from a civil authority. As statesman Robert Winthrop observed in 1852:

Men, in a word, must necessarily be controlled, either by a power within them, or by a power without them; either by the word of God, or by the strong arm of man; either by the Bible, or by the bayonet. [56]

Noah Webster had similarly noted:

There are two powers only which are sufficient to control men, and secure the rights of individuals and a peaceable administration; these are the *combined force of religion and law*, and the *force or fear of the bayonet*. [57]

The argument of whether religion is necessary to society and government is not new. The same dispute occurred between two prominent men in the founding era. The first asserted:

The legitimate powers of government extend to such acts only as are injurious to others. But it does me no injury for my neighbour to say there are twenty gods, or no god. It neither picks my pocket nor breaks my leg. [58]

William Linn, an outspoken critic of this philosophy, responded with a statement that summarized the convictions of the majority of the Founders and that has since been confirmed by experience in this country:

Let my neighbor once persuade himself that there is no God, and he will soon pick my pocket, and break not only my *leg* but my *neck*. If there be no God, there is no law, no future account; government then is the ordinance of man only, and we cannot be subject for conscience sake. [59]

In a nation such as ours (a democratic-republic), it is imperative that religion and morality be maintained, encouraged, and promoted:

Freedom belongs only to people who are morally responsible. It is not possible for a people to be corrupt and conniving liars, cheaters, and thieves, stealing from one another, and still remain free. To have a good country we have to build a nation of good people.

If we as a nation do not soon return our official public policy to the Christian consensus of our Founding Fathers and the Biblical principles of law that have provided the freedoms we've enjoyed for over two hundred years, it is just a matter of time before we lose those freedoms. [60]

It *does* make a difference which standards of morality are applied! The real danger lies in believing that one set of standards is just as good as another. It is moral suicide to believe that ethics are merely subject to the "eye of the beholder." When that belief is embraced, any motivation to restore former standards becomes paralyzed. As Puritan Nathaniel Ward stated:

Nothing is easier than to tolerate when you do not seriously believe that differences matter. [61]

The decision by the Courts to reject God, the Bible, and natural law was not purely a philosophical decision, it was actually a religious one:

Behind every system of law there is a god. To find the god in any system, look for the source of law in that system. If the source of law is the individual, then the individual is the god of that system. . . . If our source of law is the court, then the court is our god. If there is no higher law beyond man, then man is his own god. . . . When you choose your authority, you choose your god, and where you look for your law, there is your god. [62]

The Biblical book of Proverbs proclaims what our Founders also asserted concerning morality: morality is vital to the success and prosperity of both nations and individuals. The first nine chapters of Proverbs present the rewards of attaining wisdom and include such benefits as security, stability, no fear of disaster, abundance, the promise of Providential assistance, etc. Those nine chapters expounding wisdom contain 254 individual verses, of which 76 (30 percent) directly stress morality. Nearly one-third of the Biblical requirements to obtain the benefits needed, desired, and hoped for by the people of this nation involve maintaining morality— individual and national morality!

~18~
The Solution

It required decades for the Supreme Court to dispose of natural law, gradually relativism, discard God from public affairs, and redistribute governmental powers among the branches. These actions were slow, but steady; gradual, but systematic. Therefore, correcting what has happened in and to America will not necessarily occur within a single year or through a singular act.

Even though the Court's aforementioned "achievements" seem to be unrelated, they do have a common denominator: had not the public acquiesced to judicial supremacy, none of these "accomplishments" could have occurred. If the public had known American history and the role intended for the Supreme Court, the Court could never have forced the view of the 3 percent upon the 97 percent. Consequently, the solution must focus on correcting our knowledge and thus our thinking; as we change what we know, we change what we believe, and then our actions change correspondingly.

Changing our thinking involves three steps: removing wrong information from the mind, replacing it with correct information, then placing the new information into action. This book can satisfy only the second step: the input of new, correct information. The other two steps (discarding the wrong information and acting on the new) must be accomplished by the reader. This final chapter will offer four areas in which correct attitudes should be formed and four areas in which specific action can be taken.

The first attitude to be adopted involves learning to view governmental action in light of the Biblical principle of accountability. Recall that most of the original state constitutions included a stipulation that each member of government must verbalize a belief in future rewards and punishments. This requirement was beneficial both for government and for the people, because it forced each public official to recognize and acknowledge that one day he would answer to God for his actions taken while in office. Such a declaration helped maintain a long-term perspective: each official was facing and accepting the fact that there will be a reckoning for the long-term consequences of the decisions and actions he made while in office, whether for good or for bad; he must therefore behave responsibly before God. Warnings like the following one from Noah Webster helped keep the nation's leaders cognizant both of their responsibility to society and of their personal accountability to God:

The principles of all genuine liberty, and of wise laws and administrations are to be drawn from the Bible and sustained by its authority. *The man therefore who weakens or destroys the divine authority of that book may be accessory to all the public disorders which society is doomed to suffer.* [1] (emphasis added)

Unfortunately, our political leaders are no longer required either to face or to accept personal responsibility for the long-term consequences of their actions. Contemporary politicians often look no further than 2, 4, or 6 years into the future, depending on the term of their office. Consequently, their own short-term decisions (often taken to help ensure re-election) frequently jeopardize the people's long-term security and prosperity.

In natural law, it is a principle that short-term and long-term objectives generally oppose rather than complement each other. Whether in business, agriculture, religion, etc., the attainment of immediate, short-term success often compromises long-term security. For example, financial investments with short-term gains rarely provide productive long-term benefits. Conversely, investments yielding excellent long-term results typically provide poor paybacks in the short-term. In forestry, harvesting all the trees produces a good short-term profit, but seriously jeopardizes future yields. Maintaining an on-going supply of lumber requires a well-conceived long-term plan coupled with short-term restraint. Immediate decisions must always be made in view of the long-term consequences.

Decisions made by our leaders *do* have potentially serious repercussions and will eventually affect every individual in the nation, whether for good or for bad. As explained by George Mason, a Virginia delegate at the Constitutional Convention:

> As nations can not be rewarded or punished in the next world they must be in this. By an inevitable chain of causes & effects, providence punishes national sins, by national calamities. [2]

Nations, like individuals, _will_ be recompensed for the actions and stands they take under the watchful eye of God. Puritan leader John Winthrop, author of *A Model of Christian Charity,* warned of the consequences which arise from a nation's actions toward God:

> If we shall deal falsely with our God in this work we have undertaken and so cause him to withdraw his present help

from us, we shall be made a story and a byword through the world. [3]

Lincoln, too, stressed the importance of a nation's relationship toward God:

> It is the duty of nations . . . to own [admit] their dependence upon the overruling power of God . . . and to recognize the sublime truth, announced in the Holy Scriptures and proven by all history, that *those nations only are blessed whose God is the Lord.* [4] (emphasis added)

Lincoln, fully understanding this principle, attempted to conduct the nation's affairs in a manner so as to receive God's blessing rather than His opposition. Once, upon overhearing a clergyman quip that he hoped "the Lord was on the Union's side" in the Civil War, Lincoln quickly confronted the thinking behind that statement:

> I am not at all concerned about that, for I know that the Lord is always on the side of the right. But it is my constant anxiety and prayer that *I and this nation should be on the Lord's side.* [5] (emphasis added)

Collectively, this nation's leaders have allowed the Supreme Court to reject the standards delivered to us by our Founders and to take stands which God cannot bless but must rather oppose. We must again learn to view governmental actions from God's viewpoint:

> Man's law is important, but it must reflect God's law to be truly valid. . . . What a gift our forefathers have given us. By their example we learn that it is our right and duty as citizens to judge the laws and the lawmakers of this nation by the laws of God in the created order and in God's Word, and then to act. [6]

Our national policy must not be one of the denial of God, nor of apathy toward Him. It should, as formerly, "press on to acknowledge God" (Hosea 6:3, NIV), recognizing that the nation who acknowledges Him will be honored, and the nation who disregards Him will be dishonored (1 Samuel 2:30, Luke 9:26). Taking the right, or wrong, stand *does* have an effect:

> Righteousness exalts a nation, but sin is a reproach to any people. *Proverbs 14:34*

> When the righteous are in authority, the people rejoice; when the wicked rule, the people mourn. *Proverbs 29:2*

> Happy is the nation whose God is the Lord. *Psalms 144:15*

Second, we must recall our foundation and former values and establish in our thinking the conviction that this nation's institutions must return to their original foundation—the principles expressed through the Bible—because:

> It is impossible to enslave mentally or socially a Bible-reading people. The principles of the Bible are the groundwork of human freedom. [7] *Horace Greely*

> But for [the Bible] we could not know right from wrong. All things most desirable for man's welfare . . . are to be found portrayed in it. [8] *President Abraham Lincoln*

> The basis of our Bill of Rights comes from the teachings we get from Exodus and St. Matthew, from Isaiah and St. Paul. I don't think we emphasize that enough these days. If we don't have a proper fundamental moral background, we will finally end up with a . . . government which does not believe in rights for anybody except the State! [9] *President Harry S. Truman*

From a purely pragmatic viewpoint, the inclusion of religious principles within government has tangible social and civil benefits:

> Both Old and New Testament standards create a law of the heart. Whether one lives life by the Ten Commandments of the Old Testament or the fruit of God's Spirit in the New, the law of the heart helps regulate your response to the laws of this nation. Imagine how different the world would be without these biblically based constraints. Imagine what might happen to *this nation* without them. [10]

In this nation, religious principles in public and civil affairs have proven their benefits for so long and have produced such a history of international respect and national stability as to demand their continued inclusion. When one considers the benefits which religion has provided to this nation, an observation by Montaigne is worthy of contemplation:

> Were I not to follow the straight road for its straightness, I should follow it for having found by experience that, in the end, it is commonly the happiest and most useful track. [11]

Religious arguments aside, it makes good sense to return to the philosophy which so long produced nationwide moral, emotional, and social stability. As President Woodrow Wilson so astutely observed:

> A nation which does not remember what it was yesterday, does not know what it is today, nor what it is trying to do. We are trying to do a futile thing if we do not know where we came from or what we have been about. . . . The Bible . . . is the one supreme source of revelation of the meaning of life, the nature of God and . . . nature and needs of men. It is the only guide of life which really leads the spirit in the way of peace and salvation. [12]

Third, we must rekindle the understanding of the form of government that our Founders delivered to us. We were conceived and born a republic, never a democracy nor an oligarchy; we were designed for three co-sovereign branches, not one supreme branch. Only by neglect and abdication of personal responsibilities does a republic deteriorate into an oligarchy. If we do not return our government to its roots and original intent, we will have placed ourselves under a new constitution. The old one will be gone, and the new one will become whatever the Court determines:

> If a judge can interpret the Constitution or laws to mean something obviously not intended by the original makers . . . then the nation's Constitution and laws are meaningless. [13]

We must _not_ allow our foundations to be destroyed. In the words of the rhetorical question posed in Psalms 11:3:

> If the foundations be destroyed, what can the righteous do?

In early Biblical manuscripts, "foundations" were defined as the "political and moral supports." Indeed, if our "political and moral supports" are destroyed by the courts, what can the people do? If the foundation is gone, what will uphold the structure? We must protect our foundation! To help preserve that foundation, we must follow the advice given in Isaiah 1:26:

> Restore our judges as at the first, and our counsellors [lawyers] as at the beginning.

To return to being a nation of morality and Godliness, our judges and political counselors must return to the respect for God and His

values which their predecessors held. Appointing judges who interpret and administer law by the natural law principles of their
forefathers is something recommended in Ezra 7:25:

> Appoint [and elect] magistrates and judges . . . which know
> the laws of God.

Fourth, we must correct our attitude toward the possibility—even
the probability—of national reform. Although it seems at times that
there is an unstoppable tide rising toward the complete eradication of
God in public affairs, that movement has been initiated and
maintained by a very small minority of the nation. For this reason,
there remains hope—a strong hope. All that is needed to restore
what has been lost in this republic is for the majority to rise up and
take its proper place. Alexis de Tocqueville accurately described the
dilemma which now faces this country:

> The Christian nations of our age seem to me to present a
> most alarming spectacle; the impulse which is bearing them
> along is so strong that it cannot be stopped, but it is not yet
> so rapid that it cannot be guided: their fate is in their hands;
> yet a little while and it may be no longer. [14]

Our fate *is* still in our hands; however, unless we act, it will soon
pass completely beyond our control. As Edmund Burke stated:

> All that is necessary for evil to triumph is for good men to do
> nothing. [15]

Ironically, we can find solace in the fact that our current condition
has been caused through our own neglect:

> If our nation's problems were the result of some conspiracy
> of men, then the solution would be beyond the reach of
> most of us, and thus fatalism, apathy and despair would
> prevail. However, since . . . the real problem began with
> our neglect, then the power for change is also within [our]
> grasp. . . . If we accept our responsibility and do our duty,
> we have grounds for hope. [16]

This encouragement should inspire our thinking and turn our
thoughts in the right direction. Simply changing the way we think _will_
make a difference. As Harvard Professor Raoul Berger explained it:

How long can public respect for the Court, on which its power ultimately depends, survive if the people become aware that the tribunal which condemns the acts of others as unconstitutional is itself acting unconstitutionally? [17]

We must become indignant over and reject the Court's unprecedented attempts to rule the nation and to impose its own political and religious philosophies on the people. As Jefferson insisted, we must:

Carry ourselves back to the time when the Constitution was adopted, recollect the spirit manifested in the debates, and instead of trying what meaning may be squeezed out of the text, or invented against it, conform to the probable one in which it was passed. [18]

— — — • • • — — —

We must not stop with merely changing our thinking in the previous four areas—there are definite actions we should also take. The first action, while it may seem overly simple, is very profound: *read the Constitution*. As explained by one attorney:

I spent three years getting my law degree at Yale Law School. From the moment I enrolled, I was assigned huge, leather-bound editions of legal cases to study and discuss. I read what lawyers and judges, professors and historians said about the Constitution. But never once was I assigned the task of reading the Constitution itself. . . .

Over the last decade, however, I have become a student of the Constitution, searching each line for its meaning and intent. Studying the Constitution is like studying the Bible. It is amazing how much more you will learn when you quit studying *about* it and pick it up to read it for yourself. [19]

If we will personally examine the Constitution (a copy of which is provided in Appendix A), we can judge the current actions and statements of our government against the original blueprint delivered by the Founding Fathers. Once you have read the Constitution, obtain a copy of *The Federalist Papers* and read it. *The Federalist Papers*—authored by James Madison, John Jay, and Alexander Hamilton—expounds on the Founders' original intent for each branch of government. Reading the Constitution and *The Federalist Papers* will take you back to the original source and will remove the 200 years of haze and speculation which now often seem to confuse and distort both the Constitution and its intent.

Encourage your children (and others) to familiarize themselves with these two works, thus helping prepare them for the intelligent and effective fulfillment of their future civic responsibilities. To become a true republic again, we must individually accept the responsibility of citizenship and become involved, giving time and effort into the rebuilding of the nation and the reeducation of its people.

Second, we must aggressively resist the efforts of philosophical minorities who have implemented the policies which have destroyed educational success; for too long we have backed off into complacency and non-involvement about the nations schools. We must *not* give up the schools; rather, we must stand and fight for them! Abraham Lincoln asserted that schools *are* the future:

> The philosophy of the school room in one generation will be the philosophy of government in the next. [20]

Martin Luther expressed even more forcefully the impact that schools have on a nation by explaining what would happen if educational systems moved away from Biblical truths:

> I am much afraid that schools will prove to be the great gates of hell unless they diligently labor in explaining the Holy Scriptures, engraving them in the hearts of youth. I advise no one to place his child where the scriptures do not reign paramount. Every institution in which men are not increasingly occupied with the Word of God must become corrupt. [21]

Noah Webster perceptively described not only the importance of a good educational system, but the ingredients necessary in that system:

> The education of youth should be watched with the most scrupulous attention. Education . . . forms the moral characters of men, and morals are the basis of government. Education should therefore be the first care of . . . . political regulations; for it is much easier to introduce and establish an effectual system for preserving morals, than to correct by penal statutes the ill effects of a bad system. . . . The goodness of a heart is of infinitely more consequence to society than an elegance of manners. . . . The education of youth . . . lays the foundations on which both law and gospel rest for success. [22]

Morality—acquired *only* from religious principles—must again become an emphasis in education. The education of youth is now on the wrong foundation, evidenced not only by the lack of morality it has produced in students, but by the fact that it no longer provides support for the law (indicated by the 544 percent increase in violent crime occurring since the Court barred God and religious principles from education, and from the fact that 65 percent of *all* crimes are currently committed by school-age children). [23] Our educational philosophy which previously was highly successful and internationally respected has been overthrown by a revolution—a Court-initiated revolution. The very principles which brought America to the summit of the educational world are now disallowed. Action must be taken to *un*-reform education and to return it to the foundation which produced success.

The third area in which action must be taken is described by Charles Finney, a famous and respected American minister and lawyer from the early 1800's:

> The Church must take right ground in regard to politics. . . .
> The time has come that Christians must vote for honest men,
> and take consistent ground in politics or the Lord will curse
> them. . . . God cannot sustain this free and blessed country,
> which we love and pray for, unless the Church will take right
> ground. Politics are a part of a religion in such a country as
> this, and Christians must do their duty to the country as a part
> of their duty to God. . . . [God] will bless or curse this nation,
> according to the course [Christians] take [in politics]. [24]

Noah Webster delivered a similar warning to young people to impress on them the important responsibilities of citizenship:

> When you become entitled to exercise the right of voting for
> public officers, let it be impressed on your mind that *God
> commands you to choose for rulers just men who will rule
> in the fear of God. The preservation of a republican
> government depends on the faithful discharge of this duty;*
> if the citizens neglect their duty and place unprincipled men
> in office, the government will soon be corrupted; laws will
> be made, not for the public good, so much as for selfish or
> local purposes; corrupt or incompetent men will be appointed
> to execute the laws; the public revenues will be squandered
> on unworthy men; and the rights of the citizens will be

violated or disregarded. If a republican government fails to secure public prosperity and happiness, it must be because the citizens neglect the divine commands, and elect bad men to make and administer the laws. [25] (emphasis added)

President James Garfield, in an address celebrating the centennial of the Declaration of Independence, delivered a comparable admonition:

Now, more than ever before, the people are responsible for the character of their Congress. If that body be ignorant, reckless, and corrupt, it is because the people tolerate ignorance, recklessness, and corruption. If it be intelligent, brave, and pure, it is because the people demand these high qualities to represent them in the national legislature. . . . If the next centennial does not find us a great nation . . . it will be because those who represent the enterprise, the culture, and the morality of the nation do not aid in controlling the political forces. [26]

Elections are a matter of vital importance. We must actively participate in them! We *can* make a difference if we will get involved. Proof of this came in 1986 in five separate U.S. Senate races. The five candidates who stood for returning God to public affairs were narrowly defeated by a collective total of only 57,000 votes, an average of less than 12,000 votes per state. Yet, in those five states, there were over *5 million Christians who did not even vote!* If only *one percent* of those had voted for the candidate supporting God in public affairs, those five candidates would have been elected; five votes against Godly principles would have been replaced with five votes supporting them, creating a ten-vote swing in the Senate! Those candidates were not defeated by anti-God activists—they were defeated by inactive Christians!

One of the simplest solutions for returning the nation to its original foundation is changing the men in office. But this will never occur as long as the church is inactive at the polls and as long as less than 5 percent of Godly Americans are involved in party politics on the local level. [27]

In elections, the candidate's party affiliation must *not* be the deciding factor. Investigate the position of each individual candidate apart from his party. There are good and bad candidates in each party, but important votes are wasted if they are cast for a poor candidate solely because they were cast in support of a party. George Washington's offered this advice against excessive party allegiance in his Farewell Address:

> I have already intimated to you the danger of parties. . . . Let me now . . . warn you in the most solemn manner against the baneful effects of the spirit of party. . . . The common and continual mischiefs of the spirit of party are sufficient to make it the interest and duty of a wise people to discourage and restrain it. It serves always to distract the public councils and enfeeble the public administrations. It agitates the community with ill-founded jealousies and false alarms; kindles the animosity of one part against another. . . . There is an opinion that parties in free countries are useful checks upon the administration of the government, and serve to keep alive the spirit of liberty. This . . . is probably true . . . in governments [of monarchs]. . . . But . . . in governments purely elective, it is a spirit not to be encouraged. [28]

The fourth area in which action can be taken pertains to improving the composition of the federal, state, and local courts. This area can be directly affected not only by electing good officials to state and local judicial positions, but by electing good representatives and senators to federal positions. It is those federal representatives and senators who first recommend and then confirm the appointment of federal judges.

When investigating a federal candidate prior to an election, investigate his *personal* views on the courts. Specifically ask him *his* feelings on judicial policy-making, judicial legislation, and judicial supremacy; ask him his views on natural and Divine law vs. relativism. If a candidate accepts judicial supremacy, then his selections and recommendations for judicial appointments will only strengthen the power of the courts. However, if the candidate opposes court rulership, then he will select and recommend justices who also oppose judicial supremacy.

Federally elected representatives and senators must be accountable at the ballot box for the type of judges they appoint. Our politicians and representatives must work to maintain our republic, not capitulate to an oligarchy! We must require our officials to appoint constitutional judges, not relativists. We *do* have control over the judiciary through the candidates we elect to office.

Politically active minorities whose philosophical viewpoint opposes that of the majority realize that the judiciary is now the primary battlefield:

> When the ultra-liberals lose elections, they fight all the more desperately for control of our third branch, the courts. Why? Because the courts control the constitution and the constitution is the "trump card" in politics. That's why this war is crucial. Now, there are only two sides really in this struggle. Either the constitution controls the judges, or the judges rewrite the constitution. [29]

Remember, ultimately, in every issue, the enemy is not "them"; the enemy is "inactivity." While complacency rules, wrong principles and policies will abound. Only when the majority changes its thinking and actions and begins to act like a majority will this nation return to its former greatness, both internally and externally. We must get involved if we are to recover our roots. It is vital that we protect our foundations:

> The French historian, Francois Guizot, asked James Russell Lowell: "How long will the American Republic endure?" Lowell replied, "As long as the ideas of the men who founded it continue dominant." [30]

Let's get involved and protect "the ideas of the men who founded it":

> Our Founding Fathers did their part. They gave us a Constitution for the ages. Now it is up to us to do everything we can to keep it. [31]

Appendix A

The Declaration of Independence

When in the Course of human events, it becomes necessary for one people to dissolve the political bands which have connected them with another, and to assume among the powers of the earth, the separate and equal station to which the Laws of Nature and of Nature's God entitles them, a decent respect to the opinions of mankind requires that they should declare the causes which impel them to the separation.

We hold these truths to be self-evident, that all men are created equal, that they are endowed by their Creator with certain unalienable Rights, that among these are Life, Liberty and the pursuit of Happiness. That to secure these rights, Governments are instituted among Men, deriving their just powers from the consent of the governed. That whenever any Form of Government becomes destructive of these ends, it is the Right of the People to alter or to abolish it, and to institute new Government, laying its foundation on such principles and organizing its powers in such form, as to them shall seem most likely to effect their Safety and Happiness. Prudence, indeed, will dictate that Governments long established should not be changed for light and transient causes; and accordingly all experience hath shown that mankind are more disposed to suffer, while evils are sufferable, than to right themselves by abolishing the forms to which they are accustomed. But when a long train of abuses and usurpations, pursuing invariably the same Object evinces a design to reduce them under absolute Despotism, it is their right, it is their duty, to throw off such Government, and to provide new Guards for their future security. Such has been the patient sufferance of these Colonies; and such is now the necessity which constrains them to alter their former Systems of Governments. The history of the present King of Great Britain is a history of repeated injuries and usurpations, all having in direct object the establishment of an absolute Tyranny over these States. To prove this, let Facts be submitted to a candid world.

He has refused his Assent to Laws, the most wholesome and necessary for the public good.

He has forbidden his Governors to pass Laws of immediate and pressing importance, unless suspended in their operation till his

Assent should be obtained; and when so suspended, he has utterly neglected to attend to them.

He has refused to pass other Laws for the accommodation of large districts of people, unless those people would relinquish the right of Representation in the Legislature, a right inestimable to them and formidable to tyrants only.

He has called together legislative bodies at places unusual, uncomfortable, and distant from the depository of their public Records, for the sole purpose of fatiguing them into compliance with his measures.

He has dissolved Representative Houses repeatedly, for opposing with manly firmness his invasion on the rights of the people.

He has refused for a long time, after such dissolutions, to cause others to be elected; whereby the Legislative powers, incapable of Annihilation, have returned to the People at large for their exercise; the state remaining in the meantime exposed to all the dangers of invasion from without, and convulsions within.

He has endeavored to prevent the population of these States; for that purpose obstructing the Laws for Naturalization of Foreigners; refusing to pass others to encourage their migrations hither, and raising the conditions of new Appropriations of Lands.

He has obstructed the Administration of Justice, by refusing his Assent to Laws for establishing Judiciary Powers.

He has made Judges dependent on his Will alone, for the tenure of their offices, and the amount and payment of their salaries.

He has erected a multitude of New Offices, and sent hither swarms of Officers to harass our people, and eat out their substance.

He has kept among us, in times of peace, Standing Armies without the Consent of our legislature.

He has affected to render the Military independent of and superior to the Civil power.

He has combined with others to subject us to a jurisdiction foreign to our constitution, and unacknowledged by our laws; giving his Assent to their Acts of pretended Legislation:

For Quartering large bodies of armed troops among us:

For protecting them, by a mock trial, from punishment for any Murders which they should commit on the Inhabitants of these States:

For cutting off our Trade with all parts of the world:

For imposing Taxes on us without our Consent:

For depriving us in many cases of the benefits of Trial by Jury:

For transporting us beyond Seas to be tried for pretended offenses:

For abolishing the free System of English Laws in a neighboring Province, establishing therein an Arbitrary government, and enlarging its Boundaries so as to render it at once an example and fit instrument for introducing the same absolute rule into these Colonies:

For taking away our Charters, abolishing our most valuable Laws, and altering fundamentally the Forms of our Government:

For suspending our own Legislatures, and declaring themselves invested with power to legislate for us in all cases whatsoever.

He has abdicated Government here, by declaring us out of his Protection and waging War against us.

He has plundered our seas, ravaged our Coasts, burnt our towns, and destroyed the lives of our people.

He is at this time transporting large Armies of foreign Mercenaries to complete the works of death, desolation and tyranny, already begun with circumstances of Cruelty and perfidy scarcely paralleled in the most barbarous ages, and totally unworthy the Head of a civilized nation.

He has constrained our fellow Citizens taken Captive on the high Seas to bear Arms against their Country, to become the executioners of their friends and Brethren, or to fall themselves by their Hands.

He has excited domestic insurrections amongst us, and has endeavored to bring on the inhabitants of our frontiers, the merciless Indian Savages, whose known rule of warfare, is an undistinguished destruction of all ages, sexes and conditions.

In every stage of these Suppressions We have Petitioned for Redress in the most humble terms. Our repeated Petitions have been answered only by repeated injury. A Prince, whose character is thus marked by every act which may define a Tyrant, is unfit to be the ruler of a free people.

Nor have We been wanting in attention to our British brethren. We have warned them from time to time of attempts by their legislature to extend an unwarrantable jurisdiction over us. We have reminded them of the circumstances of our emigration and settlement here. We have appealed to their native justice and magnanimity, and we have conjured them by the ties of our common kindred to disavow these usurpations, which would inevitably interrupt our connections and correspondence. They too have been deaf to the voice of justice and of consanguinity. We must, therefore, acquiesce in the necessity, which denounces our Separation, and hold them, as we hold the rest of mankind, Enemies in War, in Peace Friends.

We, Therefore, the Representatives of the United States of America, in General Congress, Assembled, appealing to the Supreme Judge of the world for the rectitude of our intentions, do, in the Name, and by the Authority of the good People of these Colonies, solemnly publish and declare, That these United Colonies are, and of Right ought to be Free and Independent States; that they are Absolved from all Allegiance to the British Crown, and that all political connection between them and the State of Great Britain, is and ought to be totally dissolved; and that as Free and Independent States, they have full Power to levy War, conclude Peace, contract Alliance, establish Commerce, and to do all other Acts and Things which Independent States may of right do. And for the support of this Declaration, with a firm reliance on the protection of Divine Providence, we mutually pledge to each other our Lives, our Fortunes, and our sacred Honor.

Appendix B

The Constitution of the United States of America

Preamble to the Constitution of the United States

We the people of the United States, in order to form a more perfect Union, establish justice, insure domestic tranquility, provide for the common defence, promote the general welfare, and secure the blessings of liberty to ourselves and our posterity, do ordain and establish this Constitution for the United States of America.

ARTICLE I

Section 1. All legislative powers herein granted shall be vested in a Congress of the United States, which shall consist of a Senate and House of Representatives.

Section 2. The House of Representatives shall be composed of members chosen every second year by the people of the several States, and the electors in each State shall have the qualifications requisite for electors of the most numerous branch of the State legislature.

No person shall be a Representative who shall not have attained to the age of twenty-five years, and been seven years a citizen of the United States, and who shall not, when elected, be an inhabitant of that State in which he shall be chosen.

∞ [Representatives and direct taxes shall be apportioned among the several States which may be included within this Union, according to their respective numbers, which shall be determined by adding to the whole number of free persons, including those bound to service for a term of years, and excluding Indians not taxed, three fifths of all other persons.] The actual enumeration shall be made within three years after the first meeting of the Congress of the United States, and within every subsequent term of ten years, in such manner as they shall by law direct. The number of Representatives shall not exceed one for every thirty thousand, but each State shall have at least one Representative; and until such enumeration shall be made, the State of New Hampshire shall be entitled to choose three, Massachusetts eight, Rhode Island and Providence Plantations one, Connecticut five, New York six; New Jersey four, Pennsylvania eight, Delaware one, Maryland six, Virginia ten, North Carolina five, South Carolina five, and Georgia three.

∞ (The preceding portion in brackets is amended by the Fourteenth Amendment, Section 2).

Section 3. The Senate, of the United States shall be composed of two Senators from each State, chosen by the legislature thereof, for six years; and each Senator shall have one vote.

Immediately after they shall be assembled in consequence of the first election, they shall be divided as equally as may be into three classes. The seats of the Senators of the first class shall be vacated at the expiration of the second year, of the second class at the expiration of the fourth year, and of the third class at the expiration of the sixth year, so that one-third may be chosen every second year; and if vacancies happen by resignation, or otherwise, during the recess of the legislature of any State, the Executive thereof may make temporary appointments until the next meeting of the legislature, which shall then fill such vacancies.

No person shall be a Senator who shall not have attained to the age of thirty years, and been nine years a citizen of the United States, and who shall not, when elected, be an inhabitant of that State for which he shall be chosen.

The Vice-President of the United States shall be President of the Senate, but shall have no vote, unless they be equally divided.

The Senate shall choose their other officers, and also a President pro tempore, in the absence of the Vice-President, or when he shall exercise the office of President of the United States

The Senate shall have the sole power to try all impeachments. When sitting for that purpose, they shall be on oath or affirmation. When the President of the United States is tried, the Chief Justice shall preside: And no person shall be convicted without the concurrence of two thirds of the members present.

Judgment in cases of impeachment shall not extend further than to removal from office, and disqualification to hold and enjoy any office of honor, trust or profit under the United States: but the party convicted shall nevertheless be liable and subject to indictment, trial, judgment and punishment, according to Law.

Section 4. The times, places and manner of holding elections for Senators and Representatives, shall be prescribed in each State by the legislature thereof; but the Congress may at any time by law make or alter such regulations, except as to the places of choosing Senators.

The Congress shall assemble at least once in every year, and such meeting shall be on the first Monday in December, unless they shall by law appoint a different day.

Section 5. Each House shall be the judge of the elections, returns and qualifications of its own members, and a majority of each shall constitute a quorum to do business; but a smaller number may adjourn from day to day, and may be authorized to compel the attendance of absent members, in such manner, and under such penalties as each House may provide.

Each House may determine the rules of its proceedings, punish its members for disorderly behavior, and, with the concurrence of two thirds, expel a member.

Each House shall keep a Journal of its proceedings, and from time to time publish the same, excepting such parts as may in their judgment require secrecy; and the yeas and nays of the members of either House on any question shall, at the desire of one fifth of those present, be entered on the Journal.

Neither House, during the session of Congress, shall, without the consent of the other, adjourn for more than three days, nor to any other place than that in which the two Houses shall be sitting.

Section 6.   The Senators and Representatives shall receive a compensation for their services, to be ascertained by law, and paid out of the Treasury of the United States. They shall in all cases, except treason, felony and breach of the peace, be privileged from arrest during their attendance at the session of their respective Houses, and in going to and returning from the same; and for any speech or debate in either House, they shall not be questioned in any other place.

No Senator or Representative shall, during the time for which he was elected, be appointed to any civil office under the authority of the United States, which shall have been created, or the emoluments whereof shall have been increased during such time; and no person holding any office under the United States, shall be a member of either House during his continuance in office.

Section 7. All bills for raising revenue shall originate in the House of Representatives; but the Senate may propose or concur with amendments as on other bills.

Every bill which shall have passed the House of Representatives and the Senate, shall, before it becomes a law, be presented to the President of the United States; If he approve he shall sign it, but if not he shall return it, with his objections to that House in which it shall have originated, who shall enter the objections at large on their Journal, and proceed to reconsider it. If after such reconsideration two thirds of that House shall agree to pass the bill, it shall be sent, together with the objections, to the other House, by which it shall likewise be reconsidered, and if approved by two thirds of that House, it shall become a law. But in all such cases the votes of both Houses shall be determined by yeas and nays, and the names of the persons voting for and against the bill shall be entered on the journal of each House respectively. If any bill shall not be returned by the President within ten days (Sundays excepted) after it shall have been presented to him, the same shall be a law, in like manner as if he had signed it, unless the Congress by their adjournment prevent its return, in which case it shall not be a law.

Every order, resolution, or vote to which the concurrence of the Senate and House of Representatives may be necessary (except on a question of adjournment) shall be presented to the President of the United States; and before the same shall take effect, shall be approved by him, or being disapproved by him, shall be repassed by two thirds of the Senate and House of Representatives, according to the rules and limitations prescribed in the case of a bill.

Section 8.   The Congress shall have power to lay and collect taxes, duties, imposts and excises, to pay the debts and provide for the common defense and general welfare of the United States; but all duties, imposts and excises shall be uniform throughout the United States;

To borrow money on the credit of the United States;

To regulate commerce with foreign nations, and among the several States, and with the Indian tribes;

To establish an uniform rule of naturalization, and uniform laws on the subject of bankruptcies throughout the United States;

To coin money, regulate the value thereof, and of foreign coin, and fix the standard of weights and measures;

To provide for the punishment of counterfeiting the securities and current coin of the United States;

To establish post offices and post roads;

To promote the progress of science and useful arts, by securing for limited times to authors and inventors the exclusive rights to their respective writings and discoveries;

To constitute tribunals inferior to the Supreme Court;

To define and punish piracies and felonies committed on the high seas, and offences against the law of nations;

To declare war, grant letters of marque and reprisal, and make rules concerning captures on land and water;

To raise and support armies, but no appropriation of money to that use shall be for a longer term than two years;

To provide and maintain a Navy;

To make rules for the government and regulation of the land and naval Forces;

To provide for calling forth the militia to execute the laws of the Union, suppress insurrections and repel invasions;

To provide for organizing, arming, and disciplining, the militia, and for governing such part of them as may be employed in the service of the United States, reserving to the States respectively, the appointment of the officers, and the authority of training the militia according to the discipline prescribed by Congress;

To exercise exclusive legislation in all cases whatsoever, over such district (not exceeding ten miles square) as may, by cession of particular States, and the acceptance of Congress, become the seat of the government of the United States, and to exercise like authority over all places purchased by the consent of the legislature of the State in which the same shall be, for the erection of forts, magazines, arsenals, dock-yards, and other needful buildings;—and

To make all laws which shall be necessary and proper for carrying into execution the foregoing powers, and all other powers vested by this Constitution in the government of the United States, or in any department or officer thereof.

Section 9. The migration or importation of such persons as any of the States now existing shall think proper to admit, shall not be prohibited by the Congress prior to the year one thousand eight hundred and eight, but a tax or duty may be imposed on such importation, not exceeding ten dollars for each person.

The privilege of the writ of Habeas Corpus shall not be suspended, unless when in cases of rebellion or invasion the public safety may require it.

No bill of attainder or ex post facto law shall be passed.

No capitation, or other direct, tax shall be laid, unless in proportion to the census or enumeration herein before directed to be taken.

No tax or duty shall be laid on articles exported from any State.

No preference shall be given by any regulation of commerce or revenue to the ports of one State over those of another: nor shall vessels bound to, or from, one State, be obliged to enter, clear, or pay duties in another.

No money shall be drawn from the Treasury, but in consequence of appropriations made by law; and a regular statement and account of the receipts and expenditures of all public money shall be published from time to time.

No title of nobility shall be granted by the United States: And no person holding any office of profit or trust under them, shall, without the consent of the Congress, accept of any present, emolument, office, or title, of any kind whatever, from any king, prince, or foreign State.

Section 10. No State shall enter into any treaty, alliance, or confederation; grant letters of marque and reprisal; coin money, emit bills of credit; make any thing but gold and silver coin a tender in payment of debts; pass any bill of attainder, ex post facto law, or law impairing the obligation of contracts, or grant any title of nobility.

No State shall, without the consent of the Congress, lay any imposts of duties on imports or exports, except what may be absolutely necessary for executing its inspection laws: and the net produce of all duties and imposts, laid by any State on imports or exports, shall be for the use of the Treasury of the United States; and all such laws shall be subject to the revision and control of the Congress.

No State shall, without the consent of Congress, lay any duty of tonnage, keep troops, or ships of war in time of peace, enter into any agreement or compact with another State, or with a foreign power, or engage in war, unless actually invaded, or in such imminent danger as will not admit of delay.

ARTICLE II

Section 1. The executive power shall be vested in a President of the United States of America. He shall hold his office during the term of four years, and, together with the Vice-President, chosen for the same term, be elected, as follows:

Each State shall appoint in such manner as the legislature thereof may direct, a number of electors, equal to the whole number of Senators and Representatives to which the State may be entitled in the Congress: but no Senator or Representative, or person holding an office of trust or profit under the United States, shall be appointed an elector.

∞ ["The electors shall meet in their respective States, and vote by ballot for two persons, of whom one at least shall not be an inhabitant of the same State with themselves. And they shall make a list of all the persons voted for, and of the number of votes for each; which list they shall sign and certify, and transmit sealed to the seat of the government of the United States, directed to the President of the Senate. The President of the Senate shall, in the presence of the Senate and House of Representatives, open all the certificates, and the votes shall then be counted. The person having the greatest number of votes shall be the President, if such number be a majority of the whole number of electors appointed; and if there be more than one who have such majority, and have an equal number of votes, then the House of Representatives shall immediately choose by ballot one of them for President; and if no person have a majority, then from the five highest on the list the said House shall in like manner choose the President. But in choosing the President, the votes shall be taken by States, the representation from each State having one vote; a quorum for this purpose shall consist of a member or members from two-thirds of the States, and a majority of all the States shall be necessary to a choice. In every case, after the choice of the President, the person having the greatest number of votes of the electors shall be the Vice-President. But if there should remain two or more who have equal votes, the Senate shall choose from them by ballot the Vice-President."]

∞ (The preceding section has been superseded by the Twelfth Amendment).

The Congress may determine the time of choosing the electors, and the day on which they shall give their votes; which day shall be the same throughout the United States.

No person except a natural born citizen, or a citizen of the United States, at the time of the adoption of this Constitution, shall be eligible to the office of President; neither shall any person be eligible to that office who shall not have attained to the age of thirty-five years, and been fourteen years a resident within the United States.

In case of the removal of the President from office, or of his death, resignation, or inability to discharge the powers and duties of the said office, the same shall devolve on the Vice-President, and the Congress may by law provide for the case of removal, death, resignation, or inability, both of the President and Vice-President, declaring what officer shall then act as President, and such officer shall act accordingly, until the disability be removed, or a President shall be elected.

The President shall, at stated times, receive for his services, a compensation, which shall neither be increased nor diminished during the period for which he shall have been elected, and he shall not receive within that period any other emolument from the United States, or any of them.

Before he enter on the execution of his office, he shall take the following oath or affirmation: — "I do solemnly swear (or affirm) that I will faithfully execute the office of President of the United States, and will to the best of my ability, preserve, protect and defend the Constitution of the United States."

Section 2. The President shall be Commander in Chief of the Army and Navy of the United States, and of the militia of the several States, when called into the actual service of the United States; he may require the opinion, in writing, of the principal officer in each of the executive departments, upon any subject relating to the duties of their respective offices, and he shall have power to grant reprieves and pardons for offenses against the United States, except in cases of impeachment.

He shall have power, by and with the advice and consent of the Senate, to make treaties, provided two thirds of the Senators present concur; and he shall nominate, and by and with the advice and consent of the Senate, shall appoint Ambassadors, other public Ministers and Consuls, Judges of the Supreme Court, and all other Officers of the United States, whose appointments are not herein otherwise provided for, and which shall be established by law: but the Congress may by law vest the appointment of such inferior Officers, as they think proper, in the President alone, in the Courts of law, or in the heads of departments.

The President shall have power to fill up all vacancies that may happen during the recess of the Senate, by granting commissions which shall expire at the end of their next session.

Section 3. He shall from time to time give to the Congress information of the State of the Union, and recommend to their consideration such measures as he shall judge necessary and expedient; he may, on extraordinary occasions, convene both Houses, or either of them, and in case of disagreement between them, with respect to the time of adjournment, he may adjourn them to such time as he shall think proper; he shall receive Ambassadors and other public Ministers; he shall take care that the laws be faithfully executed, and shall commission all the officers of the United States.

Section 4. The President, Vice-President and all civil officers of the United States, shall be removed from office on impeachment for, and conviction of, treason, bribery, or other high crimes and misdemeanors.

ARTICLE III

Section 1. The judicial power of the United States, shall be vested in one Supreme Court, and in such inferior Courts as the Congress may from time to time ordain and establish. The Judges, both of the Supreme and inferior Courts, shall hold their offices during good behaviour, and shall, at stated times, receive for their services, a compensation, which shall not be diminished during their continuance in office.

Section 2. The judicial power shall extend to all cases, in law and equity, arising under this Constitution, the laws of the United States, and treaties made, or which shall be made, under their authority:—to all cases affecting Ambassadors, other public Ministers and Consuls;—to all cases of admiralty and maritime jurisdiction;—to controversies to which the United States shall be a party;—to controversies between two or more States;—between a State and citizens of another State;—between citizens of different States,—between citizens of the same State claiming lands under grants of different States, and between a State, or the citizens thereof, and foreign States, citizens or subjects.

In all cases affecting Ambassadors, other public Ministers and Consuls, and those in which a State shall be party, the Supreme Court shall have original jurisdiction. In all the other cases before mentioned, the Supreme Court shall have appellate jurisdiction, both as to law and fact, with such exceptions, and under such regulations as the Congress shall make.

The trial of all crimes, except in cases of impeachment, shall be by jury; and such trial shall be held in the State where the said crimes shall have been committed; but when not committed within any State, the trial shall be at such place or places as the Congress may by law have directed.

Section 3. Treason against the United States, shall consist only in levying war against them, or in adhering to their enemies, giving them aid and comfort. No person shall be convicted of treason unless on the testimony of two witnesses to the same overt act, or on confession in open court.

The Congress shall have power to declare the punishment of treason, but no attainder of treason shall work corruption of blood, or forfeiture except during the life of the person attainted.

ARTICLE IV

Section 1. Full faith and credit shall be given in each State to the public acts, records, and judicial proceedings of every other State. And the Congress may by general laws prescribe the manner in which such acts, records and proceedings shall be proved, and the effect thereof.

Section 2. The citizens of each State shall be entitled to all privileges and immunities of citizens in the several States.

A person charged in any State with treason, felony, or other crime, who shall flee from justice, and be found in another state, shall on demand of the executive authority of the State from which he fled, be delivered up to be removed to the State having jurisdiction of the crime.

No person held to service or labour in one State, under the laws thereof, escaping into another, shall, in consequence of any law or regulation therein, be discharged from such service or labour, but shall be delivered up on claim of the party to whom such service or labour may be due.

Section 3. New States may be admitted by the Congress into this Union; but no new State shall be formed or erected within the jurisdiction of any other State; nor any State be formed by the junction of two or more States, or parts of States, without the consent of the legislatures of the States concerned as well as of the Congress.

The Congress shall have power to dispose of and make all needful rules and regulations respecting the territory or other property belonging to the United States; and nothing in this Constitution shall be so construed as to prejudice any claims of the United States, or of any particular State.

Section 4. The United States shall guarantee to every State in this Union a republican form of government, and shall protect each of them against invasion; and on application of the legislature, or of the Executive (when the legislature cannot be convened) against domestic violence.

ARTICLE V

The Congress, whenever two thirds of both Houses shall deem it necessary, shall propose amendments to this Constitution, or, on the application of the legislatures of two thirds of the several States, shall call a convention for proposing amendments, which, in either case, shall be valid to all intents and purposes, as part of this Constitution, when ratified by the legislatures of three fourths of the several States, or by conventions in three fourths thereof, as the one or the other mode of ratification may be proposed by the Congress; provided that no amendment which may be made prior to the year one thousand eight hundred and eight shall in any manner affect the first and fourth clauses in the ninth section of the first article; and that no State, without its consent, shall be deprived of its equal suffrage in the Senate.

ARTICLE VI

All debts contracted and engagements entered into, before the adoption of this Constitution, shall be as valid against the United States under this Constitution, as under the Confederation.

This Constitution, and the laws of the United States which shall be made in pursuance thereof; and all treaties made, or which shall be made, under the authority of the United States, shall be the supreme law of the land; and the judges in every State shall be bound thereby, any thing in the Constitution or laws of any State to the contrary notwithstanding.

The Senators and Representatives before mentioned, and the members of the several State legislatures, and all executive and judicial officers, both of the United States and of the several States, shall be bound by oath or affirmation, to support this Constitution; but no religious test shall ever be required as a qualification to any office or public trust under the United States.

ARTICLE VII

The ratification of the conventions of nine States, shall be sufficient for the establishment of this Constitution between the States so ratifying the same.

DONE in convention by the unanimous consent of the States present the seventeenth day of September in the Year of our Lord one thousand seven hundred and eighty seven, and of the independence of the United States of America the twelfth.

Amendments to the Constitution

AMENDMENT I

(First ten amendments adopted June 15, 1790)

Congress shall make no law respecting an establishment of religion, or prohibiting the free exercise thereof; or abridging the freedom of speech, or of the press; or the right of the people peaceably to assemble, and to petition the Government for a redress of grievances.

AMENDMENT II

A well regulated militia, being necessary to the security of a free State, the right of the people to keep and bear arms, shall not be infringed.

AMENDMENT III

No soldier shall, in time of peace be quartered in any house, without the consent of the owner, nor in time of war, but in a manner to be prescribed by law.

AMENDMENT IV

The right of the people to be secure in their persons, houses, papers, and effects, against unreasonable searches and seizures, shall not be violated, and no warrants shall issue, but upon probable cause, supported by oath or affirmation, and particularly describing the place to be searched, and the persons or things to be seized.

AMENDMENT V

No person shall be held to answer for a capital, or otherwise infamous crime, unless on a presentment or indictment of a grand jury, except in cases arising in the land or naval forces, or in the militia, when in actual service in time of war or public danger; nor shall any person be subject for the same offence to be twice put in jeopardy of life or limb; nor shall be compelled in any criminal case to be a witness against himself, nor be deprived of life, liberty, or property, without due process of law; nor shall private property be taken for public use, without just compensation.

AMENDMENT VI

In all criminal prosecutions, the accused shall enjoy the right to a speedy and public trial, by an impartial jury of the State and district wherein the crime shall have been committed, which district shall have been previously ascertained by law, and to be informed of the nature and cause of the accusation; to be confronted with the witnesses against him; to have compulsory process for obtaining witnesses in his favor, and to have the assistance of counsel for his defence.

AMENDMENT VII

In suits at common law, where the value in controversy shall exceed twenty dollars, the right of trial by jury shall be preserved, and no fact tried by a jury shall be otherwise re-examined in any Court of the United States, than according to the rules of the common law.

AMENDMENT VIII

Excessive bail shall not be required, nor excessive fines imposed, nor cruel and unusual punishments inflicted.

AMENDMENT IX

The enumeration in the Constitution, of certain rights, shall not be construed to deny or disparage others retained by the people.

AMENDMENT X

The powers not delegated to the United States by the Constitution, nor prohibited by it to the States, are reserved to the States respectively, or to the people.

AMENDMENT XI

(Adopted January 8, 1798)

The judicial power of the United States shall not be construed to extend to any suit in law or equity, commenced or prosecuted against one of the United States by citizens of another State, or by citizens or subjects of any foreign State.

AMENDMENT XII

(Adopted September 25, 1804)

The electors shall meet in their respective states, and vote by ballot for President and Vice-President, one of whom, at least, shall not be an inhabitant of the same state with themselves; they shall name in their ballots the person voted for as President, and in distinct ballots the person voted for as Vice-President, and they shall make distinct lists of all persons voted for as President, and of all persons voted for as Vice-President, and of the number of votes for each, which lists they shall sign and certify, and transmit sealed to the seat of the government of the United States, directed to the President of the Senate;—the

President of the Senate shall, in the presence of the Senate and House of Representatives, open all the certificates and the votes shall then be counted;—the person having the greatest number of votes for President, shall be the President, if such number be a majority of the whole number of electors appointed; and if no person have such majority, then from the persons having the highest numbers not exceeding three on the list of those voted for as President, the House of Representatives shall choose immediately, by ballot, the President. But in choosing the President, the votes shall be taken by states, the representation from each state having one vote; a quorum for this purpose shall consist of a member or members from two-thirds of the states, and a majority of all the states shall be necessary to a choice. And if the House of Representatives shall not choose a President whenever the right of choice shall devolve upon them, before the fourth day of March next following, then the Vice-President shall act as President, as in the case of the death or other constitutional disability of the President. The person having the greatest number of votes as Vice-President, shall be the Vice-President, if such number be a majority of the whole number of electors appointed, and if no person have a majority, then from the two highest numbers on the list, the Senate shall choose the Vice-President; a quorum for the purpose shall consist of two-thirds of the whole number of Senators, and a majority of the whole number shall be necessary to a choice. But no person constitutionally ineligible to the office of President shall be eligible to that of Vice-President of the United States.

AMENDMENT XIII

(Adopted December 18, 1865)

Section 1. Neither slavery nor involuntary servitude, except as a punishment for crime whereof the party shall have been duly convicted, shall exist within the United States, or any place subject to their jurisdiction.

Section 2. Congress shall have power to enforce this article by appropriate legislation.

AMENDMENT XIV

(Adopted July 21, 1868)

Section 1. All persons born or naturalized in the United States, and subject to the jurisdiction thereof, are citizens of the United States and of the State wherein they reside. No State shall make or enforce any law which shall abridge the privileges or immunities of citizens of the United States; nor shall any State deprive any person of life, liberty, or property, without due process of law; nor deny to any person within its jurisdiction the equal protection of the laws.

Section 2.   Representatives shall be apportioned among the several States according to their respective numbers, counting the whole number of persons in each State, excluding Indians not taxed. But when the right to vote at any election for the choice of electors for President and Vice-President of the United States, Representatives in Congress, the Executive and Judicial officers of a State, or the members of the Legislature thereof, is denied to any of the male inhabitants of each State, being twenty-one years of age, and citizens of the United States, or in any way abridged, except for participation in rebellion, or other crime, the basis of representation therein shall be reduced in the proportion which the number of such male citizens shall bear to the whole number of male citizens twenty-one years of age in such State.

Section 3.   No person shall be a Senator or Representative in Congress, or elector of President and Vice-President, or hold any office, civil or military, under the United States, or under any State, who, having previously taken an oath, as a member of Congress, or as an officer of the United States, or as a member of any State legislature, or as an executive or judicial officer of any State, to support the Constitution of the United States, shall have engaged in insurrection or rebellion against the same, or given aid or comfort to the enemies thereof. But Congress may by a vote of two-thirds of each House, remove such disability.

Section 4.   The validity of the public debt of the United States, authorized by law, including debts incurred for payment of pensions and bounties for services in suppressing insurrection or rebellion, shall not be questioned. But neither the United States nor any State shall assume or pay any debt or obligation incurred in aid of insurrection or rebellion against the United States, or any claim for the loss or emancipation of any slave; but all such debts, obligations and claims shall be held illegal and void.

Section 5.   The Congress shall have power to enforce, by appropriate legislation, the provisions of this article.

AMENDMENT XV
(Adopted March 30, 1870)

Section 1.   The right of citizens of the United States to vote shall not be denied or abridged by the United States or by any State on account of race, color, or previous condition of servitude.

Section 2. The Congress shall have power to enforce this article by appropriate legislation.

AMENDMENT XVI
(Adopted February 25, 1913)

The Congress shall have power to lay and collect taxes on incomes, from whatever source derived, without apportionment among the several States, and without regard to any census or enumeration.

AMENDMENT XVII
(Adopted May 31, 1913.)

The Senate of the United States shall be composed of two Senators from each State, elected by the people thereof, for six years; and each Senator shall have one vote. The electors in each State shall have the qualifications requisite for electors of the most numerous branch of the State legislatures.

When vacancies happen in the representation of any State in the Senate, the executive authority of such State shall issue writs of election to fill such vacancies; *Provided,* That the legislature of any State may empower the executive thereof to make temporary appointments until the people fill the vacancies by election as the legislature may direct.

This amendment shall not be so construed as to affect the election or term of any Senator chosen before it becomes valid as a part of the Constitution.

AMENDMENT XVIII
(Adopted January 29, 1919)

Section 1. After one year from the ratification of this article the manufacture, sale, or transportation of intoxicating liquors within, the importation thereof into, or the exportation thereof from the United States and all territory subject to the jurisdiction thereof for beverage purposes is hereby prohibited.

Section 2. The Congress and the several States shall have concurrent power to enforce this article by appropriate legislation.

Section 3. This article shall be inoperative unless it shall have been ratified as an amendment to the Constitution by the legislatures of the several States, as provided in the Constitution, within seven years from the date of the submission hereof to the States by the Congress.

AMENDMENT XIX

(Adopted August 26, 1920)

The right of citizens of the United States to vote shall not be denied or abridged by the United States or by any State on account of sex.

Congress shall have power to enforce this article by appropriate legislation.

AMENDMENT XX

(Adopted January 23, 1933)

Section 1. The terms of the President and Vice-President shall end at noon on the 20th day of January, and the terms of Senators and Representatives at noon on the 3rd day of January, of the years in which such terms would have ended if this article had not been ratified; and the terms of their successors shall then begin.

Section 2. The Congress shall assemble at least once in every year, and such meeting shall begin at noon on the 3rd day of January, unless they shall by law appoint a different day.

Section 3. If, at the time fixed for the beginning of the term of the President, the President elect shall have died, the Vice-President elect shall become President. If a President shall not have been chosen before the time fixed for the beginning of his term, or if the President elect shall have failed to qualify, then the Vice-President elect shall act as President until a President shall have qualified; and the Congress may by law provide for the case wherein neither a President elect nor a Vice-President elect shall have qualified, declaring who shall then act as President, or the manner in which one who is to act shall be selected, and such person shall act accordingly until a President or Vice-President shall have qualified.

Section 4. The Congress may by law provide for the case of the death of any of the persons from whom the House of Representatives may choose a President whenever the right of choice shall have devolved upon them, and for the case of the death of any of the persons from whom the Senate may choose a Vice-President whenever the right of choice shall have devolved upon them.

Section 5. Sections 1 and 2 shall take effect on the 15th day of October following the ratification of this article (Oct., 1933).

Section 6. This article shall be inoperative unless it shall have been ratified as an amendment to the Constitution by the Legislatures of three-fourths of the several States within seven years from the date of its submission.

AMENDMENT XXI

(Adopted December 5, 1933)

Section 1.   The eighteenth article of amendment to the Constitution of the United States is hereby repealed.

Section 2.   The transportation or importation into any State, Territory, or Possession of the United States for delivery or use therein of intoxicating liquors, in violation of the laws thereof, is hereby prohibited.

Section 3.   This article shall be inoperative unless it shall have been ratified as an amendment to the Constitution by conventions in the several States, as provided in the Constitution, within seven years from the date of the submission hereof to the States by the Congress.

AMENDMENT XXII

(Adopted February 27, 1951)

Section 1.   No person shall be elected to the office of the President more than twice, and no person who has held the office of President, or acted as President, for more than two years of a term to which some other person was elected President shall be elected to the office of the President more than once.   But this Article shall not apply to any person holding the office of President when this Article was proposed by the Congress, and shall not prevent any person who may be holding the office of President, or acting as President, during the term within which this Article becomes operative from holding the office of President or acting as President during the remainder of such term.

Section 2.   This article shall be inoperative unless it shall have been ratified as an amendment to the Constitution by the Legislatures of three-fourths of the several States within seven years from the date of its submission to the States by the Congress.

AMENDMENT XXIII

(Adopted March 29, 1961)

Section 1.   The District constituting the seat of Government of the United States shall appoint in such manner as the Congress may direct:

A number of electors of President and Vice-President equal to the whole number of Senators and Representatives in Congress to which the District would be entitled if it were a State, but in no event more than the least populous State; they shall be in addition to those appointed by the States, but they shall be considered, for the purposes of the election of President and Vice-President, to be electors appointed by a State; and they shall meet in the District and perform such duties as provided by the twelfth article of amendment.

Section 2. The Congress shall have power to enforce this article by appropriate legislation.

Amendment XXIV

(Adopted January 23, 1964)

Section 1. The right of citizens of the United States to vote in any primary or other election for President or Vice-President, for electors for President or Vice-President, or for Senator or Representative in Congress, shall not be denied or abridged by the United States or any State by reason of failure to pay any poll tax or other tax.

Section 2. The Congress shall have power to enforce this article by appropriate legislation.

AMENDMENT XXV

(Adopted February 10, 1965)

Section 1. In case of the removal of the President from office or of his death or resignation, the Vice-President shall become President.

Section 2. Whenever there is a vacancy in the office of the Vice-President, the President shall nominate a Vice-President who shall take office upon confirmation by a majority vote of both houses of Congress.

Section 3. Whenever the President transmits to the President pro tempore of the Senate and the Speaker of the House of Representatives his written declaration that he is unable to discharge the powers and duties of his office, and until he transmits to them a written declaration to the contrary, such powers and duties shall be discharged by the Vice-President as Acting President.

Section 4. Whenever the Vice-President and a majority of either the principal officers of the executive departments or of such other body as Congress may by law provide, transmit to the President pro tempore of the Senate and the Speaker of the House of Representatives their written declaration that the President is unable to discharge the powers and duties of his office, the Vice-President shall immediately assume the powers and duties of the office as Acting President

Thereafter, when the President transmits to the President pro tempore of the Senate and the Speaker of the House of Representatives his written declaration that no inability exists, he shall resume the powers and duties of his office unless the Vice-

President and a majority of either the principal officers of the executive department or of such other body as Congress may by law provide, transmit within four days to the President pro tempore of the Senate and the Speaker of the House of Representatives their written declaration that the President is unable to discharge the powers and duties of his office. Thereupon Congress shall decide the issue, assembling within forty-eight hours for that purpose if not in session. If the Congress, within twenty-one days after receipt of the latter written declaration, or, if Congress is not in session, within twenty-one days after Congress is required to assemble, determines by two-thirds vote of both houses that the President is unable to discharge the powers and duties of his office, the Vice-President shall continue to discharge the same as Acting President; otherwise, the President shall resume the powers and duties of his office.

AMENDMENT XXVI

(Adopted July 1, 1971)

Section 1. The right of citizens of the United States, who are 18 years of age or older, to vote shall not be denied or abridged by the United States or any state on account of age.

Section 2. The Congress shall have the power to enforce this article by appropriate legislation.

AMENDMENT XXVII

(Adopted May 7, 1992)

No law, varying the compensation for the services of the Senators and Representatives, shall take effect, until an election of Representatives shall have intervened.

Appendix C

List of Cases Cited

Abington v. *Schempp;* 374 U.S. 203 (1963)

American Federation of Labor v. *American Sash & Door Co.;* 335 U.S. 538 (1949)

Anderson v. *Salt Lake City Corporation;* 475 F.2d 29 (10th Cir. 1973), *cert. denied,* 414 U.S. 879

Baer v. *Kolmorgen;* 181 N.Y.S.2d 230 (Sup.Ct.N.Y. 1958)

Barron v. *Baltimore;* 32 U.S. 243 (1833)

Bishop v. *Colaw;* 450 F.2d 1069 (Ct.App.Mo. 1972)

Board of Education of Westside Community Schools v. *Mergens;* —U.S.—, 110 L.Ed.2d 191 (1990)

Bogen v. *Doty;* 598 F.2d 1110 (1979)

Brandon v. *Board of Education of Guilderland Central School District;* 487 F.Supp. 1219, *affirmed,* 635 F.2d 971 (2nd Cir. 1980), *cert. denied,* 454 U.S. 1123 (1980)

Cantwell v. *State of Connecticut;* 310 U.S. 296 (1940)

Chambers v. *Marsh;* 675 F.2d 228 (8th Cir. 1982); *review allowed,* 463 U.S. 783 (1984)

Cherokee Nation v. *Georgia;* 5 Pet. 1 (1831)

Church of the Holy Trinity v. *U. S.;* 143 U.S. 457 (1892)

City of Charleston v. *S. A. Benjamin;* 2 Strob. 508 (Sup.Ct.S.C. 1846)

Cohen v. *California;* 403 U.S. 15 (1971)

Collins v. *Chandler Unified School District;* 644 F.2d 759 (9th Cir. 1981), *cert. denied,* 454 U.S. 863, (1981)

Commissioner of Education v. *School Committee of Leyden;* 267 N.E.2d 226 (Sup.Ct.Mass. 1971), *cert. denied,* 404 U.S. 849

Committee for Public Education v. *Nyquist;* 413 U.S. 756 (1973)

Commonwealth v. *Abner Kneeland;* 37 Mass. (20 Pick) 206 (Sup.Ct.Mass. 1838)

Commonwealth v. *Jesse Sharpless and Others;* 2 Serg. & R. 91 (Sup.Ct.Penn. 1815)

Commonwealth v. *Wolf;* 3 Serg. & R. 48 (Sup.Ct.Penn. 1817)

County of Allegheny v. *ACLU;* —U.S.—, 106 L.Ed.2d 472 (1989)

Davis v. *Beason;* 133 U.S. 333 (1890)

DeSpain v. *DeKalb County Community School District;* 255 F.2d 655 (N.D.Ill. 1966), *cert. denied,* 390 U.S. 906 (1967)

Dred Scott v. *Sanford,* 60 U.S. 393 (1857)

Engel v. *Vitale;* 370 U.S. 421 (1962)

Epperson v. *Arkansas;* 393 U.S. 97 (1968)

Erznoznik v. *City of Jacksonville;* 422 U.S. 205 (1975)

Everson v. *Board of Education;* 330 U.S. 1 (1947)

Finot v. *Pasadena City Board of Education;* 58 Cal.Rptr. 520 (Ct.App.2nd Dist.Cal. 1967)

Florey v. *Sioux Falls School District;* 464 F.Supp. 911 (D.C.S.D. 1979), 619 F.2d 1311 (8th Cir. 1980), *cert. denied,* 449 U.S. 987 (1980)

Graham v. *Central Community School District of Decatur County;* 608 F.Supp. 531 (D.C.S.D.Iowa 1985)

Graves v. *New York ex. rel. O'Keefe;* 306 U.S. 466 (1939)

Grove v. *Mead School District* 753 F.2d 1528 (9th Cir. 1985), *cert. denied,* 474 U.S. 826

Kay v. *Douglas School District;* 719 P.2d 875 (Or.App. 1986), *review allowed,* 727 P.2d 977 (1986)
Lanner v. *Wimmer;* 662 F.2d 1349 (10th Cir. 1981)
Lemon v. *Kurtzman;* 403 U.S. 602 (1971)
Levitt v. *Committee for Public Education;* 413 U.S. 472 (1973)
Lowe v. *City of Eugene;* 451 P.2d 117 (1969), *cert. denied,* 434 U.S. 876
Lynch v. *Donnelly;* 465 U.S. 668 (1985)
Malnak v. *Yogi;* 440 F.Supp. 1285 (D.C.N.J. 1977)
Marbury v. *Madison;* 1 Cranch 137 (1803)
Marsh v. *Chambers;* 463 U.S. 783 (1982)
McCollum v. *Board of Education;* 333 U.S. 203 (1948)
M'Creery's Lessee v. *Allender;* 4 H. & Mett. 259 (1799)
McCulloch v. *Maryland;* 4 Wheaton 316 (1819)
McGowan v. *Maryland;* 366 U.S. 420 (1960)
Murdock v. *Pennsylvania;* 319 U.S. 105 (1943)
Murphy v. *Ramsey;* 144 U.S. 15 (1885)
New York Trust Co. v. *Eisner;* 256 U.S. 345 (1921)
Osborn v. *United States Bank;* 9 Wheaton 738 (1824)
People v. *Ruggles;* 8 Johns 545 (Sup.Ct.N.Y. 1811)
Pierce v. *Society of Sisters;* 268 U.S. 510 (1925)
Reed v. *van Hoven;* 237 F.Supp. 48 (W.D.Mich. 1965)
Rex v. *Woolston;* 2 Strange 834 (93 E.R. 881), Fitz-g. 64 (94 E.R. 655) (1731)
Reynolds v. *U. S.;* 98 U.S. 145 (1878)
Ring v. *Grand Forks Public School District;* 483 F.Supp. 272 (D.C.N.D. 1980)
Runkel v. *Winemiller;* 4 Harris & McHenry 276 (Sup.Ct.Md. 1799)
State Board of Education v. *Board of Education of Netcong;* 262 A.2d 21 (Sup.Ct.N.J. 1970), *cert. denied,* 401 U.S. 1013
State of Ohio v. *Whisner;* 351 N.E.2d 750 (Sup.Ct.Ohio 1976)
State v. *Smith Clark;* 5 Dutcher (29 N.J. Law) 96 (Sup.Ct.N.J. 1860)
Stein v. *Oshinsky;* 348 F.2d 999 (2nd Cir. 1965), *cert. denied,* 382 U.S. 957
Stone v. *Graham;* 449 U.S. 39 (1980)
Swann v. *Pack;* 527 S.W.2d 99 (Sup.Ct.Tn. 1975)
Theriault v. *Silber;* 453 F.Supp. 254 (W.D.Tex. 1978)
Trietley v. *Board of Education of the City of Buffalo;* 409 N.Y.S.2d 912 (Sup.Ct.N.Y. 1978)
Trop v. *Dulles;* 356 U.S. 86 (1958)
Union Pacific Railway Co. v. *Botsford;* 141 U.S. 250 (1891)
United States v. *Kirby;* 74 U.S. 482 (1868)
United States v. *Macintosh;* 283 U.S. 605 (1931)
Updegraph v. *The Commonwealth;* 11 Serg. & R. 393 (Sup.Ct.Penn. 1824)
Vidal v. *Girard's Executors;* 43 U.S. 126 (1844)
Wallace v. *Ford;* 346 F.Supp. 156 (D.C.Ark. 1972)
Wallace v. *Jaffree;* 472 U.S. 38 (1985)
Walz v. *Tax Commission;* 397 U.S. 664 (1970)
Worcester v. *Georgia;* 6 Pet. 515 (1832)
Zorach v. *Clauson;* 343 U.S. 306 (1952)

Footnotes

Chapter 1
The Way It Is

1. *Everson* v. *Board of Education;* 330 U.S. 1, 18 (1947).

2. *Engel* v. *Vitale;* 370 U.S. 421 (1962).

3. *Abington* v. *Schempp;* 374 U.S. 203 (1963).

4. *Commissioner of Education* v. *School Committee of Leyden;* 267 N.E.2d 226 (Sup.Ct.Mass. 1971), *cert. denied,* 404 U.S. 849.

5. *Stein* v. *Oshinsky;* 348 F.2d 999 (2nd Cir. 1965), *cert. denied,* 382 U.S. 957.

6. *Collins* v. *Chandler Unified School District;* 644 F.2d 759 (9th Cir. 1981), *cert. denied,* 454 U.S. 863.

7. *Reed* v. *van Hoven;* 237 F.Supp. 48 (W.D.Mich. 1965).

8. *DeSpain* v. *DeKalb County Community School District;* 255 F.Supp. 655 (N.D.Ill. 1966), *cert. denied,* 390 U.S. 906 (1967).

9. *Lowe* v. *City of Eugene;* 451 P.2d 117 (1969), *cert. denied,* 434 U.S. 876.

10. *State Board of Education* v. *Board of Education of Netcong;* 262 A.2d 21 (Sup.Ct.N.J. 1970), *cert. denied,* 401 U.S. 1013.

11. *State of Ohio* v. *Whisner;* 351 N.E.2d 750 (Sup.Ct.Ohio 1976).

12. *Florey* v. *Sioux Falls School District;* 464 F.Supp. 911 (D.C.S.D. 1979), *cert. denied,* 449 U.S. 987 (1980).

13. *Stone* v. *Graham;* 449 U.S. 39 (1980).

14. *Ring* v. *Grand Forks Public Sch. Dist.;* 483 F.Supp. 272 (D.C.N.D. 1980).

15. *Lanner* v. *Wimmer;* 662 F.2d 1349 (10th Cir. 1981) .

16. *Wallace* v. *Jaffree;* 472 U.S. 38 (1985).

17. *Id.*

18. *Graham* v. *Central Community School District of Decatur County;* 608 F.Supp. 531 (D.C.Iowa 1985).

19. *Kay* v. *Douglas School District;* 719 P.2d 875 (Or.App. 1986).

20. William Murray, "America Without God," *The New American,* June 20, 1988, p. 19.

21. John Eidsmoe, *Christianity and the Constitution* (MI: Baker Book House, 1987), p. 406.

22. Tim LaHaye, *Faith of Our Founding Fathers* (Brentwood, TN: Wolgemuth & Hyatt, Publishers, Inc., 1987), p. 27.

23. *The Washington Times,* December 12, 1988, "Parent silences teaching of carols," "School officials deny banning Bible . . . "

24. *IFA Newsletter,* Feb. 1989, "Fifth Grader Sues for Right to Read Bible."

25. *Walz* v. *Tax Commission;* 397 U.S. 664, 701, 703 (1970).

26. *Id.* at 702, 703.

27. *Id.* at 702.

28. Lawrence A. Cremin, *1963 Yearbook,* World Book Encyclopedia, p. 38.

29. *Baer* v. *Kolmorgen;* 181 N.Y.S.2d 230, 237 (Sup.Ct.N.Y. 1958).

30. Robert Flood, *The Rebirth of America* (Philadelphia: The Arthur S. DeMoss Foundation, 1986), p. 12.

31. *Wallace* v. *Jaffree;* 472 U.S. 38 (1985).

32. Stephen K. McDowell and Mark A. Beliles, *America's Providential History* (Charlottesville, VA: Providence Press, 1989), p. 95.

33. *Trietley* v. *Board of Education of the City of Buffalo;* 409 N.Y.S.2d 912 (Sup.Ct.N.Y. 1978).

34. *Brandon* v. *Board of Education of Guilderland Central School District;* 635 F.2d 971 (2nd Cir. 1980), *cert. denied,* 454 U.S. 1123.

35. Eidsmoe, *Christianity and the Constitution* , p. 405.

36. "The Speech That Shook the Nation," *Forerunner,* Dec. 1984, p. 12.

37. Nadine Strossen, "A Constitutional Analysis of the Equal Access Act's Standards Governing Public School Student Religious Meetings," *Harvard Journal on Legislation,* Winter 1987, Vol. 24:117, p. 118.

38. *Board of Education of Westside Community Schools* v. *Mergens;* — U.S.—, 110 L.Ed.2d 191 (1990)

39. *Stone* v. *Graham;* 449 U.S. 39, 46 (1980).

40. Paul C. Vitz, *Censorship: Evidence of Bias in Our Children's Textbooks* (Ann Arbor, MI: Servant Books, 1986), p. 1.

41. *Id.* at 11.

42. *Id.* at 79-80.

43. *Id.* at 18-19.

44. "The Speech That Shook the Nation," *Forerunner,* Dec. 1984, p. 12.

Chapter 2
The Way It Was—
The Building of the Constitution and the First Amendment

1. M.E. Bradford, *A Worthy Company* (NH: Plymouth Rock Foundation, 1982), p. x.

2. *Church of the Holy Trinity* v. *U. S.;* 143 U.S. 457, 469-470 (1892). See also *The Constitutions of the Several Independent States of America, Published by Order of Congress* (Boston: Norman & Bowen, 1785), pp. 99-100.

3. Bradford, *A Worthy Company,* Table of Contents.

4. *The Constitutions of the Several Independent States of America, Published by Order of Congress* (Boston: Norman & Bowen, 1785), p. 81.

5. Bradford, *A Worthy Company,* Table of Contents.

6. *Supra* note 4 at 31.

7. *Id.* at 138.

8. *Id.* at 108.

9. Bradford, *A Worthy Company,* p. viii-ix.

10. Steve C. Dawson, *God's Providence in America's History* (Rancho Cordova, CA: Steve C. Dawson, 1988), p. 9:6.

11. *Annals of the Congress of the United States—First Congress* (Washington, D.C.: Gales & Seaton, 1834), Vol. I, p. 434.

12. *Id.* at 729, 731.

13. *Id.* at 766.

14. *Sources and Documents Illustrating the American Revolution, 1764-1788, and the Formation of the Federal Constitution,* S. E. Morison, ed. (New York: Oxford University Press, 1923), p. 158.

15. *Id.* at 157-158.

16. *Annals of the Congress,* Vol. I, p. 731.

17. *Supra* note 4 at 6-7.

18. *Id.* at 3-4. See also *The Constitutions of the United States of America with the Latest Amendments* (Trenton: Moore & Lake, 1813), pp. 37-38.

19. *Supra* note 4 at 152.

20. Noah Webster, *American Dictionary of the English Language, 1828* (San Francisco: Foundation for American Christian Education, 1967), see "religion."

21. *Id.*

22. B. F. Morris, *The Christian Life and Character of the Civil Institutions of the United States* (Philadelphia: George W. Childs, 1864), pp. 324, 327.

23. *Id.* at 317, 320-321.

24. Joseph Story, *A Familiar Exposition of the Constitution of the United States* (New York: Harper & Brothers, 1854), p. 259 § 441, p. 261 § 444.

25. Alexis de Tocqueville, *The Republic of the United States of America and Its Political Institutions, Reviewed and Examined,* Henry Reeves, trans. (Garden City, NY: A. S. Barnes & Co., 1851), Vol. I, p. 335.

26. *Id.* at 334.

27. *The Constitutions of the United States of America with the Latest Amendments* (Trenton: Moore & Lake, 1813), pp. 342, 344.

28. *Church of the Holy Trinity* v. *U. S.;* 143 U.S. 457, 469-470 (1892). See also *supra* note 4 at 99-100.

29. *Supra* note 4 at 108.

30. Edwin Gaustad, *Faith of Our Fathers* (San Francisco: Harper & Row, 1987), pp. 173-174. See also Anson Phelps Stokes, *Church and State in the United States* (NY: Harper & Brothers, 1950), Vol. I, p. 441.

31. Verna M. Hall, *The Christian History of the Constitution of the United States of America* (San Francisco: Foundation for American Christian Education, 1966), p. 262A.

32. Christopher Collier, *Roger Sherman's Connecticut* (Middletown, CT: Wesleyan University Press, 1979), p. 129.

33. John Jay, *The Correspondence and Public Papers of John Jay,* Henry P. Johnston, ed. (New York: G.P. Putnam's Sons, 1890), Vol. IV, p. 393, Oct. 12, 1816.

34. John Eidsmoe, *Christianity and the Constitution* (MI: Baker Book House, 1987), pp. 215-217.

35. *Annals of Congress,* Vol. I, p. 660.

36. *Id.* at 56.

37. *Acts Passed at a Congress of the United States of America* (Hartford: Hudson & Goodwin, 1791), p. 104.

38. *Supra* note 27 at 364.

39. *Id.*

40. Apr. 30, 1802, c. 40, 2 Stat. 173 at 174.

41. *Supra* note 27 at 334.

42. Apr. 13, 1816, c. 56, 3 Stat. 289.

43. Mar. 1, 1817, c. 23, 3 Stat. 348 at 349.

44. *The Constitutions of All the United States According to the Latest Amendments* (Lexington, KY: Thomas T. Skillman, 1817), p. 389.

45. For example, see Alabama, Mar. 2, 1819, c. 47, 3 Stat. 489; Illinois, Dec. 3, 1818, 3 Stat. 536; plus numerous others.

46. M. B. C. True, *A Manual of the History and Civil Government of the State of Nebraska* (Omaha: Gibson, Miller, & Richardson, 1885), p. 34.

47. Robert Flood, *The Rebirth of America* (Philadelphia: The Arthur S. DeMoss Foundation, 1986), p. 20.

Chapter 3
The Origin of the Phrase
"Separation of Church and State"

1. Thomas Jefferson, *Jefferson Writings,* Merrill D. Peterson, ed. (NY: Literary Classics of the United States, Inc., 1984), p. 510, January 1, 1802; see also *Reynolds* v. *U. S.;* 98 U.S. 164 (1878).

2. John Eidsmoe, *Christianity and the Constitution* (MI: Baker Book House, 1987), p. 243.

3. *Documents of American History,* Henry S. Commager, ed. (NY: Appleton-Century-Crofts, Inc., 1948), p. 179.

4. James D. Richardson, *A Compilation of the Messages and Papers of the Presidents, 1789-1897* (Published by Authority of Congress, 1899), Vol. 1, p. 379, March 4, 1805.

5. Thomas Jefferson, *The Writings of Thomas Jefferson,* Albert Bergh, ed. (Washington, D. C.: The Thomas Jefferson Memorial Association, 1904), Vol. XI, p. 428, letter on January 23, 1808.

6. *Everson* v. *Board of Education;* 330 U.S. 1 (1947).

7. *Reynolds* v. *U. S.;* 98 U.S. 145 (1878).

8. Eidsmoe, *Christianity and the Constitution,* pp. 242-243.

9. J. M. O'Neill, *Religion and Education Under the Constitution* (NY: Harper & Brothers, 1949), p. 4.

10. Amos J. Peaslee, *Constitutions of Nations* (Concord, NH: The Rumford Press, 1950), Vol. III, p. 280.

11. Tim LaHaye, *Faith of Our Founding Fathers* (Brentwood, TN: Wolgemuth & Hyatt, Publishers, Inc., 1987), p. 3.

Chapter 4
The Court's Early Rulings

1. *Church of the Holy Trinity* v. *U. S.;* 143 U.S. 457, 458 (1892).

2. *Id.* at 465, 471.

3. *Id.* at 465-468.

4. *Id.* at 470-471.

5. *Id.* at 470.

6. *Updegraph* v. *The Commonwealth;* 11 Serg. & R. 393, 394 (1824).

7. *Id.* at 396. See also Sir William Blackstone, *Commentaries on the Laws of England* (Oxford: Clarendon Press, 1769), Vol. IV, p. 59

8. Robert K. Dornan and Csaba Vedlik, Jr., *Judicial Supremacy: The Supreme Court on Trial* (MA: Plymouth Rock Foundation, 1986), p. 10.

9. John Eidsmoe, *Christianity and the Constitution* (MI: Baker Book House, 1987), p. 57.

10. Donald S. Lutz, *The Origins of American Constitutionalism* (Baton Rouge, LA: Louisiana State University Press, 1988), p. 142

11. *Updegraph* v. *The Commonwealth;* 11 Serg. & R. 393, 398-399 (1824).

12. *Id.* at 399, 402-403, 404-407.

13. *People* v. *Ruggles;* 8 Johns 545 (1811).

14. *Id.*

15. *Id.*

16. *Id.* at 545-547.

17. *Id.* at 547.

18. *Commonwealth* v. *Abner Kneeland;* 37 Mass. (20 Pick) 206, 216-17 (1838).

19. *Id.* at 208.

20. *Id.* at 210.

21. *Id.* at 213.

22. *Id.* at 217.

23. *Id.* at 218.

24. *Id.* at 219.

25. *Vidal* v. *Girard's Executors;* 43 U.S. 126, 132 (1844).

26. *Id.* at 143.

27. *Id.* at 152.

28. *Id.* at 153, 170.

29. *Id.* at 175.

30. *Id.* at 198.

31. *Id.* at 205-206.

32. *M'Creery's Lessee* v. *Allender;* 4 H. & Mett. 259 (1799).

33. *Id.*

34. *Runkel* v. *Winemiller;* 4 Harris & McHenry 276, 288 (Sup.Ct.Md. 1799).

35. Dr. Sterling Lacy, *Valley of Decision* (Texarkana: Dayspring Productions, 1988), pp. 7-8.

36. *Id.* at 6-7.

37. *Commonwealth* v. *Jesse Sharpless and Others;* 2 Serg. & R. 91, 92 (1815).

38. *Id.* at 97, 101, 102.

39. *Id.* at 103, 104.

40. *Davis* v. *Beason;* 133 U.S. 333, 341-343, 348 (1890).

41. *Id.* at 343.

42. The information about the books *Planned Parenthood* recommends comes from a packet of informational materials dated January 15, 1987, and prepared by California Assemblyman Bill Bradley of the 76th District.

43. Wardell B. Pomeroy, Ph.D., *Boys and Sex* (NY: Delacorte Press, 1981).

44. Wardell B. Pomeroy, Ph.D., *Girls and Sex* (NY: Delacorte Press, 1981).

45. Rocky Mountain Planned Parenthood, *You've Changed the Combination* (Denver: RAJ Publications, 1977).

46. Stephen K. McDowell and Mark A. Beliles, *America's Providential History* (Charlottesville, VA: Providence Press, 1989), p. 179.

47. Abraham Lincoln, *Letters and Addresses of Abraham Lincoln* (NY: Unit Book Publishing Co., 1907), p. 8, January 27, 1837.

48. *Murphy* v. *Ramsey;* 144 U.S. 15, 45 (1885).

49. "Governor Signs Abstinence Bill," California Voter's Guide, Vol. 5, No. 10 (Sacramento: California Coalition for Traditional Values), Fall 1988.

50. *Reynolds* v. *U.S.;* 98 U.S. 145, 165 (1878).

51. *City of Charleston* v. *S. A. Benjamin;* 2 Strob. 508 (1846).

52. *Id.* at 518-520.

53. *Id.* at 521.

54. *Id.* at 522-524.

55. *Id.* at 527, 529.

56. *Commonwealth* v. *Wolf;* 3 Serg. & R. 48, 50 (1817).

57. *United States* v. *Macintosh;* 283 U.S. 605, 625 (1931).

58. *Zorach* v. *Clauson;* 343 U.S. 306, 312-314 (1952).

59. *Id.* at 315.

60. John Jay, *The Correspondence and Public Papers of John Jay,* Henry P. Johnston, ed. (New York: G.P. Putnam's Sons, 1890), Vol. IV, p. 393, Oct. 12, 1816.

61. *Updegraph* v. *The Commonwealth;* 11 Serg. & R. 393, 403 (1824).

62. Joseph Story, *Commentaries on the Constitution* (Boston: Hilliard, Gray & Co., 1833), Vol. III, p. 700, § 988. See also Joseph Story, *A Familiar Exposition of the Constitution of the United States* (New York: Harper & Brothers, 1854), p. 259 § 441, p. 261 § 444.

63. Story, *Commentaries,* Vol. III, p. 700, § 989.

64. Albert J. Beveridge, *The Life of John Marshall* (Boston: Houghton Mifflin, 1919, 1947), Vol. IV, pp. 70-71.

65. Alexis de Tocqueville, *The Republic of the United States of America and Its Political Institutions, Reviewed and Examined,* Henry Reeves, trans. (Garden City, NY: A. S. Barnes & Co., 1851), Vol. I, p. 12.

66. *Id.* at 334.

Chapter 5
Other "Organic Utterances"

1. *Church of the Holy Trinity* v. *U. S.;* 143 U.S. 457, 465, 470-471 (1892).

2. Christopher Columbus, *Christopher Columbus's Book of Prophecies: Reproduction of the Original Manuscript with English Translation,* Kay Brigham, translator (Barcelona, Spain: CLIE, 1990; Ft. Lauderdale: TSELF, 1991), pp. 178-179, 182-183.

3. *Historical Collections: Consisting of State Papers and other Authentic Documents: Intended as Materials for an History of the United States of America,* Ebenezer Hazard, ed. (Philadelphia: T. Dobson, 1792), Vol. I, pp. 50-51.

4. *Id.* at 72.

5. *Church of the Holy Trinity* v. *U. S.;* 143 U.S. 457, 466 (1892). See also note 3 at Vol. I, p. 119.

6. *Supra* note 3 at Vol. I, p. 252.

7. *Democracy, Liberty, and Property: Readings in the American Political Tradition,* Francis W. Coker, ed. (NY: The Macmillan Co., 1942), p. 18-19. Quoting from John Winthrop's *Model of Christian Charity.*

8. *Id.* at 20.

9. *Documentary Source Book of American History, 1606-1889,* William McDonald, ed. (New York: Macmillan Co., 1909), p. 32, and *Documents of American History,* Henry S. Commager, ed. (New York: Appleton-Century-Crofts, Inc. 1948), p. 21. See also *supra* note 3 at Vol. I, pp. 327-328.

10. J. Moss Ives, *The Ark and the Dove* (NY: Cooper Square Publishers, Inc., 1936, 1969), p. 119. See also Joseph Banvard, *Tragic Scenes in the History of Maryland and the Old French War* (Boston: Gould and Lincoln, 1856), p. 32.

11. William Bradford, *History of Plymouth Plantation* (Boston: Little, Brown, and Company, 1856), p. 24.

12. *North Carolina History,* Hugh Talmage Lefler, ed. (Chapel Hill: University of North Carolina Press, 1934, 1956), p. 16.

13. *Supra* note 3 at Vol. II, p. 612.

14. Steve McDowell & Mark Beliles, *America's Providential History* (Charlottesville, VA: Providence Press, 1989), pp. 82-83.

15. *Supra* note 3 at Vol. II, pp. 597-605. See also B. F. Morris, *The Christian Life and Character of the Civil Institutions of the United States* (Philadelphia: George W. Childs, 1864), pp. 65-68.

16. *Id.* at 70-72, 235.

17. *Id.* at 90-91, 234-235.

18. John Fiske, *The Beginnings of New England* (Boston: Houghton, Mifflin & Co., 1898), pp. 127-128.

19. J. Wingate Thornton, *The Pulpit of the American Revolution* (Boston: Gould and Lincoln, 1860), pp. XIX-XX.

20. *The Code of 1650, Being a Compilation of the Earliest Laws and Orders of the General Court of Connecticut* (Hartford: Silus Andrus, 1822), p. 2. See also *Church of the Holy Trinity* v. *U. S.;* 143 U.S. 457, 467 (1892).

21. *Id.*

22. *Supra* note 3 at Vol. I, p. 463.

23. McDonald, p. 46, and Commager, p. 26.

24. Russ Walton, *Biblical Principles of Importance to Godly Christians* (NH: Plymouth Rock Foundation, 1984), p. 356. See also Fiske, p. 136.

25. George Bancroft, *Bancroft's History of the United States* (Boston: Little,

Brown & Co., 1859), Vol. II, pp. 145, 390.

26.   Peter G. Mode, *Sourcebook and Bibliographical Guide for American Church History* (Menasha, WI: George Banta Publishing Co., 1921), pp. 194-195.

27. *Id.* at p. 133.

28. William J. Buck, *William Penn in America* (Philadelphia: William J. Buck, 1888), p. 20. See also *Remember William Penn, 1644-1944, Tercentenary Memorial* (Harrisburg, PA: The Commonwealth of Pennsylvania and Pennsylvania Historical Commission, 1944), and Thomas Clarkson, *Memoirs of the Private and Public Life of William Penn* (London: Longman, Hunt, Rees, Orme, & Brown, 1813), Vol. I, p. 280.

29. Mode, p. 163. See also Clarkson, Vol. I, p. 287.

30. McDowell and Beliles, *America's Providential History*, p. 90. See also Hildegarde Dolson, *William Penn: Quaker Hero* (NY: Random House, 1961), p. 155.

31. Verna M. Hall, *The Christian History of the Constitution of the United States of America* (San Francisco: Foundation for American Christian Education, 1966), p. 262A. See also note 25 at Vol. II, p. 385, and Mason Locke Weems, *The Life of William Penn* (Philadelphia: Uriah Hunt, 1836), p. 121.

32. McDowell and Beliles, *America's Providential History*, p. 90.

33. James Adolph Lesftwich, "Meet Sir George Carterete: Story of the State Seals of New Jersey," *Carterete News* (Trenton: The Carterete Club), June 1953, Vol. II, No. 6.

34. *The Code of 1650*, pp. 92-93.

35. Mode, pp. 74-75. See also John Elliot, *New England First Fruits* (London: R.O. & G.D., 1643).

36. McDowell and Beliles, *America's Providential History*, p. 109.

37. Walton, p. 356.

38. Mode, p. 109.

39. McDowell and Beliles, *America's Providential History*, p. 111.

40. *Documentary History of Yale University*, Franklin B. Dexter, ed. (NY: Arno Press & The New York Times, 1969), p. 32.

41. McDowell and Beliles, *America's Providential History*, p. 111.

42. Richard Patrick McCormick, *Rutgers: A Bicentennial History* (NJ: Rutgers University Press, 1966).

43. George Washington, *The Writings of Washington*, John C. Fitzpatrick, ed. (Washington, D. C.: U. S. Government Printing Office, 1932), Vol. XV, p. 55, from speech to the Delaware Indian Chiefs on May 12, 1779.

44. *Id.*

45. McDowell and Beliles, *America's Providential History*, p. 109.

46. *Id.* at 100.

47. *American Patriotism: Speeches, Letters, and Other Papers Which Illustrate the Foundation, the Development, the Preservation of the United States of America*, Selim H. Peabody, ed. (NY: American Book Exchange, 1880), p. 34.

48. McDowell and Beliles, *America's Providential History*, p. 179.

49. John Eidsmoe, *Christianity and the Constitution* (MI: Baker Book House, 1987), p. 251. Quoting C. K. Shipton, *Sibley's Harvard Graduates*, Vol. IV, pp. 84-85.

50. Richard Frothingham, *Rise of the Republic of the United States* (Boston: Little, Brown & Co., 1872), p. 458.

51. *Id.* at 393.

52. *Id.*

53. *Adams Family Correspondence*, L. H. Butterfield, ed. (Cambridge, MA: The Belknap Press of Harvard University Press, 1963), Vol. I, p. 323, from Abigail Adams to Mercy Warren, circa Nov. 5, 1775.

54. Washington, *The Writings of Washington*, Vol. XI, p. 343, May 2, 1778.

55. Bancroft, Vol. VI, p. 440-441.

56. Verna M. Hall and Rosalie J. Slater, *The Bible and the Constitution of the United States of America* (San Francisco: Foundation for American Christian Education, 1983), p. 31.

57. Bancroft, Vol. VII, p. 99.

58. Hall & Slater, *The Bible and the Constitution*, p. 31.

59. Hezekiah Niles, *Principles and Acts of the Revolution in America* (Baltimore: William Ogden Niles, 1822), p. 418.

60. Cushing Strout, *The New Heavens and the New Earth* (NY: Harper & Row, 1974), p. 59. See also Clifford K. Shipton, *Sibley's Harvard Graduates* (Boston: Massachusetts Historical Society, 1965), Vol. XIII, p. 475-476, quoting from Election Sermon by Peter Powers, *Jesus Christ the King* (Newburyport, 1778).

61. McDowell and Beliles, *America's Providential History*, p. 149.

62. John and Abigail Adams, *Letters of John Adams, Addressed To His Wife*, Charles Francis Adams, ed. (Boston: Charles C. Little and James Brown, 1841), Vol. I, p. 128, July 3, 1776.

63. William V. Wells, *The Life and Public Services of Samuel Adams* (Boston: Little, Brown & Co., 1865), Vol. III, p. 408, quoting from *An Oration Delivered at the State House, in Philadelphia, to a very numerous audience; on Thursday the 1st of August, 1776*, London: E. Johnson, 1776. Although this oration published in London was purported to be a reprint of one delivered by Samuel Adams, no original was ever found and most historians believe that no such oration ever existed. See Wells, Vol. II, pp. 439-440.

64. *The Journals of the Continental Congress, 1774-1789*, (Washington, D. C.: Government Printing Office, 1905), Vol. II, 1775, p. 87.

65. *Id.* at p. 91, n. 1.

66. *Id.* at p. 91.

67. *Id.* at p. 92.

68. Washington, *The Writings of Washington*, Vol. V, p. 245, July 9, 1776. This statement of George Washington was also used by Abraham Lincoln in his November 15, 1862, order to his troops to maintain regular sabbath observances. See Abraham Lincoln, *Letters and Addresses and Abraham Lincoln* (NY: Unit Book Publishing Co., 1907), p. 261.

69. *Id.* at Vol. XII, p. 343, May 2, 1778.

70. George Washington, *The Writings of Washington*, Jared Sparks, editor (Boston: American Stationers' Company, 1838), Vol. XVIII, p. 452, from a letter on June 8, 1783.

71. Benjamin Franklin, *Works of the Late Doctor Benjamin Franklin Consisting of His Life, Written by Himself, Together with Essays, Humorous, Moral & Literary, Chiefly in the Manner of the Spectator*, Richard Price, ed. (Dublin: P. Wogan, P. Byrne, J. Moore, and W. Jones, 1793), p. 289.

72. *Journals of the Continental Congress* at Vol. I, 1774, p. 26.

73. *Id.* at 27.

74. John and Abigail Adams, Vol. I, pp. 23-24.

75. Edward C. Reynolds, *The Maine Scholars Manual* (Portland, ME: Dresser, McLellan & Co. 1880).

76. Thomas Y. Rhoads, *The Battle-fields of the Revolution* (Philadelphia: J. W. Bradley, 1860), pp. 36-37.

77. Proclamation of John Hancock from Concord, April 15, 1775, from an

original in the Evans collection, #14220, by the American Antiquarian Society. See also *The Journals of Each Provincial Congress of Massachusetts, 1774-1775,* William Lincoln, editor (Boston: Dutton & Wentworth, 1838), pp. 144-145.

78. *Journals of the Continental Congress* at Vol. II, 1775, p. 192.

79. *Id.* at Vol. IV, 1776, pp. 208-209.

80. *Id.* at Vol. V, 1776, p. 530.

81. John and Abigail Adams, Vol. I, p. 152.

82. *Id.*

83. Washington, *The Writings of Washington,* Vol. V, pp. 244-245, July 9, 1776.

84. *Journals of the Continental Congress* at Vol. VIII, 1777, p. 734.

85. *Id.* at Vol. IX, 1777, pp. 854-855.

86. Washington, *The Writings of Washington,* Vol. XX, pp. 94-95, September 26, 1780.

87. *Journals of the Continental Congress* at Vol. XVIII, p. 950-951.

88. Memorial of Robert Aitken to Congress, 21 January, 1781, obtained from the National Archives, Washington D. C.

89. *Journals of Continental Congress* at Vol. XXIII, 1782, p. 574. See also cover page for the "Bible of the Revolution," either the 1782 original or the 1968 reprint by Arno Press, NY.

90. Proclamation of John Hancock from Boston, November 8, 1783, from an original in the Evans collection, #18025, by the American Antiquarian Society.

91. James Madison, *The Records of the Federal Convention of 1787,* Max Farrand, ed. (New Haven: Yale Univ. Press, 1911), Vol. I, pp. 450-452, June 28, 1787.

92. E. C. M'Guire, *The Religious Opinions and Character of Washington* (NY: Harper & Brothers, 1836), p. 151.

93. Madison, *supra* note 91 at Vol. I, p. 452.

94. *Id.*

95. M'Guire, p. 152.

96. Morris, pp. 253-254.

97. Peter Marshall and David Manuel, *The Light and the Glory* (New Jersey: Fleming H. Revell Co., 1977), p. 343.

98. Tim LaHaye, *Faith of Our Founding Fathers* (Brentwood, TN: Wolgemuth & Hyatt, Publishers, Inc., 1987), p. 71.

99. Morris, p. 326.

100. *City of Charleston v. S. A. Benjamin;* 2 Strob. 508, 521 (Sup.Ct.S.C. 1846).

101. *McGowan v. Maryland;* 366 U.S. 420, 437 (1960).

102. Morris, p. 272.

103. *Annals of Congress, 1789-1791* (Washington, D. C.: Gales & Seaton, 1834), Vol. I, p. 25.

104. *Id.* at Vol. I, p. 232.

105. James D. Richardson, *A Compilation of the Messages and Papers of the Presidents, 1789-1897* (Published by Authority of Congress, 1899), Vol. 1, pp. 52-53, April 30, 1789.

106. *Annals of Congress,* Vol. I, p. 29.

107. Washington, *The Writings of Washington,* Vol. XXX, p. 321 n., May 10, 1789.

108. *Id.* at p. 432.

109. Henry Halley, *Halley's Bible Handbook* (Grand Rapids, MI: Zondervan, 1927, 1965), p. 18.

110. George Washington, *The Writings of Washington,* Jared Sparks, editor (Boston: American Stationers' Company, 1838), Vol. XVIII, p. 452, from a letter to John Armstrong on March 11, 1792.

111. *Annals of Congress,* Vol. I, p. 914.

112. *Id.*

113. Richardson, *Messages of the Presidents,* Vol. 1, p. 64, October 3, 1789.

114. *Id.* at Vol. 1, p. 220, September 17, 1796.

115. McDowell and Beliles, *America's Providential History,* p. 179.

116. William V. Wells, *The Life and Public Services of Samuel Adams* (Boston: Little, Brown & Co., 1865), Vol. III, p. 301. Taken from *Four Letters: Being an Interesting Correspondence Between . . . John Adams . . . and Samuel* Adams (Boston: Adams & Rhoades, 1802). Also cited in John Adams, *The Works of John Adams, Second President of the United States,* Charles Francis Adams, ed. (Boston: Little, Brown & Co., 1854), Vol. VI, p. 414.

117. *Id.* at 304.

118. John Witherspoon, *The Works of the Rev. John Witherspoon* (Philadelphia: William W. Woodard, 1802), Vol. III, p. 46.

119. *Id.*

120. Steve C. Dawson, *God's Providence in America's History* (Rancho Cordova, CA: Steve C. Dawson, 1988), p. I:5.

121. William Wirt Henry, *Patrick Henry: Life, Correspondence and Speeches* (New York: Charles Scribner's Sons, 1891), Vol. II, p. 621.

122. Eidsmoe, p. 314.

123. William Wirt, *The Life and Character of Patrick Henry* (Philadelphia: James Webster, 1818), p. 402.

124. John Jay, *The Correspondence and Public Papers of John Jay,* Henry P. Johnston, ed. (New York: G.P. Putnam's Sons, 1890), Vol. IV, p. 393, Oct. 12, 1816. See also B. F. Morris, *The Christian Life and Character of the Civil Institutions of the United States* (Philadelphia: George W. Childs, 1864), p. 153.

125. Morris, p. 154.

126. McDowell and Beliles, *America's Providential History,* p. 111.

127. James Madison, *The Papers of James Madison,* Robert Rutland, ed. (Chicago: University of Chicago Press, 1973), Vol. VIII, pp. 299, 304, June 20, 1785.

128. Harold K. Lane, *Liberty! Cry Liberty!* (Boston: Lamb and Lamb Tractarian Society, 1939), pp. 32-33. See also Fredrick Nyneyer, *First Principles in Morality and Economics: Neighborly Love and Ricardo's Law of Association* (South Holland: Libertarian Press, 1958), p. 31.

129. Jared Sparks, *The Life of Governeur Morris* (Boston: Gray and Bowen, 1832), Vol. III, p. 483.

130. Christopher Collier, *Roger Sherman's Connec*ticut (Middleton, CT: Wesleyan University Press, 1971), p. 185.

131. *Id.* at 129.

132. John Adams, *The Works of John Adams, Second President of the United States,* Charles Francis Adams, ed. (Boston: Little, Brown, 1854), Vol. IX, p. 564, from letter of John Adams to Dr. Prince, April 19, 1790.

133. *Id.* at Vol. IX, p. 229, October 11, 1798.

134. *Id.* at Vol. IX, p. 401, June 21, 1776.

135. John Adams, *Diary and Autobiography of John Adams,* L. H. Butterfield, ed. (Cambridge, MA: Belknap Press of Harvard University Press, 1961), Vol. III, p. 234, from Adams' diary entry for July 26, 1796.

136. *Id.* at Vol, I, p. 9, from Adams' diary entry for February 22, 1756.

137. Adams, *The Works of John Adams,* Vol. IX, p. 636, August 28, 1811.

138. Richardson, *Messages of the Presidents,* Vol. 1, p. 220, September 17, 1796.

139. Alexander Hamilton, *Selected Writings and Speeches of Alexander Hamilton*, Morton J. Frisch, ed. (Washington, D. C.: American Enterprise Institute for Public Policy Research, 1985), p. 511, April 16-21, 1802. See also Claude G. Bowers, *Jefferson and Hamilton: The Struggle for Democracy in America* (Boston: Houghton Mifflin Co., 1925, 1937), p. 40.

140. John Quincy Adams, *The Writings of John Quincy Adams,* Worthington C. Ford, editor (NY: The Macmillan Co., 1914), Vol. IV, p. 215, from a letter on September 8, 1811.

141. John Quincy Adams, *An Oration Delivered Before the Inhabitants of the Town of Newburyport at their Request on the Sixty-First Anniversary of the Declaration of Independence* (Newburyport: Charles Whipple, 1837), pp. 5-6.

142. Noah Webster, *History of the United States* (New Haven: Durrie & Peck, 1832), p. 300, ¶ 578.

143. *Id.* at p. 339, ¶ 53.

144. Noah Webster, *American Dictionary of the English Language, 1828* (San Francisco: Foundation for American Christian Education, 1967), preface, p. 12.

145. *Id.* at 22.

146. Verna Hall and Rosalie Slater, *The Bible and the Constitution* (San Francisco: Foundation for American Christian Education, 1966), p. 28.

147. Verna M. Hall, *The Christian History of the American Revolution* (San Francisco: Foundation for American Christian Education, 1976), p. 21.

148. Jedediah Morse's Election Sermon given at Charleston, Mass. on April 25, 1799, taken from an original in the Evans collection compiled by the American Antiquarian Society.

149. William H. McGuffey, *McGuffey's Eclectic Third Reader* (Cincinnati: Winthrop B. Smith & Co., 1848), p. 5, preface.

150. *Id.*

151. William H. McGuffey, *McGuffey's Eclectic Fourth Reader* (Cincinnati: Winthrop B. Smith & Co., 1853), p. 3, preface.

152. Wells, p. 116.

153. Sparks, *supra* note 129 at Vol. III, p. 483.

154. J. O. Wilson, *Records of the Columbia Historical Society* (Washington, D. C.: Columbia Historical Society, 1897), Vol. I, pp. 119-170, see especially pp. 122-127 from the article "Eighty Years of the Public Schools of Washington—1805 to 1885," delivered before the society on May 4, 1896.

155. Herbert Lockyer, *Last Words of Saints and Sinners* (Grand Rapids: Kregel, 1969), p. 98.

156. Commager, p. 131.

157. Alexis de Tocqueville, *The Republic of the United States of America and Its Political Institutions, Reviewed and Examined,* Henry Reeves, trans. (Garden City, NY: A. S. Barnes & Co., 1851), Vol. I, p. 337.

158. Morris, p. 318, see also John Holmes, *The Statesman* (Augusta: Severance & Dorr, 1840), p. 92.

159. *Id.* at 326.

160. Dr. Sterling Lacy, *Valley of Decision* (Texarkana: Dayspring Productions, 1988), p. 37. Quoted from *The New American,* September 29, 1986, p. 28.

161. Information from Project Literacy U.S. (PLUS). Cited in *America: To Pray or Not To Pray?* by David Barton (Aledo, TX: WallBuilder Press, 1991), p. 107.

162. *Education Week,* June 13, 1985, p. 28.

163. Lacy, p. 160.

164. de Tocqueville, Vol. I, p. 332.

165. Morris, pp. 324, 326, 327.

166. *Id.* at 317, 320, 321, 323.

167. *Id.* at 328.

168. Daniel Webster, *The Works of Daniel Webster* (Boston: Little, Brown and Company, 1853), Vol. I, p. 22.

169. *Id.* at 48.

170. de Tocqueville, Vol. I, 337.

171. *Id.* at Vol. I, p. 335.

172. *Id.* at Vol. I, p. 334.

173. *Id.* at Vol. I, p. 328.

174. *Id.* at Vol. I, p. 334.

175. *Id.* at Vol. I, p. 333.

176. Morris, p. 11.

177. Rosalie Slater, *Teaching and Learning America's Christian History* (San Francisco: Foundation for American Christian Education, 1975), p. ix, quoting from historian Emma Willard, 1843.

178. McDowell and Beliles, *The Spirit of the Constitution.*

179. *Church of the Holy Trinity* v. *U. S.*; 143 U.S. 457, 465, 470, 471 (1892).

180. Associated Press, *Dallas Times Herald,* August 6, 1988, B-5.

Chapter 6
Protection from the Absurd

1. *Church of the Holy Trinity* v. *U. S.*; 143 U.S. 457, 458 (1892).

2. *Id.* at 459.

3. *Id.* at 460, 461.

4. *Id.* at 465.

5. *State* v. *Smith Clark;* 5 Dutcher (29 N.J. Law) 96, 97, 98 (Sup.Ct.N.J. 1860).

6. *Id.* at 97.

7. *Id.* at 99, 100, 101.

8. *United States* v. *Kirby;* 74 U.S. 482, 483-484 (1868).

9. *Id.* at 484.

10. *Id.* at 486, 487.

11. *Church of the Holy Trinity* v. *U. S.;* 143 U.S. 457, 472 (1892).

12. *Updegraph* v. *The Commonwealth;* 11 Serg. & R. 393, 400, 401, 402 (Sup.Ct.Penn. 1824).

13. *The Constitutions of the Several Independent States of America, Published by Order of Congress* (Boston: Norman & Bowen, 1785), p. 81.

14. *Id.* at 99-100. See also *Church of the Holy Trinity* v. *U. S.;* 143 U.S. 457, 469-470.

15. *Id.* at 138.

16. George Washington, *The Writings of Washington,* John C. Fitzpatrick, ed. (Washington, D. C.: U. S. Government Printing Office, 1932), Vol. XXX, p. 321 n, May 10, 1789.

17. B. F. Morris, *The Christian Life and Character of the Civil Institutions of the United States* (Philadelphia: George W. Childs, 1864), pp. 320-321.

Chapter 7
The Absurd Becomes Reality

1. *Engel* v. *Vitale;* 370 U.S. 421, 422 (1962).

2. *Id.* at 423.

3. *State Board of Education* v. *Board of Education of Netcong;* 262 A.2d 21, 30 (Sup.Ct.N.J. 1970), *cert. denied,* 401 U.S. 1013.

4. *Engel* v. *Vitale;* 370 U.S. 421, 430, 425 (1962).

5. *Id.* at 431.

6. George Washington, *The Writings of Washington,* John C. Fitzpatrick, ed. (Washington, D. C.: U. S. Government Printing Office, 1932), Vol. XXX, p. 432 n., October 9, 1789.

7. John Adams, *The Works of John Adams, Second President of the United States,* Charles Francis Adams, ed. (Boston: Little, Brown, 1854), Vol. IX, p. 636, August 28, 1811.

8. James Madison, *The Papers of James Madison,* Robert A. Rutland, ed. (Chicago: University of Chicago Press, 1973), Vol. VIII, p. 304, June 20, 1785. Quoting from Madison's "Memorial and Remonstrance."

9. John Witherspoon, *The Works of the Rev. John Witherspoon* (Philadelphia: William W. Woodard, 1802), Vol. III, p. 46.

10. Adams, *The Works of John Adams,* Vol. IX, p. 229.

11. *Engel* v. *Vitale;* 370 U.S. 421, 436 (1962).

12. *Abington* v. *Schempp;* 374 U.S. 203, 220-221 (1963).

13. *Id.* at 220.

14. See the individual biographies of each Justice provided in Congressional Quarterly's *Guide to the Supreme Court, 2nd Edition* (Washington, D. C.: Congressional Quarterly, 1990).

15. *Engel* v. *Vitale;* 370 U.S. 421, 431 (1962).

16. *Abington* v. *Schempp;* 374 U.S. 203, 213 (1963).

17. *Id.* at 211, note 4, 207.

18. *Id.* at 209.

19. Herbert Lockyer, *Last Words of Saints and Sinners* (Grand Rapids: Kregel, 1969), p. 98.

20. Henry Halley, *Halley's Bible Handbook* (Grand Rapids, MI: Zondervan, 1927, 1965), p. 18.

21. William Wirt, *The Life and Character of Patrick Henry* (Philadelphia: James Webster, 1818), p. 402.

22. John Adams, *Diary and Autobiography of John Adams,* L. H. Butterfield, ed. (Cambridge, MA: Belknap Press of Harvard University Press, 1961), Vol. I, p. 9, from Adams' diary entry for February 22, 1756.

23. Noah Webster, *The History of the United States* (New Haven: Durrie & Peck, 1832), p. 339, ¶ 53.

24. *Abington* v. *Schempp;* 374 U.S. 203, 217 (1963).

25. John Quincy Adams, *An Oration Delivered Before the Inhabitants of the Town of Newburyport at their Request on the Sixty-First Anniversary of the Declaration of Independence* (Newburyport: Charles Whipple, 1837), pp. 5-6.

26. Peter Marshall and David Manuel, *The Light and the Glory* (NJ: Fleming H. Revell Co., 1977), p. 370, n. 10.

27. B. F. Morris, *The Christian Life and Character of the Civil Institutions of the United States* (Philadelphia: George W. Childs, 1864), pp. 320-321, 323.

28. *Abington* v. *Schempp;* 374 U.S. 203, 216 (1963).

29. *Runkel* v. *Winemiller;* 4 Harris & McHenry 276, 288 (Sup.Ct.Md. 1799).

30. *Updegraph* v. *The Commonwealth;* 11 Serg. & R. 393, 399, 402 (Sup.Ct.Penn. 1824).

31. John Jay, *The Correspondence and Public Papers of John Jay,* Henry P. Johnston, ed. (New York: G.P. Putnam's Sons, 1890), Vol. IV, p. 393, Oct. 12, 1816.

32. *Abington* v. *Schempp;* 374 U.S. 203, 212 (1963).

33. Paul C. Vitz, *Censorship: Evidence of Bias in Our Children's Textbooks* (Ann Arbor, Michigan: Servant Books, 1986), p. 11.

34. *Id.* at 53-54.

35. *Stone* v. *Graham;* 449 U.S. 39, 41 (1980).

36. *Id.* at 42.

37. *Id.*

38. Harold K. Lane, *Liberty! Cry Liberty!* (Boston: Lamb and Lamb Tractarian Society, 1939), pp. 32-33. See also Fredrick Nyneyer, *First Principles in Morality and Economics: Neighborly Love and Ricardo's Law of Association* (South Holland: Libertarian Press, 1958), p. 31.

39. *State Board of Education* v. *Board of Education of Netcong;* 262 A.2d 21, 23 (Sup.Ct.N.J. 1970), *cert. denied,* 401 U.S. 1013.

40. *Id.* at 23-24.

41. *Id.* at 26.

42. *Id.* at 31, 25-26.

43. *Id.* at 22, 26.

44. *Id.* at 21-22.

45. *Walz* v. *Tax Commission;* 397 U.S. 664, 672, 680 (1970).

46. *Id.* at 716.

47. Steve C. Dawson, *God's Providence in America's History* (Rancho Cordova, CA: Steve C. Dawson, 1988), p. I:5.

48. William V. Wells, *The Life and Public Services of Samuel Adams* (Boston: Little, Brown & Co., 1865), Vol. III, p. 301. Taken from *Four Letters: Being an Interesting Correspondence Between . . . John Adams . . . and Samuel Adams* (Boston: Adams & Rhoades, 1802). See also Adams, *The Works of John Adams,* Vol. VI, p. 414.

49. Washington, *The Writings of Washington,* Vol. XV, p. 55, from speech to the Delaware Indian Chiefs on May 12, 1779.

50. Webster, *The History of the United States,* p. 300, ¶ 578.

51. Morris, p. 323.

52. *Wallace* v. *Jaffree*; 472 U.S. 38, 48, n. 30 (1984).

53. *Id.* at 43, 44, n. 22.

54. *Id.* at 41-42.

55. *DeSpain* v. *DeKalb County Community School District;* 384 F.2d 655, 836 (N.D.Ill. 1966), *cert. denied,* 390 U.S. 906 (1967).

56. *Id.* at 841.

57. *McCollum* v. *Board of Education;* 333 U.S. 203, 207-209 (1948).

58. *Id.* at 212, 231, 212.

59. *Id.* at 205.

60. *Id.* at 234-235.

61. *Id.* at 237.

Chapter 8
The Absurd Becomes The Standard

1. *Wallace* v. *Jaffree;* 472 U.S. 38 (1984).

2. *Cantwell* v. *State of Connecticut;* 310 U.S. 296 (1940).

3. *Levitt* v. *Committee for Public Education;* 413 U.S. 472 (1973).

4. *Id.* at 474.

5. *Committee for Public Education* v. *Nyquist;* 413 U.S. 756 (1973).

6. *Id.*

7. *Stone* v. *Graham;* 449 U.S. 39 (1980).

8. *Lemon* v. *Kurtzman;* 403 U.S. 602, 612 (1971).

9. *Marsh* v. *Chambers;* 463 U.S. 783 (1982).

10. *United States* v. *Macintosh;* 283 U.S. 605, 625 (1931).

11. *Zorach* v. *Clauson;* 343 U.S. 306, 313 (1952).

12. *Church of the Holy Trinity* v. *U. S.;* 143 U.S. 457, 465, 471 (1892).

13. See, for example, Elbridge S. Brooks, *Historic Americans* (NY: Thomas Y. Crowell & Co., 1899), Benson J. Lossing, *Eminent Americans* (NY: American Book Exchange, 1881), Carroll L. Judson, *The Sages And Heroes of the American Revolution* (Philadelphia: L. Carroll Judson, 1852), *Lives of the Heroes of the American Revolution* (Boston: Phillips & Sampson, 1848), and others.

14. *Abington* v. *Schempp;* 374 U.S. 203, 220 (1963).

Chapter 9
The Court's Defense of Its Position

1. *Abington* v. *Schempp;* 374 U.S. 203, 215-216 (1963).

2. *Walz* v. *Tax Commission;* 397 U.S. 664, 701, 702, 703 (1970).

3. *Barron* v. *Baltimore;* 32 U.S. 243 (1833).

4. Robert K. Dornan and Csaba Vedlik, Jr., *Judicial Supremacy: The Supreme Court on Trial* (MA: Plymouth Rock Foundation, 1986), p. 85.

5. *Everson* v. *Board of Education;* 330 U.S. 1, 13 (1947).

6. *McCollum* v. *Board of Education;* 333 U.S. 203, 218-219, n. 6 (1948).

7. *Id.* at 218-219, n. 6.

8. Thomas Jefferson, *Writings of Thomas Jefferson,* Albert Bergh, editor (Washington, D. C.: The Thomas Jefferson Memorial Association, 1904), Vol. XV, p. 449, from a letter from Jefferson to Justice William Johnson on June 12, 1823.

9. *Murdock* v. *Pennsylvania;* 319 U.S. 105, 128, 129 (1943).

10. *Walz* v. *Tax Commission;* 397 U.S. 684, 685 (1970).

11. *Everson* v. *Board of Education;* 330 U.S. 1, 13 (1947).

12. *Engel* v. *Vitale;* 370 U.S. 421, 428-429 (1962).

13. Pat Robertson, *America's Dates With Destiny* (Nashville: Thomas Nelson Publishers, 1986), p. 75.

14. *Id.*

15. *Engel* v. *Vitale;* 370 U.S. 421, 428-429 (1962).

16. B. F. Morris, *The Christian Life and Character of the Civil Institutions of the United States* (Philadelphia: George W. Childs, 1864), p. 320.

17. *Everson* v. *Board of Education;* 330 U.S. 1, 13 (1947).

18. *Annals of the Congress of the United States—First Congress* (Washington, D. C.: Gales & Seaton, 1834), Vol. I, p. 766, Aug. 20, 1789.

19. Edwin Gaustad, *Faith of Our Fathers* (San Francisco: Harper & Row, 1987), p. 158.

20. *Documents of American History*, Henry S. Commager, ed. (NY: Appleton-Century-Crofts, Inc., 1948), p. 179.

21. James D. Richardson, *A Compilation of the Messages and Papers of the Presidents, 1789-1897* (Published by Authority of Congress, 1899), Vol. 1, p. 379, March 4, 1805.

22. Jefferson, *The Writings of Thomas Jefferson,* Vol. XI, p. 428, from a letter on January 23, 1808.

23. Paul C. Vitz, *Censorship: Evidence of Bias in Our Children's Textbooks* (Ann Arbor, Michigan: Servant Books, 1986), p. 77.

24.   Stephen K. McDowell and Mark A. Beliles, *America's Providential History* (Charlottesville, VA: Providence Press, 1989), p. 183.

25.   J. O. Wilson, *Records of the Columbia Historical Society* (Washington, D. C.: Columbia Historical Society, 1897), Vol. I, pp. 119-170, see especially pp. 122-127 from the article "Eighty Years of the Public Schools of Washington—1805 to 1885," delivered before the society on May 4, 1896.

26.   Herbert Lockyer, *The Last Words of Saints and Sinners* (Grand Rapids: Kregel, 1969), p. 98.

27.   Daniel L. Driesbach, *Real Threat and Mere Shadow: Religious Liberty and the First Amendment* (Westchester, IL: Crossway Books, 1987), p. 127. See also, Richard Peters, ed., *The Public Statutes at Large of the United States of America* (Boston: Charles C. Little and James Brown, 1846), "A Treaty Between the United States and the Kaskaskia Tribe of Indians," 23 December 1803, Art. III, Vol. VII, p. 78-79, "Treaty with the Wyandots, etc.", 1805, Vol. VII, Art. IV, p. 88, "Treaty with the Cherokees," 1806, Vol. VII, Art. II, p. 102. See also, Robert L. Cord, *Separation of Church and State* (NY: Lambeta Press, 1982), p. 39.

28.   McDowell & Beliles, *America's Providential History*, p. 178.

29.   Thomas Jefferson, *Notes on the State of Virginia* (Philadelphia: Matthew Carey, 1794), Query XVIII, p. 237.

30.   James Madison, *The Papers of James Madison*, Robert Rutland, ed. (Chicago: University of Chicago Press, 1973), Vol. VIII, p. 299, June 20, 1785.

31.   Tim LaHaye, *Faith of Our Founding Fathers* (Brentwood, TN: Wolgemuth & Hyatt, Publishers, Inc., 1987), p. 127. Quoting from Galliard Hunt, *James Madison and Religious Liberty* (Washington, D. C.: American Historical Association, Government Printing Office, 1902), p. 166.

32.   Jefferson, *Writings of Thomas Jefferson*, Vol. XI, pp. 50-51, September 11, 1804.

33.   *Id.* at Vol. XV, p. 277, September 28, 1820.

34.   *Id.* at Vol. XV, pp. 331-332, August 18, 1821.

35.   Madison, *The Papers of James Madison*, Vol. VIII, pp. 299-300, June 20, 1785.

36.   *Id.* at Vol. XI, p. 293, October 15, 1788.

Chapter 10
Dilemmas for the Court

1. *Cohen* v. *California;* 403 U.S. 15, 18, 20, 25 (1971).

2. *People* v. *Ruggles;* 8 Johns 545, 546 (Sup.Ct.N.Y. 1811).

3. *Erznoznik* v. *City of Jacksonville;* 422 U.S. 205, 207 (1975).

4. *Id.* at 206, 207.

5. *Id.* at 205.

6. *Commonwealth* v. *Jesse Sharpless and Others;* 2 Serg. & R. 91, 103, 104 (Sup.Ct.Penn. 1815).

7. *Grove* v. *Mead School District;* 753 F.2d 1528, 1540 (9th Cir. 1985), *cert. denied,* 474 U.S. 826.

8. *People* v. *Ruggles;* 8 Johns 545, 546 (Sup.Ct.N.Y. 1811).

9. *Walz* v. *Tax Commission;* 397 U.S. 664, 695 (1970).

10. *Davis* v. *Beason;* 133 U.S. 333, 343 (1890).

11. *Murphy* v. *Ramsey;* 144 U.S. 15, 37, 45 (1885).

12. *Theriault* v. *Silber;* 453 F.Supp. 254 (W.D.Tex. 1978).

13. *Malnak* v. *Yogi;* 440 F.Supp. 1285, 1287 (D.C.N.J. 1977).

14. *Grove* v. *Mead School District;* 753 F.2d 1528, 1534 (9th Cir. 1985), *cert. denied,* 474 U.S. 826.

15. *Commonwealth* v. *Abner Kneeland;* 37 Mass. (20 Pick) 206, 233, 234 (Sup.Ct.Mass. 1838).

16. Noah Webster, *American Dictionary of the English Language, 1828* (San Francisco: Foundation for American Christian Education, 1967), see "religion."

17. *Id.*

18. *McGowan* v. *Maryland;* 366 U.S. 420, 436 (1960).

19. *Florey* v. *Sioux Falls School District;* 619 F.2d 1311, 1325 (D.C.S.D. 1979), *cert. denied,* 449 U.S. 987 (1980).

20. *City of Charleston* v. *S. A. Benjamin;* 2 Strob. 508, 521 (Sup.Ct.S.C. 1846).

21. B. F. Morris, *The Christian Life and Character of the Civil Institutions of the United States* (Philadelphia: George W. Childs, 1864), p. 326.

22. *Epperson* v. *Arkansas;* 393 U.S. 97 (1968).

23. *Walz* v. *Tax Commission;* 397 U.S. 664, 695 (1970).

24. *Church of the Holy Trinity* v. *U. S.;* 143 U.S. 457, 465 (1892).

Chapter 11
Double Standards

1. *Chambers* v. *Marsh;* 675 F.2d 228, 233 (8th Cir. 1982); *review allowed,* 463 U.S. 783 (1982).

2. *State Board of Education* v. *Board of Education of Netcong;* 262 A.2d 21 (Sup.Ct.N.J. 1970), *cert. denied,* 401 U.S. 1013.

3. *Anderson* v. *Salt Lake City Corporation;* 475 F.2d 29, 33, 34 (10th Cir. 1973), *cert. denied,* 414 U.S. 879.

4. *Stone* v. *Graham;* 449 U.S. 39 (1980).

5. *Bogen* v. *Doty;* 598 F.2d 1110 (1979)

6. *Chambers* v. *Marsh;* 675 F.2d 228, 234 (8th Cir. 1982); *review allowed,* 463 U.S. 783 (1982).

7. *Graham* v. *Central Community School District of Decatur County;* 608 F.Supp. 531 (S.D.Iowa 1985).

8. *Kay* v. *Douglas School District;* 719 P.2d 875 (Or.App. 1986), *review allowed,* 727 P.2d 977 (1986).

9. *Lynch* v. *Donnelly;* 465 U.S. 668, 669-670 (1985).

10. *County of Allegheny* v. *ACLU;* 106 L.Ed.2d 472, 475 (1989).

11. *Florey* v. *Sioux Falls School District;* 464 F.Supp. 911, 912, 914 (D.C.S.D. 1979), *cert. denied,* 449 U.S. 987 (1980).

12. *Baer* v. *Kolmorgen;* 181 N.Y. S. 2d 230 (Sup.Ct.N.Y. 1958).

13. *Bishop* v. *Colaw;* 450 F.2d 1069, 1072, 1075 (Ct.App.Mo 1972).

14. *Union Pacific Railway Co.* v. *Botsford;* 141 U.S. 250 (1891).

15. *Wallace* v. *Ford;* 346 F.Supp. 156, 162 (D.C.Ark. 1972).

16. *Finot* v. *Pasadena City Board of Education;* 58 Cal.Rptr. 520, 522 (Ct.App.2nd Dist.Cal. 1967).

17. *Cohen* v. *California;* 403 U.S. 15, 25 (1971).

18. *Grove* v. *Mead School District;* 753 F.2d 1528, 1540 (9th Cir. 1985), *cert. denied,* 474 U.S. 826.

19. *State of Ohio* v. *Whisner;* 351 N.E. 2d 750 (Sup.Ct.Ohio 1976).

20. *Reed* v. *van Hoven;* 237 F.Supp. 48, 56 (W.D.Mich. 1965).

21. *DeSpain* v. *DeKalb County Community School District;* 384 F.2d 655, 841 (N.D.Ill. 1966), *cert. denied,* 390 U.S. 906 (1967).

22. *Swann* v. *Pack;* 527 S.W. 2d 99, 101 (Sup.Ct.Tn. 1975).

23. *State Board of Education* v. *Board of Education of Netcong;* 262 A.2d 21, 22 (Sup.Ct.N.J. 1970), *cert. denied,* 401 U.S. 1013.

24. *Pierce* v. *Society of Sisters;* 268 U.S. 510 (1925).

25. *Reed* v. *van Hoven;* 237 F.Supp. 48, 51 (W.D.Mich. 1965).

26. *State Board of Education* v. *Board of Education of Netcong;* 262 A.2d 21, 26 (Sup.Ct.N.J. 1970), *cert. denied,* 401 U.S. 1013.

27. *Id.* at 21.

28. *Erznoznik* v. *City of Jacksonville*; 422 U.S. 205 (1975).

29. *New York Trust Co.* v. *Eisner;* 256 U.S. 345 (1921).

30. *Walz* v. *Tax Commission;* 397 U.S. 664, 681 (1970).

31. *Id.* at 702.

32. Stephen K. McDowell and Mark A. Beliles, *America's Providential History* (Charlottesville, VA: Providence Press, 1988), p. 95.

Chapter 12
Toward a New Constitution

1. James Madison, *The Records of the Federal Convention of 1787,* Max Farrand, ed. (New Haven: Yale University Press, 1911), Vol. I, p. 451, June 28, 1787.

2. John Eidsmoe, *Christianity and the Constitution* (MI: Baker Book House, 1987), p. 51, 53.

3. George Bancroft, *Bancroft's History of the United States* (Boston: Little, Brown & Co., 1859), Vol. V, p. 24.

4. Charles Montesquieu, *The Spirit of the Laws* (Worcester: Isaiah Thomas, 1802), Vol. I, pp. 125-126.

5. J. Wingate Thornton, *The Pulpit of the American Revolution* (Boston: Gould and Lincoln, 1860), p. XXVII.

6. James Madison, *Letters and Other Writings of James Madison* (New York: R. Worthington, 1884), Vol. III, p. 233, letter dated October 18, 1821.

7. Robert K. Dornan and Csaba Vedlik, Jr., *Judicial Supremacy: The Supreme Court on Trial* (Massachusetts: Plymouth Rock Foundation, 1986), p. 10.

8. Sir William Blackstone, *Commentaries on the Laws of England* (Philadelphia: Robert Bell, Union Library, 1771), Vol. I, p. 39.

9. *Id.* at Vol. I, 41-42

10. *Id.* at Vol. I, 42

11. *Id.* at Vol. I, 42

12. Eidsmoe, p. 61.

13. *Id.* at 62.

14. *Id.*

15. *Id.* at 61.

16. John Locke, *The Second Treatise on Civil Government, 1690* (reprinted Buffalo, N.Y.: Prometheus Books, 1986), p. 75.

17. *Id.* at 76, n. 1.

18. Alexander Hamilton, *The Papers of Alexander Hamilton,* Harold Syrett, ed. (New York: Columbia University Press, 1961), Vol. I, p. 86, February 23, 1775, taken from his "The Farmer Refuted."

19. Eidsmoe, pp. 62-63.

20. *Id.* at 65.

21. *Id.* at 66-67.

22. Russ Walton, *Biblical Principles of Importance to Godly Christians* (NH: Plymouth Rock Foundation, 1984), p. 358.

23. Dornan & Vedlik, p. 70.

24. Donald S. Lutz, *The Origins of American Constitutionalism* (Baton Rouge, LA: Louisiana State University Press, 1988), p. 141.

25. Stephen K. McDowell and Mark A. Beliles, *America's Providential History* (Charlottesville, VA: Providence Press, 1989), p. 186.

26. Kenneth Woodward and David Gates, "How the Bible Made America," *Newsweek*, December 27, 1982, p. 44.

27. Dornan & Vedlik, p. 27.

28. *The Encyclopedia of Religion* (NY: Macmillan Publishing Co. 1987), see "Relativism," by Richard H. Popkin.

29. John Dewey, *The Public and Its Problems* (NY: Henry Holt, 1927), p. 34.

30. Dornan & Vedlik, p. 26.

31. Eidsmoe, p. 394.

32. Oliver Wendell Holmes, Jr., "The Law in Science—Science in Law," in *Collected Legal Papers* (NY: Harcourt, Brace and Company, 1920), p. 225.

33. Oliver Wendell Holmes, Jr., *The Common Law* (Cambridge, MA: Harvard University Press, 1963), p. 5.

34. Benjamin N. Cardozo, *The Growth of the Law* (New Haven: Yale University Press, 1924), p. 49.

35. *Trop* v. *Dulles;* 356 U.S. 86, 101 (1958).

36. Benjamin N. Cardozo, *The Nature of the Judicial Process* (New Haven: Yale University Press, 1921), p. 10.

37. Dornan & Vedlik, p. xi.

38. Lawrence Patton McDonald, *We Hold These Truths* (Seal Beach, CA: '76 Press, 1976), p. 32.

39. Edwin Corwin, *The Constitution and What It Means Today* (Princeton, NJ: Princeton University Press, 1920, 1937), xxiv.

Chapter 13
Even a Child . . .

1. *Graves* v. *New York ex rel. O'Keefe;* 306 U.S. 466, 491-492 (1939).

2. Edwin Corwin, *The Constitution and What It Means Today* (Princeton, NJ: Princeton University Press, 1920, 1937), xxiv.

3. *Id.* at 398.

4. James Madison, *The Records of the Federal Convention of 1787,* Max Farrand, ed. (New Haven: Yale Univ. Press, 1911), Vol. II, p. 370, August 27, 1787.

5. *Id.* at Vol. I, pp. 451-452.

6. John Eidsmoe, *Christianity and the Constitution* (MI: Baker Book House, 1987), pp. 360-361.

7. Tim LaHaye, *Faith of Our Founding Fathers* (Brentwood, TN: Wolgemuth & Hyatt, Publishers, Inc., 1987), p. 41-42.

8. Harold O. J. Brown, *The Reconstruction of the Republic* (New Rochelle, NY: Arlington House Publishers, 1977), p. 19.

9. Robert K. Dornan and Csaba Vedlik, Jr., *Judicial Supremacy: The Supreme Court on Trial* (MA: Plymouth Rock Foundation, 1986), p. 27.

10. *Id.* at 70-71.

11. Pat Robertson, *America's Dates With Destiny* (Nashville: Thomas Nelson Publishers, 1986), p. 88.

12. John Adams, *The Works of John Adams, Second President of the United States,* Charles Francis Adams, ed. (Boston: Little, Brown, 1854), Vol. IX, p. 229, October 11, 1798.

13. Daniel Marsh, *Unto the Generations* (Buena Park, CA: ARC, 1970), p. 51.

Chapter 14
Government of the People, by the People, and for the People ...

1. Pat Robertson, *America's Dates With Destiny* (Nashville: Thomas Nelson Publishers, 1986), p. 97.

2. *Id.*

3. Albert J. Beveridge, *The Life of John Marshall* (Boston: Houghton Mifflin, 1929), Vol. III, p. 121, n.

4. Peter Marshall and David Manuel, *From Sea to Shining Sea* (NJ: Fleming H. Revell Co., 1986), pp. 197-198.

5. Robert G. McCloskey, *The American Supreme Court* (Chicago: University of Chicago Press, 1960), p. 31.

6. Charles Montesquieu, *The Spirit of the Laws* (Worcester: Isaiah Thomas, 1802), Vol. 1, p. 185.

7. Robertson, p. 98.

8. Robert K. Dornan and Csaba Vedlik, Jr., *Judicial Supremacy: The Supreme Court on Trial* (MA: Plymouth Rock Foundation, 1986), p. 10. Quoting from Blackstone's *Commentaries on the Law.*

9. James Madison, *The Papers of James Madison,* Robert Rutland, ed. (Chicago: University of Chicago Press, 1973), Vol. XI, p. 293, October 15, 1788.

10. Thomas Jefferson, *Writings of Thomas Jefferson,* Albert Bergh, editor (Washington, D. C.: Thomas Jefferson Memorial Assoc., 1904), Vol. XV, p. 277, September 28, 1820.

11. James Madison, *The Records of the Federal Convention of 1787,* Max Farrand, ed. (New Haven: Yale Univ. Press, 1911), Vol. II, p. 75, July 21, 1787.

12. *Id.* at Vol. II, p. 428, August 27, 1787.

13. *Id.* at Vol. II, p. 430, August 27, 1787.

14. Robertson, p. 98.

15. Madison, *supra* note 11 at Vol. II, p. 76, July 21, 1787.

16. *Commonwealth* v. *Abner Kneeland;* 37 Mass. (20 Pick) 206, 227, 232 (Sup.Ct.Mass. 1838).

17. John Locke, *The Second Treatise on Civil Government, 1690* (reprinted Buffalo, NY: Prometheus Books, 1986), p. 73.

18. Beveridge, Vol. III, p. 85.

19. Montesquieu, *supra* note 6, Vol. I, pp. 185, 187.

20. Dornan & Vedlik, p. 77.

21. James D. Richardson, *A Compilation of the Messages and Papers of the Presidents, 1789-1897* (Published by Authority of Congress, 1899), Vol. 1, pp. 52-53, April 30, 1789.

22. Madison, *The Papers of James Madison,* Vol. VIII, pp. 299-300, June 20, 1785.

23. Montesquieu, *supra* note 6, Vol., I, p. 181.

24. Dornan & Vedlik, p. 69.

25. Samuel Adams, Boston Gazette, Jan. 20, 1772, quoting John Locke. See Locke's *Second Treatise,* p. 74, n.

Chapter 15
Judicial Supremacy—The Three Percent Majority

1. Benjamin Rush, *Letters of Benjamin Rush,* L. H. Butterfield, ed. (Princeton: The American Philosophical Society, 1951), p. 498, to John Adams on January 22, 1789.

2. This anecdote appears in numerous works, including "America's Bill of Rights at 200 Years," by former Chief Justice Warren E. Burger, printed in *Presidential Studies Quarterly,* Vol. XXI, No. 3, Summer 1991, p. 457.

3. *Supra* note 1 at 454 to Dr. David Ramsay on March or April, 1788.

4. *Id.*

5. George Bancroft, *Bancroft's History of the United States* (Boston: Little, Brown & Co., 1859), Vol. V, p. 24.

6. *Abington* v. *Schempp;* 374 U.S. 203, 213 (1963).

7. Paul C. Vitz, *Censorship: Evidence of Bias in Our Children's Textbooks* (Ann Arbor, Michigan: Servant Books, 1986), p. 87.

8. *State Board of Education* v. *Board of Education of Netcong;* 262 A.2d 21, 28 (Sup.Ct.N.J. 1970), *cert. denied,* 401 U.S. 1013.

9. Robert K. Dornan and Csaba Vedlik, Jr., *Judicial Supremacy: The Supreme Court on Trial* (MA: Plymouth Rock Foundation, 1986), pp. 1-2.

10. *Wallace* v. *Jaffree;* 472 U.S. 38, 47, n. 26 (1984).

11. *State Board of Education* v. *Board of Education of Netcong;* 262 A.2d 21 (Sup.Ct.N.J. 1970), *cert. denied,* 401 U.S. 1013.

12. Edwin Corwin, *The Constitution and What It Means Today* (Princeton, NJ: Princeton University Press, 1920, 1937), xxiv.

13. Dornan & Vedlik, p. 76.

14. Thomas Jefferson, *Writings of Thomas Jefferson,* Albert Bergh, editor (Washington, D. C.: Thomas Jefferson Memorial Assoc., 1904), Vol. X, p. 302, to John Dickinson on December 19, 1801.

15. *Id.* at Vol. XV, pp. 331-332, letter to Charles Hammond on August 18, 1821.

16. Dornan & Vedlik, p. 4.

17. Lino A. Graglia, "Judicial Review on the Basis of 'Regime Principles': A Prescription for Government by Judges," *South Texas Law Journal,* Vol. 26, No. 3 (Fall 1985), pp. 435-452, at 441.

18. Vitz, p. 85. Quoted from Joseph Adelson, "What Happened to the Schools," *Commentary* (March 1981), p. 36-41.

19. Dornan & Vedlik, p. 3.

20. Jefferson, *Writings of Thomas Jefferson,* Vol. XV, p. 213, a letter to Judge Spencer Roane on September 6, 1819.

21. Alexis de Tocqueville, *The Republic of the United States of America and Its Political Institutions, Reviewed and Examined,* Henry Reeves, trans. (Garden City, NY: A. S. Barnes & Co., 1851), Vol. I, pp. 160-161.

22. From an address by Judge Robert H. Bork, April 23, 1988.

23. Dornan & Vedlik, p. 21.

24. Raoul Berger, *Government by Judiciary: The Transformation of the Fourteenth Amendment* (Cambridge, MA: Harvard University Press, 1977), p. 410.

Chapter 16
When Three Percent Was A Minority

1. *American Federation of Labor* v. *American Sash & Door Co.;* 335 U.S. 538, 556-557 (1949).

2. Alexis de Tocqueville, *The Republic of the United States of America and Its Political Institutions, Reviewed and Examined,* Henry Reeves, trans. (Garden City, NY: A. S. Barnes & Co., 1851), Vol. I, p. 332.

3. *Id.* at Vol. I, 104.

4. *Marbury* v. *Madison;* 1 Cranch 137 (1803).

5. Thomas Jefferson, *Writings of Thomas Jefferson,* Albert Ellery Bergh, ed. (Washington, D. C.: Thomas Jefferson Memorial Assoc., 1904), Vol. XV, p. 447, June 12, 1823.

6. *Id.* at Vol. XI, pp. 50-51, September 11, 1804.

7. *The Debates in the Several State Conventions on the Adoption of the Federal Constitution,* Jonathan Elliot, ed. (Washington: Jonathan Elliot, 1836), Vol. IV, pp. 382-383.

8. Robert K. Dornan and Csaba Vedlik, Jr., *Judicial Supremacy: The Supreme Court on Trial* (MA: Plymouth Rock Foundation, 1986), p. 60.

9. *Id.* at 61.

10. Albert J. Beveridge, *The Life of John Marshall* (Boston: Houghton Mifflin, 1919), Vol. III, p. 158.

11. Edward Corwin, *Court Over Constitution* (Princeton, NJ: Princeton University Press, 1938), pp. 13-14.

12. *Dred Scott* v. *Sanford;* 60 U.S. 393 (1857)

13. J. G. Holland, *The Life of Abraham Lincoln* (Springfield, MA: Gurdon Bill, 1866), p. 175.

14. Beveridge, Vol. III, p. 85.

15. See *Cherokee Nation* v. *Georgia;* 5 Pet. 1 (1831), and *Worcester* v. *Georgia;* 6 Pet. 515 (1832).

16. Beveridge, Vol. IV, p. 551.

17. James D. Richardson, *A Compilation of the Messages and Papers of the Presidents, 1789-1897* (Published by Authority of Congress, 1899), Vol. II, p. 582, January 10, 1832.

18. *The Debates in the Several State Conventions,* Vol. IV, p. 399.

19. See *McCulloch* v. *Maryland;* 4 Wheaton 316 (1819), and *Osborn* v. *United States Bank;* 9 Wheaton 738 (1824).

20. Holland, *supra* note 13.

21. Beveridge, Vol. VI, p. 9.

22. *The Debates and Proceedings of the Second Session of the Thirty-Seventh Congress,* John C. Rives, ed. (Washington, D. C.: Congressional Globe Office, 1862), Vol. III, p. 2618, June 9, 1962.

23. Dornan & Vedlik, p. 48. Quoted from Edward S. Corwin, "Curbing the Court," *The Annals of the American Academy of Political and Social Science 185,* May 1936, pp. 51, 55.

24. Charles Hodge, *Systematic Theology, 1871* (reprinted Grand Rapids, MI: Wm. B. Eerdmans Publishing Company, 1975), pp. 343-346.

25. Dornan & Vedlik, pp. 76-77.

Chapter 17
The Potential Downfall of the Republic

1. James D. Richardson, *A Compilation of the Messages and Papers of the Presidents, 1789-1897* (Published by Authority of Congress, 1899), Vol. I, p. 220, September 17, 1796.

2. John Adams, *The Works of John Adams, Second President of the United States,* Charles Francis Adams, ed. (Boston: Little, Brown, 1854), Vol. IX, p. 401, June 21, 1776.

3. Verna M. Hall, *The Christian History of the American Revolution* (San Francisco: Foundation for American Christian Education, 1976), p. 21.

4. Stephen K. McDowell and Mark A. Beliles, *America's Providential History* (Charlottesville, VA: Providence Press, 1989), p. 179. Quoting from Moody Adams, *America Is Too Young To Die,* 1976, p. 25.

5. John Witherspoon, *The Works of the Rev. John Witherspoon* (Philadelphia: William W. Woodard, 1802), Vol. III, p. 46.

6. Harold K. Lane, *Liberty! Cry Liberty!* (Boston: Lamb and Lamb Tractarian Society, 1939), pp. 32-33. See also Fredrick Nyneyer, *First Principles in Morality and Economics: Neighborly Love and Ricardo's Law of Association* (South Holland: Libertarian Press, 1958), p. 31.

7. *Supra* note 4 at 112, quoting from historian B. F. Morris, 1864.

8. Thomas Jefferson, *Notes on the State of Virginia* (Philadelphia: Matthew Carey, 1794), Query XVIII, p. 237.

9. Jared Sparks, *The Life of Governeur Morris* (Boston: Gray and Bowen, 1832), Vol. III, p. 483.

10. William V. Wells, *The Life and Public Service of Samuel Adams* (Boston: Little, Brown, & Co., 1865), Vol. I, p. 22, quoting from a political essay by Samuel Adams published in *The Public Adviser, 1749.*

11. Alexis de Tocqueville, *The Republic of the United States of America and Its Political Institutions, Review and Examined,* Henry Reeves, trans. (Garden City, NY: A. S. Barnes & Co., 1851), Vol. I, p. 44.

12. Timothy Dwight, *Travels; in New England and New York* (New Haven: Timothy Dwight, 1822), Vol. IV, pp. 403-404.

13. Noah Webster, *The History of the United States* (New Haven: Durrie & Peck, 1832), p. 6.

14. George Washington, *The Writings of Washington,* John C. Fitzpatrick, ed. (Washington, D. C.: U. S. Government Printing Office, 1932), Vol. XXX, p. 432 n., from his address to the Synod of the Dutch Reformed Church in North America, October 9, 1789.

15. Rosalie J. Slater, *Teaching and Learning America's Christian History* (San Francisco: Foundation for American Christian Education, 1965), p. 251.

16. Benjamin Franklin, *The Writings of Benjamin Franklin,* Jared Sparks, ed. (Boston: Tappan, Whittemore and Mason, 1840), Vol. X, p. 297, April 17, 1787.

17. Adams, *The Works of John Adams,* Vol. IX, p. 229.

18. Abraham Lincoln, *Letters and Addresses of Abraham Lincoln* (NY: Unit Book Publishing Co., 1907), p. 8, January 27, 1837.

19. *Warren-Adams Letters* (Boston, MA: Massachusetts Historical Society, 1917), Vol. I, p. 222.

20. Daniel Webster, *The Works of Daniel Webster* (Boston: Little, Brown, & Co., 1853), Vol. II, p. 615, July 4, 1851.

21. Witherspoon, p. 42.

22. *Church of the Holy Trinity* v. *U. S.;* 143 U.S. 457, 469 (1892).

23. *Updegraph* v. *Commonwealth;* 11 Serg. & R. 393, 405 (Sup.Ct.Penn 1824).

24. *People* v. *Ruggles;* 8 Johns 545, 546 (Sup.Ct.N.Y. 1811).

25. *Church of the Holy Trinity* v. *U. S.;* 143 U.S. 457, 469 (1892).

26. *Commonwealth* v. *Jesse Sharpless and Others;* 2 Serg. & R. 91, 103 (Sup.Ct.Penn. 1815).

27. Thomas Clarkson, *Memoirs of the Private and Public Life of William Penn* (London: Longman, Hurst, Rees, Orme, & Grown, 1813), Vol. I, p. 303.

28. John Adams, *Diary and Autobiography of John Adams,* L. H. Butterfield, ed. (Cambridge, MA: Belknap Press of Harvard University Press, 1961), Vol. IV, p. 123, from diary entry on June 2, 1778 while in Paris.

29. Joseph Story, *Commentaries on the Constitution* (Boston: Hilliard, Gray & Co., 1833), Vol. III, p. 700, § 989.

30. Henry Halley, *Halley's Bible Handbook* (Grand Rapids, MI: Zondervan, 1927, 1965), p. 18.

31. Webster, *The History of the United States,* p. 339, ¶ 53.

32. Adams, *Diary and Autobiography,* Vol. I, p. 9, from Adams' diary entry for February 22, 1756.

33. *Adams Family Correspondence,* L. H. Butterfield, ed. (Cambridge, MA: The Belknap Press of Harvard University Press, 1963), Vol. I, p. 323, from Abigail Adams to Mercy Warren, circa Nov. 5, 1775.

34. Robert Flood, *The Rebirth of America* (Philadelphia: The Arthur S. DeMoss Foundation, 1986), p. 37.

35. "The Speech That Shook the Nation," *Forerunner,* Dec. 1984, p. 12.

36. *American Patriotism: Speeches, Letters, and Other Papers Which Illustrate the Foundation, the Development, the Preservation of the United States of America,* Selim H. Peabody, ed. (NY: American Book Exchange, 1880), p. 142

37. Webster, *The Works of Daniel Webster,* Vol. I, p. 44.

38. Marshall and Manuel, *The Light and the Glory,* p. 370, n. 10. Quoting from Charles E. Kistler, *This Nation Under God* (Boston: Richard G. Badger, The Gorham Press, 1924), p. 83.

39. Jedediah Morse's Election Sermon given at Charleston, Mass. on April 25, 1799, taken from an original in the Evans collection compiled by the American Antiquarian Society.

40. *Vidal* v. *Girard's Executors;* 43 U.S. 126, 153 (1844).

41. *Updegraph* v. *Commonwealth;* 11 Serg. & R. 393, 404 (Sup.Ct.Penn. 1824).

42. *People* v. *Ruggles;* 8 Johns 545, 546 (Sup.Ct.N.Y. 1811).

43. *Church of the Holy Trinity* v. *U. S.;* 143 U.S. 457, 471 (1892).

44. *City of Charleston* v. *S.A. Benjamin;* 2 Strob. 508, 520 (Sup.Ct.S.C. 1846).

45. *Id.* at 523.

46. *Updegraph* v. *Commonwealth;* 11 Serg. & R. 393, 398, 399 (Sup.Ct.Penn. 1824).

47. *People* v. *Ruggles;* 8 Johns 545, 546 (Sup.Ct.N.Y. 1811).

48. B. F. Morris, *The Christian Life and Character of the Civil Institutions of the United States* (Philadelphia: George W. Childs, 1864), p. 323.

49. Noah Webster, *American Dictionary of the English Language,* 1828 (San Francisco: Foundation for American Christian Education, 1967), preface, p. 12.

50. *Updegraph* v. *Commonwealth;* 11 Serg. & R. 393, 406 (Sup.Ct.Penn. 1824).

51. Morris, p. 328.

52. Dr. Sterling Lacy, *Valley of Decision* (Texarkana: Dayspring Productions, 1988), pp. 7-8.

53. *Id.* at 6-7.

54. Steve C. Dawson, *God's Providence in America's History* (Rancho Cordova, CA: Steve C. Dawson, 1988), p. 5:4.

55. William Linn, *The Life of Thomas Jefferson* (Ithaca, NY: Mack & Andrus, 1834), p. 265.

56. Robert Winthrop, *Addresses and Speeches on Various Occasions* (Boston: Little, Brown & Co., 1852), p. 172 from his "Either by the Bible or the Bayonet."

57. Hall, *supra* note 3 at 21.

58. Jefferson, *supra* note 8, Query XVII, p. 231.

59. Thomas Jefferson, *Jefferson's Extracts from the Gospels,* Dickinson W. Adams, ed. (Princeton: Princeton University Press, 1983), p. 11. Quoting from William Linn, *Serious Considerations on the Election of a President: Addressed to the Citizens of the United States* (NY, 1800), p. 19.

60. Tim LaHaye, *Faith of Our Founding Fathers* (Brentwood, TN: Wolgemuth & Hyatt, Publishers, Inc., 1987), p. 196.

61. Cushing Strout, *The New Heavens and New Earth* (NY: Harper and Row, 1974), p. 79.

62. John Eidsmoe, *Christianity and the Constitution* (MI: Baker Book House, 1987), p. 409.

Chapter 18
The Solution

1. Verna M. Hall, *The Christian History of the American Revolution* (San Francisco: Foundation for American Christian Education, 1976), p. 21.

2. James Madison, *Records of the Federal Convention of 1787,* Max Farrand, ed. (New Haven: Yale University Press, 1911), Vol. II, p. 370, August 22, 1787.

3. *Democracy, Liberty, and Property: Readings in the American Political Tradition,* Francis W. Coker, ed. (NY: The Macmillan Co., 1942), p. 20. Quoting from John Winthrop's *Model of Christian Charity.*

4. James D. Richardson, *A Compilation of the Messages and Papers of the Presidents, 1789-1897* (Published by Authority of Congress, 1899), Vol. VI, p. 164, March 30, 1863.

5. *Abraham Lincoln's Stories and Speeches,* J. B. McClure, ed. (Chicago: Rhodes & McClure Pub. Co., 1896), pp. 185-186; John Wesley Hill, *Abraham Lincoln—Man of God* (NY: G. P. Putnam's Sons, 1920), p. 330.

6. Pat Robertson, *America's Dates With Destiny* (Nashville: Thomas Nelson Publishers, 1986), p. 72.

7. Henry Halley, *Halley's Bible Handbook* (Grand Rapids, MI: Zondervan, 1927, 1965), p. 19.

8. Abraham Lincoln, *The Collected Works of Abraham Lincoln,* Roy P. Basler, ed. (New Brunswick, NJ: Rutgers Union Press, 1853), p. 542, September 7, 1864. See also Clarence E. Macartney, *Lincoln and the Bible* (NY: Abingdon-Cokesbury Press, 1949), p. 35.

9. Steve C. Dawson, *God's Providence in America's History* (Rancho Cordova, CA: Steve C. Dawson, 1988), p. 13:1.

10. Robertson, pp. 94-95.

11. Alexis de Tocqueville, *The Republic of the United States of America and Its Political Institutions, Reviewed and Examined,* Henry Reeves, trans. (Garden City, NY: A. S. Barnes & Co., 1851), Vol. II, p. 130.

12. Dawson, p. 11:7.

13. Lawrence Patton McDonald, *We Hold These Truths* (Seal Beach, CA: '76 Press, 1976) p. 32.

14. de Tocqueville, Vol. I, p. 5.

15. John Bartlett, *Familiar Quotations* (Boston: Little, Brown & Co., 1980), p. 374.

16. Stephen K. McDowell and Mark A. Beliles, *America's Providential History* (Charlottesville, VA: Providence Press, 1989), p. 248.

17. Raoul Berger, *Government by Judiciary: The Transformation of the Fourteenth Amendment* (Cambridge, MA: Harvard University Press, 1977), p. 410.

18. Thomas Jefferson, *Writings of Thomas Jefferson,* Albert Bergh, editor (Washington, D. C.: Thomas Jefferson Memorial Assoc., 1904), Vol. XV, p. 449, in a letter from Jefferson to Justice William Johnson on June 12, 1823.

19. Robertson, p. 95.

20. McDowell & Beliles, *America's Providential History,* p. 95.

21. Robert Flood, *The Rebirth of America* (Philadelphia: The Arthur S. DeMoss Foundation, 1986), p. 127

22. H. R. Warfel, *Noah Webster, Schoolmaster to America* (NY: Macmillan Co, 1936), pp. 181-82.

23. Percentage increase in violent crime calculated from raw data provided by United States Department of Justice (see chart on p. 210 this book); 65 percent of all crime committed by minors was reported in various news broadcasts on April 29, 1991.

24. Charles G. Finney, *Revival Lectures* (reprinted Old Tappan, NJ: Fleming Revell Co., 1970), Lecture XV, pp. 336-337.

25. Noah Webster, *History of the United States* (New Haven: Durrie & Peck, 1832), pp. 336-337, ¶ 49.

26. John M. Taylor, *Garfield of Ohio: The Available Man* (NY: W. W. Norton and Company, Inc.), p. 180. Quoted from "A Century of Congress," by James A. Garfield, published in *Atlantic,* July 1877.

27. McDowell & Beliles, *America's Providential History,* p. 262.

28. Richardson, *Messages and Papers,* Vol. 1, pp. 218-219, Sept. 17, 1796.

29. From an address by Judge Robert H. Bork, April 23, 1988.

30. Daniel Marsh, *Unto The Generations* (Buena Park, CA: ARC, 1970), p. 51.

31. Tim LaHaye, *Faith of Our Founding Fathers* (Brentwood, TN: Wolgemuth & Hyatt, Publishers, Inc., 1987), p. 201.

Bibliography
Books

Adams. *Adams Family Correspondence*, L. H. Butterfield, editor. Cambridge, MA: The Belknap Press of Harvard University Press, 1963.

Adams, John. *Diary and Autobiography of John Adams*, L. H. Butterfield, editor. Cambridge, MA: Belknap Press of Harvard University Press, 1961.

Adams, John. *The Works of John Adams, Second President of the United States*, Charles Francis Adams, editor. Boston: Little, Brown & Co., 1854.

Adams, John and Abigail. *Letters of John Adams, Addressed To His Wife*, Charles Francis Adams, editor. Boston: Charles C. Little and James Brown, 1841.

Adams, John and Adams, Samuel. *Four Letters: Being an Interesting Correspondence Between those Eminently Distinguished Characters, John Adams, Later President of the United States; and Samuel Adams, Late Governor of Massachusetts, on the Important Subject of Government.* Boston: Adams & Rhoades, 1802.

Adams, John Quincy. *The Writings of John Quincy Adams*, Worthington C. Ford, editor. New York: The Macmillan Co., 1914.

Adams, John Quincy. *An Oration Delivered before the Inhabitants of the City of Newburyport at their Request on the Sixty-First Anniversary of the Declaration of Independence.* Newburyport: Charles Whipple, 1837.

Adams, Samuel. *An Oration Delivered at the State House, in Philadelphia, to a very numerous audience; on Thursday the 1st of August, 1776.* London: E. Johnson, 1776.

Bancroft, George. *Bancroft's History of the United States.* Boston: Little, Brown & Co., 1859.

Banvard, Joseph. *Tragic Scenes in the History of Maryland and the Old French War.* Boston: Gould and Lincoln, 1856.

Bartlett, John. *Familiar Quotations.* Boston: Little, Brown & Co., 1980.

Barton, David. *America: To Pray or Not To Pray?* Aledo, TX: WallBuilder Press, 1991.

Berger, Raoul. *Government by Judiciary: The Transformation of the Fourteenth Amendment.* Cambridge, MA: Harvard University Press, 1977.

Beveridge, Albert J. *The Life of John Marshall.* Boston: Houghton Mifflin, 1919, 1947.

Blackstone, Sir William. *Commentaries on the Laws of England.* Oxford: Clarendon Press, 1769.

Bowers, Claude G. *Jefferson and Hamilton: The Struggle for Democracy in America.* Boston: Houghton Mifflin Co., 1925, 1937.

Bradford, M. E. *A Worthy Company.* NH: Plymouth Rock Foundation, 1982.

Bradford, William. *History of Plymouth Plantation.* Boston: Little, Brown & Co., 1856.

Brooks, Elbridge S. *Historic Americans.* NY: Thomas Y. Crowell & Co., 1899.

Brown, Harold O. J. *The Reconstruction of the Republic.* New Rochelle, NY: Arlington House Publishers, 1977.

Buck, William J. *William Penn in America.* Philadelphia: William J. Buck, 1888.

Cardozo, Benjamin N. *The Growth of the Law.* New Haven: Yale University Press, 1924.

Cardozo, Benjamin N. *The Nature of the Judicial Pro*cess. New Haven: Yale University Press, 1921.

Clarkson, Thomas. *Memoirs of the Private and Public Life of William Penn.* London: Longman, Hunt, Rees, Orme, & Brown, 1813.

Coker, Francis W., editor. *Democracy, Liberty, and Property: Readings in the American Political Tradition.* NY: The Macmillan Co., 1942.

Collier, Christopher. *Roger Sherman's Connecticut.* Middletown, CT: Wesleyan University Press, 1979.

Columbus, Christopher. *Christopher Columbus's Book of Prophecies: Reproduction of the Original Manuscript with English Translation,* Kay Brigham, trans. Fort Lauderdale: TSELF, 1991.

Commager, Henry S. editor. *Documents of American History.* NY: Appleton-Century-Crofts, Inc., 1948.

Congressional Quarterly. *Guide to the Supreme Court.* Washington, D. C.: Congressional Quarterly, 1990.

Cord, Robert L. *Separation of Church and State.* NY: Lambeta Press, 1982.

Corwin, Edward. *Court Over Constitution.* Princeton, NJ: Princeton Universtiy Press, 1938.

Corwin, Edwin. *The Constitution and What It Means Today.* Princeton, NJ: Princeton University Press, 1920, 1937.

Dawson, Steve C. *God's Providence in America's History.* CA: Steve C. Dawson, 1988.

de Tocqueville, Alexis. *The Republic of the United States of America and Its Political Institutions, Reviewed and Examined,* Henry Reeves, translator. Garden City, NY: A. S. Barnes & Co., 1851.

Dewey, John. *The Public and Its Problems.* NY: Henry Holt, 1927.

Dexter, Franklin B., editor. *Documentary History of Yale University.* NY: Arno Press & The New York Times, 1969.

Dolson, Hildegarde. *William Penn: Quaker Hero.* NY: Random House, 1961.

Dornan, Robert K. and Vedlik, Jr., Csaba. *Judicial Supremacy: The Supreme Court on Trial.* MA: Plymouth Rock Foundation, 1986.

Driesbach, Daniel L. *Real Threat and Mere Shadow: Religious Liberty and the First Amendment.* Westchester, IL: Crossway Books, 1987.

Dwight, Timothy. *Travels; in New England and New York.* New Haven, 1821-1822.

Eidsmoe, John. *Christianity and the Constitution.* MI: Baker Book House, 1987.

Elliot, Jonathan, editor. *The Debates in the Several State Conventions on the Adoption of the Federal Constitution.* Washington: Jonathan Elliot, 1836.

Elliot, John. *New England First Fruits.* London: R. O. & G. D., 1643.

Finney, Charles G. *Revival Lectures.* Old Tappan, NJ: Fleming Revell Co., reprinted 1970.

Fiske, John. *The Beginnings of New England*. Boston: Houghton, Mifflin & Co., 1898.

Flood, Robert. *The Rebirth of America*. Philadelphia: The Arthur S. DeMoss Foundation, 1986.

Franklin, Benjamin. *Works of the Late Doctor Benjamin Franklin Consisting of His Life, Written by Himself, Together with Essays, Humorous, Moral & Literary, Chiefly in the Manner of the Spectator*, Richard Price, editor. Dublin: P. Wogan, P. Byrne, J. Moore, and W. Jones, 1793.

Franklin, Benjamin. *The Writings of Benjamin Franklin*, Jared Sparks, ed. Boston: Tappan, Whittemore and Mason, 1840.

Frothingham, Richard. *Rise of the Republic of the United States*. Boston: Little, Brown & Co., 1872.

Gaustad, Edwin. *Faith of Our Fathers*. San Francisco: Harper & Row, 1987.

Hall, Verna M. *The Christian History of the Constitution of the United States of America*. San Francisco: The Foundation for American Christian Education, 1966.

Hall, Verna M. *The Christian History of the American Revolution*. San Francisco: Foundation for American Christian Education, 1976.

Hall, Verna M. and Slater, Rosalie J. *The Bible and the Constitution of the United States of America*. San Francisco: The Foundation for American Christian Education, 1983.

Halley, Henry. *Halley's Bible Handbook*. Grand Rapids, MI: Zondervan, 1927, 1965.

Hamilton, Alexander. *Selected Writings and Speeches of Alexander Hamilton*, Morton J. Frisch, editor. Washington, D. C.: American Enterprise Institute for Public Policy Research, 1985.

Hamilton, Alexander. *The Papers of Alexander Hamilton*, Harold Syrett, ed. New York: Columbia University Press, 1961.

Hazard, Ebenezer. *Historical Collections: Consisting of State Papers and other Authentic Documents: Intended as Materials for an History of the United States of America*. Philadelphia: T. Dobson, 1792.

Henry, William Wirt. *Patrick Henry: Life, Correspondence and Speeches*. New York: Charles Scribner's Sons, 1891.

Hill, John Wesley. *Abraham Lincoln—Man of God*. NY: G. P. Putnam's Sons, 1920.

Hill, Kent R. *The Puzzle of the Soviet Church*. Portland: Multnomah, 1989.

Hodge, Charles. *Systematic Theology, 1871*. Reprinted Grand Rapids, MI: Wm. B. Eerdmans Publishing Company, 1975.

Holland, J. G. *The Life of Abraham Lincoln*. Springfield, MA: Gurdon Bill, 1866.

Holmes, John. *The Statesman*. Augusta: Severance & Door, 1840.

Holmes, Jr., Oliver Wendell. *Collected Legal Papers*. NY: Harcourt, Brace and Company, 1920.

Holmes, Jr., Oliver Wendell. *The Common Law*. Cambridge, MA: Harvard University Press, 1963.

Hunt, Galliard. *James Madison and Religious Liberty*. Washington, D. C.: American Historical Association, Government Printing Office, 1902.

Ives, J. Moss. *The Ark and the Dove*. NY: Cooper Square Publishers, Inc., 1936, 1969.

Jay, John. *The Correspondence and Public Papers of John Jay,* Henry P. Johnston, editor. New York: G. P. Putnam's Sons, 1890.

Jefferson, Thomas. *Jefferson's Extracts from the Gospels,* Dickinson W. Adams, editor. Princeton: Princeton University Press, 1983.

Jefferson, Thomas. *Notes on the State of Virginia.* Philadelphia: Matthew Carey, 1794.

Jefferson, Thomas. *Jefferson Writings,* Merrill D. Peterson, editor. NY: Literary Classics of the United States, Inc., 1984.

Jefferson, Thomas. *Writings of Thomas Jefferson,* Albert Ellery Bergh, editor. Washington, D. C.: Thomas Jefferson Memorial Assoc., 1904.

Judson, Carroll L. *The Sages And Heroes of the American Revolution.* Philadelphia: L. Carroll Judson, 1852.

Kistler, Charles E. *This Nation Under God.* Boston: Richard G. Badger, The Gorham Press, 1924.

Lacy, Dr. Sterling. *Valley of Decision.* Texarkana: Dayspring Productions, 1988.

LaHaye, Tim. *Faith of Our Founding Fathers.* Brentwood, TN: Wolgemuth & Hyatt, Publishers, Inc., 1987.

Lane, Harold K. *Liberty! Cry Liberty!* Boston: Lamb and Lamb Tractarian Society, 1939.

Lefler, Hugh Talmage, editor. *North Carolina History.* Chapel Hill: Univ. of North Carolina Press, 1934, 1956.

Lincoln, Abraham. *Abraham Lincoln's Stories and Speeches,* J. B. McClure, editor. Chicago: Rhodes & McClure Pub. Co., 1896.

Lincoln, Abraham. *The Collected Works of Abraham Lincoln,* Roy P. Basler, editor. New Brunswick, NJ: Rutgers Union Press.

Lincoln, Abraham. *Letters and Addresses of Abraham Lincoln.* NY: Unit Book Publishing Co., 1907.

Linn, William. *The Life of Thomas Jefferson.* Ithaca, NY: Mack & Andrus, 1834.

Linn, William. *Serious Considerations on the Election of a President: Addressed to the Citizens of the United States.* NY, 1800.

Locke, John. *The Second Treatise on Civil Government, 1690.* Reprinted Buffalo, NY: Prometheus Books, 1986.

Lockyer, Herbert. *Last Words of Saints and Sinners.* Grand Rapids: Kregel, 1969.

Lossing, Benson J. *Eminent Americans.* NY: American Book Exchange, 1881.

Lutz, Donald S. *The Origins of American Constitutionalism.* Baton Rouge, LA: Louisiana State University Press, 1988.

M'Guire, E. C. *The Religious Opinions and Character of Washington.* NY: Harper & Brothers, 1836.

Macartney, Clarence E. *Lincoln and the Bible.* NY: Abingdon-Cokesbury Press, 1949.

Madison, James. *The Records of the Federal Convention of 1787,* Max Farrand, ed. New Haven: Yale University Press, 1911.

Madison, James. *Letters and Other Writings of James Madison.* New York: R. Worthington, 1884.

Madison, James. *The Papers of James Madison,* Robert Rutland, editor. Chicago: University of Chicago Press, 1973.

Marsh, Daniel. *Unto the Generations*. Buena Park, CA: ARC, 1970.

Marshall, Peter and Manuel, David. *The Light and the Glory*. NJ: Fleming H. Revell Co., 1977.

Marshall, Peter and Manuel, David. *From Sea to Shining Sea*. NJ: Fleming H. Revell Co., 1986.

McCloskey, Robert G. *The American Supreme Court*. Chicago: University of Chicago Press, 1960.

McCormick, Richard Patrick. *Rutgers: A Bicentennial History*. NJ: Rutgers University Press, 1966.

McDonald, Lawrence Patton. *We Hold These Truths*. Seal Beach, CA: '76 Press, 1976.

McDonald, William. *Documentary Source Book of American History, 1606-1889*. NY: The Macmillan Company, 1909.

McDowell, Stephen K. and Beliles, Mark A. *America's Providential History*. Charlottesville, VA: Providence Press, 1989.

McDowell, Stephen K. and Beliles, Mark A. *The Spirit of the Constitution*. Charlottesville, VA: Providence Press.

McGuffey, William H. *McGuffey's Eclectic Fourth Reader*. Cincinnati: Winthrop B. Smith & Co., 1853.

McGuffey, William H. *McGuffey's Eclectic Third Reader*. Cincinnati: Winthrop B. Smith & Co., 1848.

Mode, Peter G. *Sourcebook and Bibliographical Guide for American Church History*. Menasha, WI: George Banta Publishing Co., 1921.

Montesquieu, Charles. *The Spirit of the Laws*. Worcester: Isaiah Thomas, 1802.

Morison, S. E., editor. *Sources and Documents Illustrating the American Revolution 1764-1788 and the Formation of the Federal Constitution*. NY: Oxford University Press, 1923.

Morris, B. F. *The Christian Life and Character of the Civil Institutions of the United States*. Philadelphia: George W. Childs, 1864.

Niles, Hezekiah. *Principles and Acts of the Revolution in America*. Baltimore: William Ogden Niles, 1822.

Nyneyer, Fredrick. *First Principles in Morality and Economics: Neighborly Love and Ricardo's Law of Association*. South Holland: Libertarian Press, 1958.

O'Neill, J. M. *Religion and Education Under the Constitution*. NY: Harper & Brothers, 1949.

Peabody, Selim H., editor. *American Patriotism: Speeches, Letters, and Other Papers Which Illustrate the Foundation, the Development, the Preservation of the United States of America*. NY: American Book Exchange, 1880.

Peters, Richard, editor, *The Public Statutes at Large of the United States of America*. Boston: Charles C. Little and James Brown, 1846.

Pomeroy, Wardell B., Ph.D. *Boys and Sex*. NY: Delacorte Press, 1981.

Pomeroy, Wardell B., Ph.D. *Girls and Sex*. NY: Delacorte Press, 1981.

Powers, Peter. *Jesus Christ the King*. Newburyport, 1778.

Reynolds, Edward C. *The Maine Scholars Manual*. Portland, ME: Dresser, McLellan & Co., 1880.

Rhoads, Thomas Y. *The Battle-fields of the Revolution.* Philadelphia: J. W. Bradley, 1860.

Richardson, James D., editor. *A Compilation of the Messages and Papers of the Presidents, 1789-1897.* Published by Authority of Congress, 1899.

Robertson, Pat. *America's Dates With Destiny.* Nashville: Thomas Nelson Publishers, 1986.

Rocky Mountain Planned Parenthood. *You've Changed the Combination.* Denver: RAJ Publications, 1977.

Rush, Benjamin. *The Letters of Benjamin Rush,* L. H. Butterfield, ed. Princeton: The American Philosophical Society, 1951.

Shipton, Clifford K. *Sibley's Harvard Graduates.* Boston: Massachusetts Historical Society, 1965.

Slater, Rosalie. *Teaching and Learning America's Christian History.* San Francisco: Foundation for American Christian Education, 1975.

Sparks, Jared. *The Life of Governeur Morris.* Boston: Gray and Bowen, 1832.

Stokes, Anson Phelps. *Church and State in the United States.* NY: Harper & Brothers, 1950.

Story, Joseph. *A Familiar Exposition of the Constitution of the United States.* New York: Harper & Brothers, 1854.

Story, Joseph. *Commentaries on the Constitution.* Boston: Hilliard, Gray & Co., 1833.

Strout, Cushing. *The New Heavens and the New Earth.* NY: Harper & Row, 1974.

Taylor, John M. *Garfield of Ohio: The Available Man.* NY: W. W. Norton and Company, Inc., 1970.

Thornton, J. Wingate. *The Pulpit of the American Revolution.* Boston: Gould & Lincoln, 1860.

True, M. B. C. *A Manual of the History and Civil Government of the State of Nebraska.* Omaha: Gibson, Miller, & Richardson, 1885.

Vitz, Paul C. *Censorship: Evidence of Bias in Our Children's Textbooks.* Ann Arbor, MI: Servant Books, 1986.

Walton, Russ. *Biblical Principles of Importance to Godly Christians.* NH: Plymouth Rock Foundation, 1984.

Warfel, H. R. *Noah Webster, Schoolmaster to America.* NY: Macmillan Co, 1936.

Washington, George. *The Writings of Washington,* Jared Sparks, editor. Boston: American Stationers' Company, 1838.

Washington, George. *The Writings of Washington,* John C. Fitzpatrick, editor. Washington, D. C.: U. S. Government Printing Office, 1932.

Webster, Daniel. *The Works of Daniel Webster.* Boston: Little, Brown and Company, 1853.

Webster, Noah. *American Dictionary of the English Language, 1828.* Reprinted San Francisco: The Foundation for American Christian Education, 1967.

Webster, Noah. *History of the United States.* New Haven: Durrie & Peck, 1832.

Weems, Mason Locke. *The Life of William Penn.* Philadelphia: Uriah Hunt, 1836.

Wells, William V. *The Life and Public Services of Samuel Adams*. Boston: Little, Brown & Co., 1865

Wilson, J. O. *Records of the Columbia Historical Society*. Washington, D. C.: Columbia Historical Society, 1897. See "Eighty Years of the Public Schools of Washington—1805 to 1885," October 30, 1896, Vol. I.

Winthrop, Robert. *Addresses and Speeches on Various Occasions*. Boston: Little, Brown & Co., 1852.

Wirt, William. *The Life and Character of Patrick Henry*. Philadelphia: James Webster, 1818.

Witherspoon, John. *The Works of the Rev. John Witherspoon*. Philadelphia: William W. Woodard, 1802.

———. *Acts Passed at a Congress of the United States of America*. Hartford: Hudson & Goodwin, 1791.

———. *Annals of the Congress of the United States*. Washington, D. C.: Gales & Seaton, 1834.

———. *The Bible of the Revolution, 1782*. Reprinted NY: Arno Press, 1968.

———. *The Code of 1650, Being a Compilation of the Earliest Laws and Orders of the General Court of Connecticut*. Hartford: Silus Andrus, 1822.

———. *The Constitutions of the Several Independent States of America, Published by Order of Congress*. Boston: Norman & Bowen, 1785.

———. *The Constitutions of the United States of America with the Latest Amendments*. Trenton: Moore & Lake, 1813.

———. *The Constitutions of All the United States According to the Latest Amendments*. Lexington, KY: Thomas T. Skillman, 1817.

———. *The Debates and Proceedings of the Second Session of the Thirty-Seventh Congress*, John C. Rives, ed. Wash., D. C.: Congressional Globe Office, 1862.

———. *The Journals of the Continental Congress, 1774-1789*. Washington, D. C.: Government Printing Office, 1905.

———. *The Journals of Each Provincial Congress of Massachusetts, 1774-1775*, William Lincoln, editor. Boston: Dutton & Wentworth, 1838.

———. *Lives of the Heroes of the American Revolution*. Boston: Phillips & Sampson, 1848.

———. *The Records of the Columbia Historical Society*. Washington, D.C.: Colubia Historical Society, 1896.

———. *Remember William Penn, 1644-1944, Tercentenary Memorial*. Harrisburg, PA: The Commonwealth of Pennsylvania and Pennsylvania Historical Commission, 1944.

———. *Warren-Adams Letters*. Boston, MA: Mass. Historical Society, 1917.

Special Historical Works or Documents

Adams, Samuel. *The Public Adviser*, 1749.

Adams, Samuel . *Boston Gazette*, Jan. 20, 1772.

Aitken, Robert. Memorial to Congress, 21 January, 1781, obtained from National Archives.

Hancock, John. Proclamation from Concord, April 15, 1775, from an original in the

Evans collection, #14220, by the American Antiquarian Society.

Hancock, John. Proclamation from Boston, November 8, 1783, from an original in the Evans collection, #18025, by the American Antiquarian Society.

Morse, Jedediah. Election Sermon given at Charleston, Mass. on April 25, 1799, taken from an original in the Evans collection compiled by the American Antiquarian Society.

Winthrop, John. *Model of Christian Charity.*

Articles

Joseph Adelson, "What Happened to the Schools," *Commentary,* March 1981.

Warren E. Burger, former Chief Justice, "America's Bill of Rights at 200 Years," *Presidential Studies Quarterly,* Vol. XXI, No. 3, Summer 1991.

Edward S. Corwin, "Curbing the Court," *The Annals of the American Academy of Political and Social Science 185,* May 1936, pp. 51, 55.

Lawrence A. Cremin, *1963 Yearbook,* World Book Encyclopedia, p. 38.

President James A. Garfield, "A Century of Congress," *Atlantic,* July 1877.

Lino A. Graglia, "Judicial Review on the Basis of 'Regime Principles': A Prescription for Government by Judges," *South Texas Law Journal,* Vol. 26, No. 3, Fall 1985.

James Adolph Lesftwich, "Meet Sir George Carterete: Story of the State Seals of New Jersey," *Carterete News* (Trenton: The Carterete Club), June 1953, Vol. II, No. 6.

William Murray, "America Without God," *The New American,* June 20, 1988, p. 19.

Richard H. Popkin, "Relativism," *The Encyclopedia of Religion* (NY: Macmillan Publishing Co., 1987).

Nadine Strossen, "A Constitutional Analysis of the Equal Access Act's Standards Governing Public School Student Religious Meetings," *Harvard Journal on Legislation,* Winter 1987, Vol. 24:117, p. 118.

Kenneth Woodward and David Gates, "How the Bible Made America," *Newsweek,* December 27, 1982, p. 44.

"Parent silences teaching of carols," "School officials deny banning Bible..." *The Washington Times,* December 12, 1988.

"Fifth Grader Sues for Right to Read Bible," *IFA Newsletter,* Feb. 1989.

"The Speech That Shook the Nation," *Forerunner,* Dec. 1984, p. 12.

The New American, September 29, 1986, p. 28.

Education Week, June 13, 1985, p. 28.

Associated Press, *Dallas Times Herald,* August 6, 1988, B-5.

An address by Judge Robert H. Bork, April 23, 1988.

Project Literacy U.S. (PLUS).

The information about the books *Planned Parenthood* recommends comes from a packet of informational materials dated January 15, 1987, and prepared by California Assemblyman Bill Bradley of the 76th District.

"Governor Signs Abstinence Bill," California Voter's Guide, Vol. 5, No. 10 (Sacramento: California Coalition for Traditional Values), Fall 1988.

Index

NOTES

NOTES

NOTES

NOTES

Price List

Prices subject to change without notice
Quantity and case-lot discounts available

WallBuilders, Inc.
P.O. Box 397
Aledo, TX 76008
(817) 441-6044

	Price/Copy	Quantity	Total
Books & Publications			
America: To Pray or Not To Pray?	$6.95		
A statistical look at what has happened when religious principles were separated from public affairs by the Supreme Court in 1962.			
The Myth of Separation	$7.95		
An examination of the writings of the Framers of the Constitution and of the Supreme Court's own records.			
The Bulletproof George Washington	$4.95		
An account of God's miraculous protection of Washington in the French and Indian War and of his open gratitude for God's Divine intervention.			
The New England Primer	$5.95		
A reprint of the 1777 textbook used by the Founding Fathers.			
Bible Study Course—New Testament	$4.95		
A reprint of the 1946 New Testament Summary text used by the Dallas Public High Schools.			
What Happened in Education?	$2.95		
Statistical evidence that disproves several popular educational explanations for the decline in SAT scores.			
Did Television Cause the Changes in Youth Morality?	$2.95		
This exam is very enlightening not only as to what happened in television, but when it happened, and why?			
America's Godly Heritage Transcript (See video)	$2.95		
Cassette Tapes			
"America's Godly Heritage" (See video)	$4.95		
"Education and the Founding Fathers" (See video)	$4.95		
"The Spirit of the American Revolution" (See video)	$4.95		
"The Laws of the Heavens"	$4.95		
An explanation of the eight words in the Declaration of Independence on which the nation was birthed.			
"America: Lessons from Nehemiah"	$4.95		
A look at the Scriptural parallels between the rebuilding of Jerusalem in the book of Nehemiah and that of America today.			
"The Founding Fathers"	$4.95		
Highlights accomplishments and notable quotes of prominent Founding Fathers which show their strong belief in Christian principles.			

"Keys to Good Government"	$4.95	____	____

"Keys to Good Government" $4.95   ____ ____
The Founding Fathers formula for good government.

"8 Principles for Reformation" $4.95   ____ ____
Eight Biblical guidelines for restoring Christian principles to society and public affairs.

"The Myth of Separation" (See book) $4.95   ____ ____

"America: To Pray or Not To Pray" (See book) $4.95   ____ ____

Video Cassette (VHS)

America's Godly Heritage (60 min.) $19.95   ____ ____
This clearly sets forth the beliefs of many of the famous Founding Fathers concerning the proper role of Christian principles in education, government, and the public affairs of the nation.

Education and the Founding Fathers (60 min.) $19.95   ____ ____
A look at the Bible-based educational system which produced America's great heroes.

Spirit of the American Revolution (53 min.) $19.95   ____ ____
A look at the Christian motivation of the founders throughout the American Revolution.

Foundations of American Government (18 min.) $9.95   ____ ____
Surveys the historical statements and records surrounding the drafting of the First Amendment, showing the Founders's intent.

Tax (TX only, add 7.75%): _____

Shipping (see chart at left): _____

TOTAL: _____

Shipping and Handling

Under $5.00	$1.50	$25.01-$ 40.00	$5.95
$ 5.01-$15.00	$2.95	$40.01-$ 60.00	$6.95
$15.01-$25.00	$3.95	$60.01-$100.00	$9.95

Canada orders add $5 extra.

* When shipping products to multiple addresses, please calculate shipping cost based on the dollar amount to each address—not on the order total. Thank you.

Please allow 4-6 Weeks for delivery.

Send The Above Indicated Materials To:

Name_____ Phone (____)_____

Address_____

City_____ State_____ Zip_____

"You see the distress that we are in . . . come, let us build the walls that we may no longer be a reproach." Nehemiah 2:17.

2/93